FREEDOM
AT YOUR FINGERTIPS

FREEDOM
AT YOUR FINGERTIPS

GET RAPID PHYSICAL AND EMOTIONAL RELIEF WITH THE BREAKTHROUGH SYSTEM OF TAPPING

The Ultimate Question & Answer Guidebook
For Using Emotional Freedom Techniques™
to Feel More Energized & Alive

COMPILED BY RON BALL

INROADS PUBLISHING

Printed in the United States of America.
Published in the United States of America by:

Inroads Publishing
P.O. Box 357
Fredericksburg, VA 22404-0357

E-mail: info@fayf.com

If you are unable to order this book from your local bookseller, you may order directly from the publisher. Quantity discounts for organizations are available.

ISBN 10: 0-9727671-3-4
ISBN 13: 978-0-9727671-3-2

First Edition

Co-Authors

Gloria Arenson
Ron Ball
Gwenn Bonnell
Paul & Layne Cutright
Lindsay Kenny
Dr. Alexander R. Lees
Carol Look
Angela Treat Lyon
Rebecca Marina
Betty Moore-Hafter
Carol Solomon
Loretta Sparks
Mary Stafford
Carol Tuttle
Stacey Vornbrock
Maryam Webster
Rick Wilkes
Brad Yates
Jan Yordy

Contents

> What is EFT?
>
> How was EFT developed?
>
> What is the body's *energy* system?
>
> Isn't EFT illogical?
>
> What if I'm skeptical about EFT?
>
> Is EFT something anyone can learn to do?
>
> What is the Apex problem?
>
> Is EFT part of energy medicine or energy psychology?
>
> What's the best way to learn EFT?
>
> Briefly, how do you do EFT?
>
> What are the EFT tapping points?
>
> What are the steps to doing the EFT Shortcut method?
>
> How do you do the classic or long version?
>
> When do you recommend doing the long version of EFT?
>
> Rather than learn EFT myself, the reason I bought this book was to find how EFT can help me and work with an EFT practitioner. What do you recommend?
>
> Why do some EFT practitioners use different tapping points?
>
> Can I tap on points on either side of my face or body?
>
> How should I tap?
>
> Why do some practitioners do EFT differently?
>
> How long does the change last?
>
> What if I'm doing EFT the *wrong* way?
>
> What if I believe EFT won't work for me?
>
> Why do you do the setup phrase?
>
> What are *aspects*?
>
> Do I need to *say* the EFT statement or can I just *think* it?
>
> Why don't more people know about EFT?
>
> What is Psychological Reversal?
>
> What's the difference between the Sore Spot and the Karate Chop point?
>
> Is EFT safe?
>
> Is it a good idea for me to teach other people to use EFT?

Why is the EFT affirmation negative instead of positive?
What is the Choices Method?
I've learned EFT. Why don't I remember to do it when I have a problem?

How would you define abundance? Is it only about money?
I have read many books on the subject of manifesting, and I
    am trying very hard to attract abundance into my life.
    I don't understand why it's not working and I'm not
    attracting the abundance *I say that I want*. In your
    opinion, what am I doing wrong?
What is *Prosperity Consciousness* and what does it have to
    do with attracting abundance?
What is a limiting belief?
How do I find out if I have limiting beliefs? Does everyone
    have them?
Would you please give me some good examples of typical
    limiting beliefs to attracting wealth and abundance?
I've been making about $50,000 every year for a long time.
    I definitely want and need to make more, and I believe
    I should be making more, so what is in the way?
How do I know, or how do you know, if I have a *comfort zone*?
    Maybe something else is wrong. Maybe I don't have
    enough credentials to make more money in my field.
How do I know which emotions are getting in my way? Isn't
    it normal to be anxious about money and paying the bills?
I think I understand what a *comfort zone* is, and that I
    probably have a few *limiting beliefs* from my family
    about money. However, I still don't understand why
    I am so stuck when I know I want to move forward.
    How do I stop this negative cycle?
Is being stuck the same thing as self sabotage?
And you think EFT can be used to break through these
    comfort zones and *limiting beliefs*?
So how do you use EFT as an effective tool to attract abundance?
What are some of the EFT setup phrases I might use?
What if I have concerns about being one of those "nasty"
    millionaires who doesn't care about others? What
    would some typical setup phrases be for me?
Why do so many people feel unsafe earning more money?
Do you have any final suggestions for what more I could do
    to make more money?

How successful is EFT in overcoming anxiety?
What are some of the factors that can help me be successful
    in dealing with anxiety?

What are blockages?
How do personal emotional blockages begin?
How do identify these blockages?
What are some EFT setup phrases I could use in working on
    my blockages?
What if I'm reminded of other things while tapping on my
    specific blockage?
What is the best way to end an EFT session after working
    successfully on a blockage?
Tell me some more about how I can make the right Choices.
    How do I attract what I would really rather have in my life?
I want to model success! What are the key personality traits
    of those who are consistently able to remove their own
    blockages and obstacles?
What can I expect when my blockages start to dissolve
    through using EFT?

Is EFT a technique which is safe to use with children or teens?
Why is it important for parents to tap on their own issues
    before approaching their child to do EFT tapping?
What are some parental EFT setup phrases to help work on
    or process parental issues?
What are some ways of introducing EFT to a child?
When is the best time to use EFT with a child or teen?
What does the basic setup phrase for a child look like?
What kinds of issues are most effective to process with
    children using EFT?
What is meant by surrogate tapping and how is it done?
At what age do you recommend introducing children to EFT?
    Do you have any helpful strategies for showing EFT
    to younger children?
Are there times when a parent should seek professional help
    for an issue with their child?
Do you have some tips for making EFT more successful
    for children?

What is a neuropeptide and what does it do?

Does this upgrading of information affect our emotions?

Are you saying that if we have unresolved negative emotions
we can get sick?

Does this mean I should pay more attention to my thoughts?

What are the pathways we can follow?

How do our emotional states of mind affect our progress,
and/or our health?

How exactly do we get ourselves into these states that affect
our health?

What can you do to help yourself?

What is EFT?

So the environment is constantly upgrading our software,
as it were?

What happens if I use EFT enough?

How did you get involved with EFT?

How does EFT take away pain?

How do I know EFT will work for my pain?

How do I address the pain with EFT?

What if addressing the physical symptoms doesn't work
for me?

What if I tapped for the emotion and the physical symptoms
but still have the pain?

What can I do if I can't seem to find any emotion tied to this
pain?

Should I stop tapping if the pain starts getting worse?

What do I do when the pain starts in one spot and then moves?

The pain started diminishing but there is still some left, and
it's stuck on the 0-10 level. How can I break through this
plateau?

Should I stop tapping when the pain disappears?

Still nothing is happening... how long do I tap?

What if the pain is from an accident or an emotionally
traumatic event?

Will EFT still be effective if there is a physical cause for the
pain?

What if the pain comes back?

We're trying to conceive a child. How can I use EFT for fertility problems? More specifically, how does stress affect trying to conceive?

What about teenagers dealing with the peer pressure of having sex?

Can EFT be of use if I have a different sexual orientation?

I was sexually abused. Is EFT effective for sexual abuse issues?

What about sex and aging?

What is the cause of fear of public speaking?

What is important about the shocked or distorted energy system?

What kinds of stage fright are there?

How do you know you have stage fright?

What's a good example of a fear of public-speaking?

I experience extreme nausea. How do I deal with that?

How do I get rid of my stage fright?

What do I do once I make note of my sensations, feelings, and thoughts and how they show up in my body?

How do we grow spiritually?

Do I have to use the name "God" to describe this spiritual connection?

How can I start having spiritual experiences?

Is blind faith required?

Do I have to become religious to be spiritual?

So, how do I connect with God?

How do I *ask* to grow spiritually?

How can I know that God always answers?

How do I *allow* myself to experience God and grow spiritually?

What should I expect to feel as I *allow*?

Does spiritual growth require much practice?

What are some of the practices I can use for spiritual growth?

How does meditation help?

What role does mindfulness play in spiritual growth?

What is the role of prayer?

Where do I go from here?

Once you've tapped on all the aspects and all the causes
you can find, what else can you do to make sure you're
ready to fly before you book a ticket?
How do you tap in public without drawing attention to
yourself?
How would you tap for jet lag?
What setup phrases could you use for other travel issues?

Why EFT for weight loss?
What is involved in using EFT for weight loss?
How can EFT be used most effectively for weight loss?
How can I use EFT for specific events?
How can I use EFT for food cravings?
What can I expect when I tap for food cravings?
How can I identify the emotional issues?
What are some common emotional states that lead to
overeating, and how can I address them with EFT?
How can I use EFT to stop sabotaging myself?
How can I use EFT when I am feeling stuck?
How can I use EFT to change my beliefs about weight loss?
How can I use EFT to stay motivated in my weight loss plan?

DEDICATION

This book is dedicated to you, the reader, as you are right now and all that you ever will be. By reading this book, you are opening doors to new possibilities for your physical and emotional well being. Within you are the possibilities of being anything you think or dream you can be.

DISCLAIMER

The intention of this book is to provide information for learning about EFT (Emotional Freedom Techniques™) and the ways people might use it for self-help and personal development. While it quite often produces remarkable results, EFT is still relatively new and in the experimental stage. Given that, nothing in this book should be construed as a promise of benefits, claims of cures or a guarantee of results to be achieved.

Individual chapters are based on the opinions of the respective author. The book is offered with the understanding that the authors and publisher are not engaged in rendering medical, psychological, legal or other professional advice. The reader must take complete responsibility for his or her physical health and emotional well-being.

The information, instructions or advice presented is not intended to be a substitute for professional medical or psychological care. If you are under medical or psychological supervision, consult your healthcare professional before using any of the procedures in this book. The authors and publisher disclaim any liability or loss incurred directly or indirectly as a result of the use or application of any of the contents of this book.

HOW TO USE THIS BOOK

The format of this book is different than most books which are read cover to cover. Rather, this is a convenient questions and answers guidebook. You'll want to read the chapter on what EFT is and how you can do it. After that, use *Freedom at Your Fingertips* as a reference guide. Whenever you have a problem or issue that bothers you, refer to the Contents section at the front of the book. Find your topic and question, and then go right to the section with the answer. Also, in most of the chapters you'll find actual case stories of people that have used EFT to overcome different issues.

This book is intended to be a primer on EFT and to introduce you to world class EFT experts and some of their areas of specialty. To learn EFT in depth, we highly recommend downloading the *EFT Manual*, available from www.emofree.com. Also, the best way to learn EFT is to not only read about it. You'll want to see, hear and feel how to do it.

Gary Craig, the founder of EFT, offers a selection of video sets that are excellent for learning EFT. Again, you'll find them at www.emofree.com. You'll find references throughout this book to this Website. It's the most comprehensive worldwide site for learning EFT, providing case stories and a wealth of other information on EFT.

As a guide, in many chapters of this book, the co-author has indicated examples of EFT setup phrases to use. Whenever you see this icon ▷ it's a visual indicator that the setup phrase(s) follow. Please note that these phrases are examples only. With EFT, it's important that you use setup phrases that are specific and relevant to your situation or issue.

Lastly, to complement what's in this book, we've also provided some learning tools and valuable information for you at www.fayf.com. This Website is especially set up for readers of *Freedom At Your Fingertips*.

FOREWORD
By Dr. Joseph Mercola

(New York Times Bestselling Author & Founder of Mercola.com, World's Most Popular Natural Health Website)

I have spent the last three decades studying health, with a particularly strong focus on how to best prevent disease. Like most other doctors, back in medical school I was brainwashed to believe that the toxic drug-and-surgery based approach to treating illness was the be-all and end-all to healing.

This is the dominant model today, as most people think of prescription drugs when they think of healthcare. It is an expensive and dangerous situation, as drugs and surgery both are really just mere treatments that have almost nothing to do with actual prevention or cure.

Fortunately, there are sections of conventional medicine that are starting to appreciate the importance of true preventive and curative health approaches. This is particularly true in the area of emotions. It is finally being widely recognized that emotions have a significant role in the etiology of disease; even the conservative Center for Disease Control acknowledges that over 85 percent of all diseases have an emotional component (and this is a very conservative estimate.)

The problem, of course, is that conventional medicine has no consistently effective tools that address the emotional dysfunction at its causal level. They rely primarily on a drug based model in conjunction with counseling and psychotherapy, which rarely seem to fully resolve the energetic and physiological dysfunctions that contribute to the disease.

When one carefully analyzes the various healing models in a non-biased manner, it becomes clear that energy psychology tools are one of the most powerful healing modalities available.

Those that have heard of me know that I am an information junkie and love to read scientific advances. I review hundreds of articles every week in preparation for publishing my health newsletter at Mercola.com, which has become one of the most widely read health newsletters in the world. In the many tens of thousands of articles I have reviewed and in all my twenty years of clinical experience, I have yet to encounter any healing modality that is consistently as effective in resolving human health challenges as EFT.

I used to believe exercise was the most fundamental health tool; with time I modified that to nutritional biochemistry. While both of these tools, along with sleep and optimal sun exposure, are essential for health, if I had to rely on only one tool (fortunately I don't) I would have to select EFT.

Unfortunately, it took me nearly 15 years of searching after I graduated from medical school before I encountered energy psychology. My first exposure was to EFT's precursor, TFT. However, it did not seem to be time effective in a busy clinical setting that I practiced. This prejudiced me against evaluating EFT until a close friend encouraged me to consider it.

I am so glad I did, because EFT has been the most effective healing tool I have ever encountered. As Gary Craig is fond of saying, you can use it for just about everything.

Ron Ball's book, *Freedom at Your Fingertips*, provides a powerful resource to use this tool even more effectively. He has been able to coordinate some of the best therapists in this amazing field and have them contribute a chapter on their expertise.

If you are a health care professional or just using EFT for your own or your family's benefit, this book *needs* to be in your library, as it will help you to integrate what some of the brightest people in the field have learned on the practical application of this powerful tool.

Once you become more proficient with EFT through this *exceptional book*, I would strongly encourage you to subscribe to the free newsletter at Mercola.com, as it has a variety of resources that will complement what you learn in this book, and serve as a powerful synergistic combination to achieve optimal health.

INTRODUCTION

"No pessimist ever discovered the secret of the stars, or sailed to an uncharted land, or opened a new doorway to the human spirit.... The best and most beautiful things in the world cannot be seen or even touched. They must be felt with the heart."

Helen Keller

In Malcolm Gladwell's bestselling book, *The Tipping Point,* he says that new ideas, products and changes move through a population like an *epidemic*. Ultimately, there becomes a moment of critical mass, the threshold, the boiling point, a place where the unexpected becomes expected and where radical change not only becomes a possibility but a certainty.

Perhaps we are at a tipping point in alternative treatments for *physical and emotional wellness*. According to a study released in 2004 by the National Center for Complementary and Alternative Medicine (NCCAM), one of the institutes of the National Institutes of Health, 36 percent of American adults have tried alternative therapies and treatments.

The most common reason was that adults believed that it would help them when combined with conventional treatments. Interestingly, another key reason was that 28 percent believed conventional treatments wouldn't help them with their health problems. It's also important to note that more than 75 percent of the medical schools in the United States now require some kind of complementary and alternative medicine coursework, according to the Association of American Medical Colleges.

You're about to learn an extraordinary new method called Emotional Freedom Techniques™ (EFT). In a way, it proves that everything old is new again. EFT, like other methods in energy psychology and energy medicine, is based on the belief that our bodies have energy circuits or meridians. This dates back thousands of years. When our bodies are in balance, we are healthy. When out of balance, the result is *dis-eases*.

What if emotional and physical freedom was right there at your fingertips? What if a simple, elegant and powerful cure to healing all kinds of issues was at your disposal? What's more, what if it was something you could do for yourself anytime you needed to? All you had to do was open your mind to the possibility and discover for yourself. Would you choose to do it?

Surprisingly, most people would *not*. Most adults would wait until an authority figure or official organization told them it was okay. That's contrary to what we did as kids. As children we were naturally inquisitive about everything. We didn't make assumptions. We were constantly exploring the world to discover things for ourselves. Explorers and pioneers are the champions of new ideas and possibilities.

For most adults, it's different. They stopped being curious long ago. Now, limiting beliefs about what's possible or impossible get in their way. More importantly, a method as simple and unusual as EFT challenges a lot of people's beliefs, especially in the areas of health and psychology.

Did you know that only about 16 percent of people are innovators or early adopters willing to try something new… even wondrous things life EFT? This means that eight out of ten people resist change or anything new. Look how many years it took yoga and acupuncture to be culturally accepted.

As the reader of this book, you're one of the people open to new ideas. Instead of waiting to hear about it from others, you want to be first to find out about it. These are characteristics for innovators and early adopters. Do some of these descriptions sound like you?

- You enjoy playing, trying new things and discovering for yourself.
- You like to be first.
- You seek breakthrough benefits.
- You're intrigued by advances.
- You like to *push the edge*.
- You're open to new ideas and find it easy to imagine, understand and appreciate the benefits.
- You believe that you're in charge of your life.
- You rely on your own intuition and vision in making decisions.
- You're not willing to wait for years for ideas to be accepted by others.
- You form your own beliefs by experiences.
- You're straightforward and outspoken about what you think.
- You find change can be exciting.

Welcome, you're about to learn a breakthrough self-help system for getting rapid physical and emotional relief. Based on centuries old meridian points, EFT is a method in the area of energy psychology and energy medicine. Get ready to explore and discover the possibilities.

Be prepared to learn one of the most exciting ways you can empower yourself. Not only will you have the ability to create physical and emotional freedom, you'll open the doors to *creating* more of what you desire in life. The best part is that EFT is a powerful system available right at your fingertips to use anyplace and anytime.

There are two important Websites that you'll want to refer to. The first one is by the founder of EFT, Gary Craig. His Website is the preeminent source for information and case stories on EFT. It's located at www.emofree.com.

The second Website is one that we've set up especially for readers of *Freedom At Your Fingertips*. It provides learning tools and valuable information for you. Go to www.fayf.com. Enjoy learning EFT as it opens doors for self-development and a pathway for physical and emotional freedom.

THE BASICS OF EFT
A breakthrough system for rapid physical and emotional relief

By Ron Ball

> *"Never before in history has innovation offered promise of so much to so many in so short a time."*
>
> *Bill Gates*

WHAT IS EFT?

EFT stands for Emotional Freedom Techniques™. The premise of EFT is that, unlike Western medicine's focus on our bodies as a chemical system, our bodies also have an energy system. The cause of all negative emotions is a disruption or blockage in that energy system. These blocks include fears, phobias, anger, grief, anxiety, depression, trauma, worry, guilt and other restricting emotions that also contribute to physical problems. When you clear the disruption or blockage using EFT, you have physical and emotional freedom.

HOW WAS EFT DEVELOPED?

One day, Dr. Roger Callahan, a prominent psychologist, was treating a female patient for a water phobia. She had had this fear all her life. After a year and a half, Dr. Callahan wasn't making much headway. He decided to try some new ideas he had been studying. He had his patient tap under her eyes — an energy meridian point for the stomach. When she did this, he was astonished to find her fear of water completely gone in less than two minutes. Her water phobia went away and never returned.

Gary Craig, a Stanford University graduate and engineer with a lifelong passion for studying self-development techniques, was a student of Dr. Callahan's. Craig developed the concept of EFT, a simpler algorithm.

He surmised that instead of diagnosing an issue and "prescribing" a specific energy meridian point to tap, do a "complete overhaul" by doing a round of tapping on the body's major energy meridian points. That way, a diagnosis wasn't needed.

Using an automobile for an analogy, instead of requiring a computer or other instruments to diagnose the trouble with the car engine, do a quick, complete *overhaul*. Doing a round of EFT only takes minutes. A complete *tune-up* works wonders to balance your body's energy. You can find more information on the history and background of EFT by visiting www.emofree.com.

What is the body's energy system?

Our bodies are electrical in nature. Your body constantly gets electrochemical messages to keep it informed about what's going on. Doctors use instruments to record electrical activities in your body. There's the electroencephalograph (EEG) to check the electrical activity of the brain. The electrocardiograph (EKG) records the electrical activity of the heart.

Several thousand years ago, the Chinese discovered a complex system of energy circuits, called energy meridians, running throughout the body. Meridians are the centerpiece of Eastern medicine and health practices. Recently, Western medicine has started to pay attention to energy flows and their effect on mental and physical health. EFT uses these energy meridians to clear energy blockages in your body, contributing to physical and emotional relief.

Isn't EFT illogical?

It certainly doesn't fit into what many people think is possible. When you first bring up the idea of tapping on energy meridians to clear physical and emotional issues, it's foreign to most people. It takes awhile for the idea to *sink in*. They simply don't have any frame of reference. They may have never heard of energy meridians, even though the system has been around in Chinese medicine for eons.

At first, EFT may seem weird to you. You may even think it looks and sounds ridiculous or silly. Once you try it and get results, you'll not only feel more comfortable about EFT, you'll be enthusiastic about it. Of course, if you're self-conscious, you can always use EFT. For example, you can try one of these setup phrases:

> *Even though EFT seems [ridiculous, silly or whatever description you choose], I deeply and completely accept myself anyway.*
>
> *Even though I'm self-conscious about doing EFT and tapping, I deeply and completely accept myself.*
>
> *Even though my friends and family might think I'm strange for tapping, I choose to do EFT anyway, and I deeply and completely accept myself.*

The other thing that people have trouble with is the part of the setup phrase where you say, "… I deeply and completely accept myself, " or "… I deeply and completely *love and accept myself*." That makes a lot of people uncomfortable. They don't like or accept who they are. The whole idea is quite simple. You are who you are right now in this moment. Instead of any disliking or resistance, accept who you are. This is the key to opening yourself to change.

The best thing to do is get rid of any thinking about whether or not EFT works. Just do it and discover for yourself. Then it won't matter to you whether it's illogical or not. Perhaps we need less reverence for logic and more for intuition.

WHAT IF I'M SKEPTICAL ABOUT EFT?

It's fine to be skeptical, especially with something as new and unusual as EFT. If you try EFT, you may be surprised to find that it works despite your being skeptical. Be skeptical, but allow room to keep a sense of openness and wonder too.

Is EFT something anyone can learn to do?

Yes, EFT is a great do-it-yourself tool. That's one of the key reasons we published this book. EFT is a leading-edge personal tool you can use to erase limiting emotions, beliefs and conditioning to realize more of what you want in life. Early on, many of the people who embraced EFT were psychologists and health-care professionals seeking the most effective new methods. Now, we want to make EFT known to the general public. You'll find that EFT is an incredibly versatile tool for self-development and peak performance. We recommend that you try EFT on everything.

What is the Apex problem?

The Apex problem is the tendency most people have to attribute change to their *current belief system* rather than to EFT, even though EFT was most likely responsible for the change. Most people in our culture know little, if anything, about Chinese medicine, acupuncture, acupressure, or energy meridians. These practices are foreign to their beliefs, so they don't accept that these alternative therapies work. The same is true of EFT.

When a person gets results with EFT, instead of accepting that EFT helped create a positive change, they explain, give credit to or attribute the changes produced by EFT to something else within their current belief system. Quite often people will say they got distracted or relaxed and that's why it worked instead of giving credit to EFT.

Is EFT part of energy medicine or energy psychology?

Yes, because you can use EFT to relieve physical and emotional issues. EFT is a body technique. It works with your body's energy to clear blocks or negative emotions. Energy medicine is based upon the belief that changes in the life force of the body, including the electric, magnetic and electromagnetic fields, affect human health and can promote healing. Energy psychology or therapy works as a catalyst with the body's physical energies to affect desired changes in emotions, thoughts and behaviors.

 ## WHAT'S THE BEST WAY TO LEARN **EFT?**

This book, *Freedom at Your Fingertips* is a great start. It's meant to give you a primer on EFT, convey benefits, describe the myriad of ways to use EFT and introduce you to some of the leading EFT experts. Also, several of the co-authors offer products and services to learn EFT. In our opinion, there isn't any book by itself that's going to effectively teach you how to do EFT.

You need to see, feel and hear examples of experts doing EFT. The best way to learn EFT is to get a set of videos from Gary Craig at his Website www.emofree.com. The videos are inexpensive and are loaded with examples of EFT in action.

Also, to complement what's in this book, we've also provided some special learning tools and valuable information for you at www.fayf. com. This Website has been especially set up for you and readers of *Freedom at Your Fingertips*.

 ## BRIEFLY, HOW DO YOU DO **EFT?**

EFT is like acupuncture. However, instead of using needles on specific energy meridian points, you use your fingers to tap on them. Plus, you do two other things concurrent with tapping. You concentrate on the issue that bothers you while you say a short phrase describing the issue. By doing this technique, you help erase, diminish or neutralize whatever physical or emotional issue you have. Usually, you get rapid relief.

What are the EFT tapping points?

The best way to learn the EFT points is to have someone show them to you. The next best thing is to look at the tapping diagram that follows to get a visual fix on each point. Next to each point is its abbreviation and a description of where the point is located. To facilitate learning, it's best to go in the sequence indicated.

Summary of EFT points:

EB = Beginning of the Eyebrow
SE = Side of the Eye
UE = Under the Eye
UN = Under the Nose
Ch = Chin
CB = Beginning of the Collarbone
BN = Below the Nipple (Also known as Under Breast point)
UA = Under the Arm

Th = Thumb
IF = Index Finger
MF = Middle Finger
BF = Baby Finger
KC = Karate Chop
G = Gamut Point

As a reminder, the tapping points go down the body. Each tapping point is below the next one. Although it may seem complicated at first, once you learn the points, you'll be surprised how fast you can tap through them.

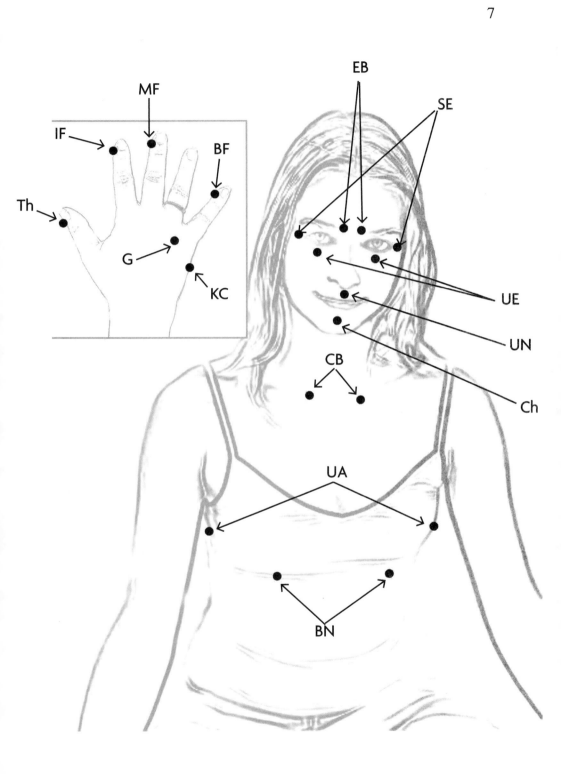

What are the steps to doing the **EFT Shortcut method?**

There's the longer, classic way of doing EFT and the Shortcut method. In this book, we'll focus on the Shortcut method because most of the time you'll get effective results using this technique. We'll also explain the other steps to doing the classic, longer EFT *recipe*.

In summary, here are the methods to doing the Shortcut method:

1. **Pick an issue.** Think of a specific thing that you would like to change using EFT. It's important to be as specific as you can.

2. **Assess intensity.** On a SUDS (Subjective Units of Distress Scale) of zero to 10, with zero being no emotional intensity and 10 being very intense, pick a number that best represents how you feel about the issue. (It's okay to guess.) Write your number down so you can measure any changes.

3. **Create a Reminder Phrase.** This is just a short description of the problem.

4. **Do the setup.** While continuously tapping the bottom of your hand (KC is the Karate Chop point) and concentrating on the issue, repeat your setup affirmation phrase aloud three times: *"Even though I have this [whatever the issue is], I deeply and completely accept myself."*

5. **Tap the sequence.** While repeating your Reminder Phrase, tap 7-10 times each on the EFT points indicated below:

    EB, SE, UE, UN, Ch, CB, UA

6. **Stop and reassess intensity.** On scale of zero to 10, is it less than the number you wrote down? If not, you may need to get more specific. If it's better, yet not at zero, repeat the steps

using a modified phrase for the setup: *"Even though I still have some remaining [whatever the issue is], I deeply and completely accept myself."* Use the reminder phrase, "remaining [whatever the issue is]."

7. **Keep tapping.** Repeat the EFT tapping procedure with subsequent rounds until you get to zero or a level that is comfortable for you.

8. **Test.** Check periodically to find if the change holds.

HOW DO YOU DO THE CLASSIC OR LONG VERSION?

If you were going to do the longer, classic method of EFT, you'd also add tapping on the finger points and a procedure called *The Nine Gamut.* Once again, most EFT practitioners now use the Shortcut method, but it's also valuable to know how to do the longer technique.

Here are the steps to the classic method:

1. **Pick an issue.** Think of a specific thing that you would like to change using EFT. It's important to be as specific as you can.

2. **Assess intensity.** On a SUDS (Subjective Units of Distress Scale) of zero to 10, with zero being no emotional intensity and 10 being very intense, pick a number that best represents how you feel about the issue. (It's okay to guess.)

3. **Create a Reminder Phrase.** This is just a short description of the problem.

4. **Do the setup.** While continuously tapping the bottom of your hand (KC is the Karate Chop point) and concentrating on the issue, repeat your setup affirmation phrase aloud three times: *"Even though I have this [whatever the issue is], I deeply and completely accept myself."*

5. **Tap the sequence.** While repeating your Reminder Phrase, tap 7-10 times each on the EFT points indicated including the finger points.

    EB, SE, UE, UN, Ch, CB, UA, Th, IF, MF, BF, KC

6. **Do the Nine Gamut.** Continuously tap on the Gamut point on your hand while doing each of these actions.

    a. *Continuously* tap on the Gamut point in a steady rhythm while doing the following in sequence.
    b. Close your eyes.
    c. Open your eyes.
    d. Quickly look down to the right toward the floor *while holding your head steady.*
    e. Do the opposite and quickly look down to the left toward the floor.
    f. Roll your eyes clockwise in a circle like your nose was in the center of a clock and you were trying to see all the numbers in order.
    g. Now roll your eyes counterclockwise in the same manner.
    h. Hum a few seconds of your favorite song.
    i. Count rapidly from one to five.
    j. Hum a few seconds of your favorite song again.
    k. Take a deep breath and notice how you feel.
    l. Repeat if necessary.

7. **Tap the sequence again (step 5).**

8. **Stop and reassess intensity.** On scale of zero to 10, is it less? If not, you may need to get more specific. If it's better, yet not at zero, repeat the steps using a modified phrase for the setup: *"Even though I still have some remaining [whatever the issue is], I deeply and completely accept myself."* Use the reminder phrase, *"remaining [whatever the issue is]."*

9. Keep tapping. Repeat the EFT tapping procedure with subsequent rounds until you get to zero or a level that is comfortable for you.

10. Test. Check periodically to find if the change holds.

WHEN DO YOU RECOMMEND DOING THE LONG VERSION OF EFT?

Most of the time, you'll get effective results using the Shortcut version of EFT. In fact, you won't see the longer version used much. If you're not making progress, perhaps you need to get more specific or do more rounds of EFT. If you still feel like you're not getting a change or shift, do the long version. Although rolling your eyes, counting and humming may seem a bit strange, the process is designed to engage both hemispheres of your brain to create changes. You can find more information on how and why the longer version works at www. emofree.

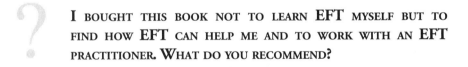

I BOUGHT THIS BOOK NOT TO LEARN EFT MYSELF BUT TO FIND HOW EFT CAN HELP ME AND TO WORK WITH AN EFT PRACTITIONER. WHAT DO YOU RECOMMEND?

All of the co-authors of this book are recognized EFT experts, usually in specialized areas. If there is an issue in which you need assistance, contact one of them. At the end of their chapters, you'll find contact information. More details about the co-authors are in the biography section at the back of the book. In many cases, the co-authors also offer books, audio/video products and other services. You can also find additional EFT practitioners at www.emofree.com.

WHY DO SOME EFT PRACTITIONERS USE DIFFERENT TAPPING POINTS?

Some EFT practitioners use different points because they've discovered what works best for them in producing results. They all use the basic

EFT points and may include others. For example, in the *EFT Manual*, Gary Craig has included the Below the Nipple (BN) point to be complete in describing the EFT points. Some people use this point. Most people don't.

There are 361 traditional Chinese acupressure points in the body. EFT uses major meridian points. One of the meridian points that you will see a lot of people use is the Top of the Head or Crown point. EFT practitioners may also use wrist and ankle points.

There's no need to get confused by all of this. Learn the EFT points as described in this book and the *EFT Manual*. As you become more proficient in EFT, you can made adaptations.

CAN I TAP ON POINTS ON EITHER SIDE OF MY FACE OR BODY?

Yes. As we said, EFT offers a lot of flexibility. Not only can you tap on either side, you can tap on two sides at once. For example, you can tap on the left and right eyebrow points simultaneously. Find out what feels best to you.

HOW SHOULD I TAP?

Tap with one to three fingers, 7-10 times on each of the points in a way that's most comfortable to you. You'll want to feel solid tapping, yet not overdo it. You don't want to feel any discomfort.

WHY DO SOME PRACTITIONERS DO EFT DIFFERENTLY? SOME OF THEM SAY ALTERNATE PHRASES AT EACH POINT.

Some practitioners do EFT differently because EFT is as much an art as a science. Following their intuition, and their successes with EFT, they discover what works best for them in producing results. Yes, there is a classic way to do EFT that is covered in this book. We recommend that you learn EFT this way. Think of learning EFT like learning to play a piece of music. There is a certain way to play the music according to the notes written, but musicians will each play the song somewhat differently because of their own feelings and styles of playing.

How long does the change last?

EFT results are usually permanent. When some problems reappear, it's often the result of different aspects of the problem showing up. The solution is to tap on these aspects. Other times, the cause may be energy toxins that are electromagnetic, chemical, food-related or other toxins that disrupt the body's energy system.

What if I'm doing EFT the *wrong* way?

One of the great things about EFT is that it's very *forgiving*. As you learn the different EFT tapping points and how to do EFT, enjoy the process. Have fun. Instead of getting uptight about doing EFT properly, relax about it. While you're learning, don't get hung up on doing it perfectly. You'll just get in the way. Like learning anything else, the more you do EFT and refine your skills, the better you'll get at it.

What if I believe EFT won't work for me?

EFT is so different, some people get judgmental about it and don't even try EFT. It's okay to be skeptical, especially about something new and unfamiliar. Just don't let that get in your way. Don't let your skepticism prevent you from doing EFT to *discover for yourself* whether it works or not. You may just be surprised because EFT works even if you think it won't.

Sometimes you may get dramatic results. At other times, doing EFT can be more subtle. You may not even notice any changes right away. Be persistent. Remember the quote about patience and persistence from

Jacob Riis. "When nothing seems to help, I go and look at a stonecutter hammering away at his rock perhaps a hundred times without as much as a crack showing in it. Yet at the hundred and first blow, it will split in two, and I know it was not that blow that did it, but all that had gone before."

Lastly, you could always tap about EFT not working:

> *Even if I think EFT won't work, I deeply and completely accept myself anyway.*

Why do you do the setup phrase?

You say the setup phrase to ensure that your energy flow is *set up* and properly oriented. By saying the setup phrase and tapping on the Karate Chop point, you take care of any Psychological Reversals or self-sabotage that may be present.

What are *aspects*?

This happens quite often in EFT. While you're tapping on clearing a specific issue, another aspect comes up. It could be part of the original issue or a completely different one. You'll need to tap on all of the aspects and tap on them as separate issues.

Do I need to *say* the EFT statement or can I just *think* it?

We recommend that you say it aloud. In fact, you may find that you get better results by being emphatic when you say it. Say it with volume in your voice. Really put your body and emotions into saying the setup statement.

Of course, if you're sitting in a seat on an airplane, instead you'll want to think it. Mentally do EFT. Do the whole process by saying the setup statement in your mind and by imagining tapping on the different points. Mental EFT can be quite effective. Find out more about it at www.emofree.com.

WHY DON'T MORE PEOPLE KNOW ABOUT EFT?

New ideas, discoveries and inventions don't take the world by storm. They bump their way in. People's beliefs about what's possible get in the way. Only about 16 percent of people are innovators or early adopters willing to try something new.

The pioneers and explorers are the champions of new ideas. The people who embrace something like EFT are innovators or early adopters, not the majority. So it's unrealistic to expect the masses to understand or try EFT yet. As with anything else, some people want to be first. Others want to wait and see.

As we said, a method as simple and unusual as EFT challenges a lot of people's beliefs about what's possible, especially in the areas of health and psychology. Even though other cultures in the world have been working with energy meridians and similar techniques for centuries, the idea of tapping on acupressure points can seem illogical or absurd at first. Even a breakthrough like EFT will take time to be accepted and hit the mainstream.

All we really want people to do is try EFT and discover the benefits for themselves. It's simple. It's safe. It's easy for anyone to learn. Quite often, the results are surprising and wondrous beyond *beliefs*.

WHAT IS PSYCHOLOGICAL REVERSAL?

Psychological Reversal is one of the most important things to understand in EFT. Basically, it means that the body's electricity or energy is reversed. It's going in the wrong direction. It's like having your batteries in backwards with the wrong polarities. Psychological Reversal (PR) is caused by negative thinking that often happens subconsciously outside of your awareness.

The result of PR is self-sabotage or subconscious resistance. Part of you wants to do something and part of you doesn't. The way to correct PR is by tapping on the Karate Chop point.

WHAT'S THE DIFFERENCE BETWEEN THE SORE SPOT AND THE KARATE CHOP POINT?

Basically, they both serve the same function — to eliminate Psychological Reversals or self sabotage. You can use either one. With the Sore Spot, you apply pressure and rub. To teach EFT to people, it's easier to use the Karate Chop point because it's a tapping point. It keeps things simple.

IS EFT SAFE?

Yes. EFT has no known negative side effects.

IS IT A GOOD IDEA FOR ME TO TEACH OTHER PEOPLE TO USE EFT?

One of the nice things about EFT is that you can learn the basics of how to do it in a short period of time. When people get quick, positive results with EFT, they get enthusiastic and want to run out and teach other people how to do it. This is a mistake. Mastering EFT takes years and it's an ongoing process.

Until you become proficient with EFT, we don't recommend you teach other people. Most likely, you'll run into a situation where you won't get the results you expect. You'll be disappointed and so will the other person. In the beginning, use EFT as a self-help tool and study EFT with the video sets from www.emofree.com. If you find someone really interested in EFT, give them a copy of this book so they can learn more about EFT for themselves.

WHY IS THE **EFT** AFFIRMATION NEGATIVE INSTEAD OF POSITIVE?

Typically, we're taught to say affirmations in the positive. EFT is focused on addressing and erasing the negative. Unless you eliminate the energy disruption, positive affirmations won't be very effective. By stating the negative and tuning into the issue, you're acknowledging the problem. *And even though there is this problem, I'm okay.* I deeply and completely accept myself… problem and all. The phrasing is integrative. Instead of dividing or conflicting, it unites. Once you erase a negative with EFT, you're ready to *tap in* a positive affirmation.

WHAT IS THE CHOICES METHOD?

The *Choices* method was developed by Dr. Patricia Carrington. In short, instead of using the classic setup phrase of *"Even though I have this [whatever the issue is], I deeply and completely accept myself,"* you make a choice instead. For example, your setup phrase might be, *"Even though I have this [whatever the issue is], I choose to feel surprisingly calm and at peace about it."*

After you learn the basics of EFT, you'll want to learn the Choices method. To find out more, go to www.emofree and search for "Dr. Carrington" or "choices." Also check Dr. Carrington's Website at www.eftupdate.com.

I'VE LEARNED **EFT.** WHY DON'T I REMEMBER TO DO IT WHEN I HAVE A PROBLEM?

Like learning anything new, it takes time to develop doing EFT into a positive habit. It's like working out or exercising. Start doing it incrementally. Do it daily. Over time, it will become a habit and you will almost automatically want to do it each day. If not, there may be some block or resistance. Use EFT to uncover it. Here are some examples:

> *Even though I don't want to do EFT, I deeply and completely accept myself.*
>
> *Even though I forget to do EFT, I deeply and completely accept myself.*
>
> *Even though I'm not motivated to do EFT, I deeply and completely accept myself.*

Through practice and results, you'll discover EFT to be one of the most important tools for your health and well being. The chapters that follow are written by some of the most talented and experienced EFT practitioners in the world. They offer you specific ways that you can use EFT to erase limiting barriers, paving the way for you to install empowering beliefs and emotions that propel you to create more of what you want in life. Welcome to the wonder of Emotional Freedom Techniques. They're right there are your fingertips, anyplace and anytime you need them.

To contact Ron Ball, his e-mail address is reb@eftblog.com. Visit Ron's Websites at www.eftzone.com, www.eustress.net, and www.stress-sucks.com. Also, please see Ron Ball's biography at the back of the book.

ABUNDANCE & PROSPERITY
Changing beliefs and feelings to attract what you want in life

By Carol Look

> *"Life begets life. Energy becomes energy. It is by spending oneself that one becomes rich."*
>
> *Sarah Bernhardt*

HOW WOULD YOU DEFINE ABUNDANCE? IS IT ONLY ABOUT MONEY?

For me, *abundance* is an attitude, a state of consciousness that, when turned on, brings into your life the money, relationships or joy and health you are seeking. Technically, the word abundance means plenty, overflowing, more than enough. Some people are looking for an abundance of money, while others are looking for an abundance of friendships. So, no, it is not just about money. The word can be used to apply to health, love, relationships, happiness etc.

The way I look at it, abundance is actually a *feeling* about prosperity and a trust that there is enough to go around for everyone. Once you have this feeling (regardless of what is in your bank account), you can relax and magnetize or attract what you want into your life. This is one of the confusions out there — that abundance is all or only about money. It should actually be all about the attitude and feeling. Without a feeling of abundance, you will not be able to attract any abundance of health, love or opportunities into your life. EFT, since it can change feelings and attitudes, has been incredibly helpful in bringing people an abundance of what they want.

For instance, I had a client who was convinced that there were "no men" in New York. That attitude of scarcity is what kept her from dating men, not any fact that there weren't enough men in New York! Another client was convinced that she would always be sick because she had a weak immune system. This was an attitude of scarcity, not a fact of reality.

I HAVE READ MANY BOOKS ON THE SUBJECT OF MANIFESTING, AND I AM TRYING VERY HARD TO ATTRACT ABUNDANCE INTO MY LIFE. I DON'T UNDERSTAND WHY IT'S NOT WORKING AND I'M NOT ATTRACTING THE ABUNDANCE *I SAY THAT I WANT*. IN YOUR OPINION, WHAT AM I DOING WRONG?

Here's how I would put it. It's not that you are doing anything wrong. You just aren't doing enough that is right to *allow* abundance into your life. If you aren't attracting the abundance of money or friendships or opportunities that you say you want, it is evidence you have some *limiting beliefs,* or that you do not have what we call *"Prosperity Consciousness."*

For instance, many people assume they are thinking about money when they are focused on the bills they need to pay. They may think they are focusing on money, but instead their focus is actually on the *lack of money.* This is what usually goes wrong for people. They read all the manifestation books but fail to get the subtle difference between worrying about money and thinking about abundance.

Hoping for more money means you don't expect it to come. Wishing for money to drop into your lap means you aren't in harmony to attracting it on an emotional level. But expecting money to show up when you need it means you have turned the corner attitudinally. You will soon be able to enjoy little surprises in your life and things will go the right direction financially. So if you are not manifesting the abundance in your life that you say you want, it means that your *vibration* (your thoughts, feelings and focus) is somehow not on what you supposedly want but on what you have been worried about or what you lack. You will definitely be able to shift this focus with EFT.

This is a personal story about me, the author of this chapter, Carol Look. I was a successful therapist in New York City, with a solid referral base for individual clients. I taught classes, sold books, and worked full time. However, two years in a row I earned the exact same amount of money running my private practice. This is nearly impossible when you take into account all of the factors of a private therapy practice: vacation time, new clients calling for appointments, old clients leaving therapy, illnesses, holidays falling on different days, etc.

What it revealed to me is that I had a previously undetected comfort zone around my salary. I used EFT on my fears of earning more money, my discomfort with other people's reactions, the conflicts around being so successful, and looking forward to the freedom earning more money could bring me. Since then, I have nearly quadrupled my salary in a few short years.

QUESTION: WHAT IS PROSPERITY CONSCIOUSNESS AND WHAT DOES IT HAVE TO DO WITH ATTRACTING ABUNDANCE?

Having *Prosperity Consciousness* means that you believe in abundance, and that, as I said previously, you trust the universe will provide for you. You know there is enough to go around. It means that you don't feel a sense of lack anywhere in your life or in the world. Wherever your consciousness is vibrating is what you will attract into your life. So as long as you believe in lack (the opposite of prosperity), you will continue to attract lack into your life.

In order to shift from a lack consciousness to prosperity consciousness, EFT is the best tool I have ever found. Once your consciousness is pointing in the right direction, you will get what you have been asking for. If you have *limiting beliefs* about your ability to attract financial resources into your life, your beliefs will reflect this back in your reality and circumstances.

You might want to ask yourself about your consciousness and level of awareness about abundance. Do you honestly believe that there is enough for everyone? Do you have some sneaking suspicions that you are the type of person who never gets what you want? Are you afraid there won't be anything left for you after everyone else takes their share?

If you answered *yes* to any of these questions, it will tell you where your consciousness is about prosperity, mainly, that your consciousness or mentality is more about lack and is getting in your way. Remember not to blame yourself for this. You have learned a lot from parents, coaches, society etc., about how to think about money and abundance. The good news is that you can uncover what's in the way very quickly and efficiently and painlessly neutralize it with EFT.

 ### What is a limiting belief?

A limiting belief is a thought, belief or conviction you have about how the world works, about what's right, or about how your life is going to work out, based on previous life experiences that you claim are true. These life experiences may indeed have happened, but if you draw entire life conclusions from them, they will get in your way. Take any belief you have, and you will be able to discover its limitations. For instance, do you believe you can double your salary in one year? If the answer is "no," then no matter how practical or legitimate your list of reasons may be, it is still a limiting belief for you.

Do you believe you could land a new job in the next few months that would be a perfect fit for you? If the answer is "no," then you have uncovered another limiting belief. A client of mine was convinced she couldn't find a new job when unemployed, so she stayed miserable in an old job. While everyone has heard this bit of advice, and it may seem realistic, it is still a limiting belief. If you run your life by it, it will be true for you.

HOW DO I FIND OUT IF I HAVE LIMITING BELIEFS? DOES EVERYONE HAVE THEM?

Yes, everyone has unique limiting beliefs about every area of their life. We inherited or absorbed some of these beliefs directly from our parents, some we learned from coaches, teachers and society, and some were our own confused conclusions based on early relationships. To find out specific limiting beliefs that you can use EFT for, I recommend filling in the following statements:

1. I can't be wealthy because _____.
2. I shouldn't make more money because _____.
3. I don't really want to make more money because _____.
4. I don't believe I can make more money because _____, _____, and _____.
5. I'm afraid to earn more money because _____.

The answers to these simple statements will highlight particular beliefs you have that are impeding your progress in the area of financial abundance or relationships, health, etc. I recommend you answer these questions as honestly as possible, even if you feel uncomfortable with what you uncover. Remember, the sooner you uncover the blocks and limiting beliefs, the sooner you will be able to eliminate them and move forward in manifesting abundance into your life.

WOULD YOU PLEASE GIVE ME SOME GOOD EXAMPLES OF TYPICAL LIMITING BELIEFS TO ATTRACTING WEALTH AND ABUNDANCE?

Some simple but common examples are as follows:

- I don't believe I deserve abundance.
- No one in my family deserves abundance.
- I'm not worthy of abundance.
- I'm afraid of changes that might happen if I become wealthy.
- The economy has to be booming for me to make a lot of money.

24

- No one in my profession can become wealthy.

These statements aren't factual. They are just powered by beliefs or past experiences. For instance, let's say you believe the economy has to be booming in order for you to be wealthy. Millions of people believe this, but it is not factually true. Many people in a variety of businesses make incredible fortunes when the economy is down. It's not about the economy. It's about your attitude, your beliefs, your confidence and what you can attract to yourself when you clean up these limiting beliefs and vibrations.

I'VE BEEN MAKING ABOUT $50,000 EVERY YEAR FOR A LONG TIME. I DEFINITELY WANT AND NEED TO MAKE MORE, AND I BELIEVE I SHOULD BE MAKING MORE, SO WHAT IS IN THE WAY?

It looks like you have a *comfort zone* above which you are unwilling to climb. This means you feel good or normal within a certain range of annual income, or success, and once you are outside of it, you feel anxiety in your mind or body. You will try consciously and unconsciously to correct the balance again so that you land back in your comfort zone. A great exercise to do before using EFT to clear this problem is to picture yourself making $60,000, a 20 percent increase over your standard income. Then ask yourself how you feel.

Is there any anxiety associated with your making this leap? If so, you can use EFT to reduce the anxiety and clear the path. If there is no negative feeling associated with this increase, then move to the next level. Now picture and feel yourself earning $75,000 a year. How much anxiety or "yes, but" excuses do you feel in your body and mind? This is a very practical way for people to find out the parameters of their comfort zones and make a plan to move through them with EFT.

HOW DO I KNOW, OR HOW DO YOU KNOW, IF I HAVE A *COMFORT ZONE?* MAYBE SOMETHING ELSE IS WRONG. MAYBE I DON'T HAVE ENOUGH CREDENTIALS TO MAKE MORE MONEY IN MY FIELD.

The evidence of a comfort zone is what you have told me about your financial life. You stated that you earned $50,000 last year and for several

Consider John, a competent therapist, plugging away at a clinic feeling bored and uninspired, and tired of just making ends meet. He used EFT for every possible downside to becoming wealthier and every possible excuse for why he might be holding himself back in a comfort zone. What he discovered was that he didn't feel deserving of attracting more clients or earning more money.

His family had been quite poor and he felt guilty for rising above them on a financial level. He was happily married with a healthy son and lived in a modest home. Why should he get any more? He used EFT consistently on setup phrases about deserving abundance. As a result, he has changed his entire clinic and client base. Frustrated that he has so little time for himself and family, he's learning to use EFT to balance out his work and personal life.

years despite fluctuations in your field, changing economic conditions, or changes in personnel in your company. This would indicate that you seem to need psychologically to stay in your particular comfort zone of $50,000. It is likely that you stay there because there is some discomfort associated with moving beyond it.

Let's say you believe you don't have the right or enough credentials to move forward and earn more. Then we are back to uncovering a limiting belief, which would sound like "I can't make more money because I don't have the right credentials." This is a belief, and it helps keep you where you are, but it's not necessarily true. Some of the most successful people in the world and some of the wealthiest entrepreneurs do not have the right credentials, and it hasn't made a bit of difference.

HOW DO I KNOW WHICH EMOTIONS ARE GETTING IN MY WAY? ISN'T IT NORMAL TO BE ANXIOUS ABOUT MONEY AND PAYING THE BILLS?

Usually the emotion of *fear* blocks our ability to attract more of what we want into our lives. For some, anger at wealthy people gets in the way. For others, guilt about seeing themselves as lucky or privileged can cause them to sabotage or not feel deserving of abundance. Even if you think it is normal to be anxious about money, is that how you want to feel about money? It is typical for people to worry about money, but that doesn't mean it is normal! Anxiety has never helped anyone attract more money into a bank account, so I recommend you use EFT to neutralize the anxiety on every angle of your financial situation.

I THINK I UNDERSTAND WHAT A *COMFORT ZONE* IS, AND THAT I PROBABLY HAVE A FEW *LIMITING BELIEFS* FROM MY FAMILY ABOUT MONEY. HOWEVER, I STILL DON'T UNDERSTAND WHY I AM SO STUCK WHEN I KNOW I WANT TO MOVE FORWARD. HOW DO I STOP THIS NEGATIVE CYCLE?

Ask yourself the following questions: "What is the *downside* of attracting abundance and what might be potential *upsides* for staying in this comfort zone?" This will help uncover why you are stuck and why you keep sabotaging yourself. For instance, suppose you are afraid of someone else being jealous of your success. Then that would be a good reason to stay stuck. Let's say you are afraid of making more than your father made in his day. That would be a good reason for you to blame the economy for making the same amount of money year after year.

IS BEING STUCK THE SAME THING AS SELF SABOTAGE?

Well, being stuck can be a form of self sabotage, but sabotage behavior usually is more blatant. For instance, being late, not closing the deal, procrastinating, failing a test even though you know the material — those are all clear examples of outright sabotage. Being stuck means you aren't growing beyond your current level and keep recreating the exact same situations (or earning the exact same salary) again and again.

If you feel stuck, it is a great target for EFT treatment. Technically, when you are stuck, you aren't standing still. You just keep re-creating the same situation. The good news is, as long as you have been in motion — which you have if you are stuck — you can change your life. Being stuck means you are doing the same things over and over again because of your beliefs, your feelings and your behavior. EFT can change all three of these.

AND YOU THINK EFT CAN BE USED TO BREAK THROUGH THESE *COMFORT ZONES* **AND** *LIMITING BELIEFS?*

I know so. I have used EFT on myself and hundreds of clients for abundance issues, and I have plenty of evidence that tells me and my clients that EFT works. I have not come across any other technique or tool that can so quickly and deeply eliminate the resistance to becoming more successful in any part of your life. There is a reason people continuously read more self help books on abundance. They aren't getting the answers from the first dozen they have read! You need a tool to release the resistance, and in my opinion, after seeing so many clients and myself change dramatically as a result of using this incredible tool, EFT is the answer.

I ask my clients if they are tired of "muscling it" and if they are tired of trying so hard. When I tell them how easy EFT is for erasing limiting beliefs, they don't believe me at first. But all I have to do is help them through a few exercises, and they understand in their body and mind what I have been trying to tell them. Their energy shifts, their beliefs loosen and their attitudes become more open.

SO HOW DO YOU USE EFT AS AN EFFECTIVE TOOL TO ATTRACT ABUNDANCE?

EFT is the most effective method I have found in more than 15 years in the mental health field to eliminate comfort zones and break through limiting beliefs that are in the way of success and financial freedom. But first, I ask my clients to identify their limiting beliefs so we have something as a target for EFT. Once you have a focus for EFT, you can get started. I use EFT to eliminate comfort zones, erase limiting beliefs, expand prosperity consciousness and improve overall attitudes.

WHAT ARE SOME OF THE **EFT** SETUP PHRASES **I** MIGHT USE?

Remember that you need to personalize this treatment for you. First you need to identify some of the blocks that you have by answering some of the questions I gave you. Suppose you think that if you made more money, your friends or family members would be jealous of you. Then I would structure a setup phrase as follows:

Even though I'm afraid of their reactions to my success, I deeply and completely love and accept myself anyway.

Even though I don't want them to be jealous of me, I choose to feel comfortable making more money anyway.

Even though I know they will say something mean to me if I become wealthier, I accept who I am and how I feel.

Suppose you are afraid that, if you become wealthy, you won't have any time left for your family. This is another limiting belief. I would handle it this way:

Even though I worry about being successful because I won't have any time left, I choose to feel calm and peaceful.

Even though there's not enough time, I accept who I am and how my life is going now.

Even though I'm afraid of the changes that might happen in my life if I become wealthy, I deeply and completely love and accept myself anyway.

WHAT IF **I** HAVE CONCERNS ABOUT BEING ONE OF THOSE "NASTY" MILLIONAIRES WHO DOESN'T CARE ABOUT OTHERS? WHAT WOULD SOME TYPICAL SETUP PHRASES BE FOR ME?

Well, you have certainly identified a conflict about becoming wealthier. You might examine your beliefs about wealthy people to see what judgments come forward. Suppose you have never met a wealthy person who is nice or has integrity. Then, of course, you wouldn't want to become one of them. You could use EFT to neutralize this prejudice. For instance, you might use a setup phrase like one of these:

> *Even though I'm convinced that wealthy people are nasty, I deeply and completely love and accept who I am and who they are.*
>
> *Even though I'm afraid to become one of them, I deeply and completely love and accept who I am and who they are.*
>
> *Even though I don't want to be associated with wealthy people, I deeply and completely love and accept who I am and who they are.*

Remember, these are all your beliefs. For every person who doesn't like wealthy people, there are others who love them and have had nothing but positive experiences with them.

WHY DO SO MANY PEOPLE FEEL UNSAFE EARNING MORE MONEY?

Not feeling safe is one of the biggest blocks to attracting more abundance in your life. People worry about peer reactions, how friends and family members might act towards them, and basic envy, jealousy and judgment from strangers. Ask yourself if you have ever been the object of envy. It doesn't feel very good because people tend to act it out with hostility rather than being direct about it.

As a result, many people fear being the target of envy or jealousy. Sometimes they have had experiences of other people criticizing them for having more or for what they do with their money. Sometimes they just know people will be uncomfortable with their wealth.

If you can't get over this block, you will never earn more or reach the success in your life with friends and your health because this fear will keep you locked into a pattern and a comfort zone. People are afraid of

Ed was impatiently waiting for a business deal to close. He had been waiting for four months. He had little tolerance for more details and excuses about what was going wrong with the potential buyers. He could feel his anxiety around the money issues, irritation about not getting the money he was supposed to earn from the deals, frustration with the bills that were piling up, and the tension in general. While we were using EFT on his anxiety and anger about the fact that the deal hadn't gone through yet, he said his entire body felt different.

He reduced his anxiety and frustration in half in just two rounds of EFT. His attitude of frustration eased. He said he was able to handle this delay and felt completely different. Just then, while I was on the phone with him, his cell phone rang. It was his lawyer telling him that the deal had finally gone through. Coincidence you say? Ed didn't care. He knew that using EFT to reduce his anxiety about the money and frustration about the situation had allowed an energetic shift to take place.

standing out. If you are super rich, super famous, have tons of friends or are incredibly happy in your life, you tend to stand out in a crowd. These fears can all be neutralized with EFT.

DO YOU HAVE ANY FINAL SUGGESTIONS FOR WHAT MORE I COULD DO TO MAKE MORE MONEY?

Yes, stop trying to do more! Work on the internal beliefs and limited thinking that is getting in your way. If you don't clear these blocks with EFT, it doesn't matter what you do as far as action, you will continue to stay stuck. Be open to many possibilities. We all tend to get trapped by seeing only a few options for abundance. There are many, many channels through which the universe can bring you money, friendships, love and happiness. Be sure you are looking for them!

To contact Carol Look, her e-mail address is Carol@CarolLook.com and her telephone number is 212-477-8645. Visit Carol's Website at www.CarolLook.com. Also see Carol Look's biography at the back of the book.

ADDICTIONS
Integrating EFT into treatments for substance or behavior dependency

By Loretta Sparks

"Every form of addiction is bad, no matter whether the narcotic be alcohol or morphine or idealism."

Carl Jung

WHAT CAUSES AN ADDICTION?

At the root of all addictions is the desire to relieve or ease the pain or discomfort caused by negative emotions, particularly those emotions associated with anxiety. Addictions only temporarily mask or tranquilize problems and associated feelings. Whatever relief is experienced is fleeting.

WHAT IS THE PROBLEM WITH TEMPORARY RELIEF?

Since addictive substances or behaviors are not permanent solutions to one's negative emotions or anxiety, they must be repeated for continued relief. Soon the individual grows dependent on the substance or behavior and winds up in a self-destructive cycle, which negatively impacts on all aspects of their health and life.

WHAT IS THE DIFFERENCE BETWEEN A HABIT AND AN ADDICTION?

The terms are often used interchangeably. However, the more destructive the habit is to an individual's life, the more likely it will be referred to as an addiction.

WHAT KIND OF ADDICTIVE SUBSTANCES OR BEHAVIORS ARE THERE?

Some examples are overeating, drinking too much, abusing drugs (including over-the-counter drugs), smoking cigarettes, compulsive spending, gambling, compulsive lying, hair-pulling, self-injury, overuse of television and video games, sex addiction, etc. Even *people pleasing* and *rescuing others* can be compulsive behaviors.

WHAT KIND OF NEGATIVE EMOTIONS CAN ACTIVATE AN ADDICTION?

Any emotion that creates anxiety can activate an addiction. Anxiety is the major player. Anxiety exists on a scale ranging from concern on one end to a panic attack at the other. Some familiar terms we use for varying degrees of anxiety are: worry, nervousness, apprehension, strain, tension, jitters, butterflies (in the stomach) or uneasiness (usually about something with an uncertain outcome) and just plain fear.

When a sufficient degree of one or more negative emotion stresses the individual, it triggers cravings or urges, which in turn usually activate the addiction. Here's a setup and reminder phrase that may be used to deal with negative emotions:

> *Even though I have this negative emotion [specific emotion or feeling], I accept myself deeply and profoundly.*
> *Reminder phrase: Feeling [specific emotion or feeling]*

WHAT IF YOU ARE NOT AWARE OF ANY NEGATIVE EMOTIONS, BUT THERE ARE TIMES WHEN YOU JUST GET A CRAVING OR AN URGE?

It is not unusual for people who develop addictive patterns of coping to repress their feelings associated with anxiety and stress. Often their first clue that they are stressed or anxious is either a craving for an addictive substance or an urge to act out in some way, sometimes both. Anxious or stressed individuals who repress their feelings benefit from using EFT five or 10 times a day to relieve accumulated stress and anxiety. A setup and reminder phrase that may be used to deal with repressed stress or anxiety:

Even though I accumulate stress and anxiety outside of my awareness, I accept myself deeply and profoundly.
Reminder phrase: Stress and anxiety

How can EFT help with cravings and urges?

EFT is an extremely powerful tool in eliminating cravings and urges. It can be done very simply. Whether you have a craving for a substance or behavior, tailor the following to specifically address your craving or urge. Here's a setup and reminder phrase that may be used to deal with cravings and urges:

Even though I have this craving for [whatever it is] or urge to [whatever it is], I deeply and completely accept myself.
Reminder phrase: Craving for a cigarette or really wanting a cigarette

How can one stop repressing emotions?

Repression is a powerful defense mechanism not under our conscious control. However, there are negative behavioral clues that you are getting anxious or stressed. It would be extremely helpful to identify those behavioral clues and use EFT to balance the negative emotions associated with them.

The following are five groups of behavioral clues that indicate levels of stress. They are designed to help you identify your stress and anxiety through your feelings and behavior. Also, each clue can easily be used as a setup and reminder phrase, allowing you to treat it with EFT. The higher the group number, the greater the stress and anxiety.

Group one: barely managing

You are barely getting everything done. You need help, but you don't ask for it. You tell yourself to try harder and plan your time better. You start to let go of self-care activities. You have a hard time saying 'no,' and you are unaware stress is building. Here's an example of a setup and reminder phrase that may be used to deal with *barely managing*:

 Even though I am barely managing to get everything done, I accept myself deeply and profoundly.
Reminder phrase: Barely managing

Here's another:

 Even though I can't say no, I accept myself deeply and profoundly.
Reminder phase: Can't say no

Group two: zoning out

You start to space out by not being present in the situation at hand. You can't hear what is being said to you because of your own self-talk. You get lost in daydreams and find yourself driving on autopilot. You do not notice that stress is building in you, but other people are beginning to irritate you. A setup and reminder phrase that may be used to deal with zoning out is:

 Even though the stress is building and I am [zoning out or getting lost in daydreams], I accept myself deeply and profoundly.
Reminder phrase: Zoning out

Group three: defensive behavior

You notice others are not taking care of business. You get angry easily. You feel critical and judgmental a lot. You blame others and make excuses for yourself. You feel victimized and withdraw into silence. A setup and reminder phrase that may be used to deal with being defensive is:

After sustaining an injury in a car accident five years ago, Ben became addicted to his prescription pain medication. He had been drug-free for over a year when he started using again — this time for emotional not physical pain. After a month of using increasing amounts of pain medication on a daily basis, Ben knew he was hooked again. He made the decision to stop. While waiting to see the physician, who specialized in treating addictions, it became apparent that Ben was experiencing withdrawal symptoms. Unfortunately, his wait to see the doctor was an hour or more.

EFT was offered to him to reduce the pain and discomfort of his withdrawal while he waited. Initially he was not interested, but after waiting half-an-hour he changed his mind. In less than 15 minutes of using EFT, all signs of withdrawal were gone. First, EFT was focused on the physical symptoms of his withdrawal. Next, it was the shame and guilt he felt about relapsing. Subsequently, we were also able to treat with EFT the two major triggers leading to Ben's relapse — anger and loneliness.

> *Even though I am angry at [people/name of person you're angry at] for not taking care of business, I accept myself deeply and profoundly.*
> *Reminder phrase: Feeling angry*

Or, use this setup phrase:

> *Even though [other people/name of person(s)] are to blame for my situation, I accept myself deeply and profoundly.*
> *Reminder phrase: Blaming [name of person]*

Group four: overreactive

You jump to conclusions and are not willing to listen to others. You frequently disagree with others, are sarcastic, threatening and frustrated. When hurt or angry, you generalize saying always and never. A setup and reminder phrase that may be used to deal with being overreactive is:

Even though I don't want to listen to others [specify person if possible], I accept myself deeply and profoundly.
Reminder phrase: Don't want to listen

Or this setup phrase may be more appropriate:

Even though I am hurt and angry at [specify], I accept myself deeply and profoundly.
Reminder phrase: Hurt and angry

Group five: out of control

You're obsessed with addictive cravings or urges, including self-talk that encourages having just one because you deserve it, and besides no one will know. You engage in physical or verbal violence and/or addictive behavior — either primary or secondary — such as alcohol, drugs, food, gambling, sex, spending, obsessive relationships, work, etc. A setup and reminder phrase that may be used to deal with being out of control is:

Even though I am obsessing on my addictive behavior, I accept myself deeply and profoundly.
Reminder phrase: Wanting to use [specify]

Another setup phrase would be:

Even though I think I can have just one, I accept myself deeply and profoundly.
Reminder phrase: Just one

WHAT DOES HALT MEAN?

Literally, it means stop what you are doing and take care of yourself if you are *Hungry or Hurt, Angry, Lonely or Lustful or Tired.* Any of these, when not addressed, can create enough stress to lead to cravings and/or urges activating the addiction. Proactive planning to avoid or deal with the common life stressors identified by HALT is extremely helpful. If any issue becomes active, then it must be dealt with as soon as possible using EFT. A setup and reminder phrase that may be used to deal with HALT is:

> *Even though I am [specify], I deeply and profoundly accept myself.*
> Reminder phrase: Feeling [specify]

ARE THERE ANY CONSIDERATIONS IN USING EFT TO GET OVER AN ALCOHOL, DRUG OR CIGARETTE DEPENDENCY?

For the substance-dependent individual wanting to stop using or drinking, special medical consideration is needed. A physician with expertise in these areas must assess a person with alcohol or drug addiction or, for that matter, anyone with a serious eating disorder such as bulimia or anorexia. Once a doctor has determined that the individual is stable medically and able to participate in treatment for the addiction in question, an assessment needs to be conducted to determine the appropriate level of care needed to support recovery. For the chronically addicted, there is a higher risk of relapse so there may, initially, need to be a higher level of care provided than outpatient office visits.

WHAT DOES A HIGHER LEVEL OF CARE MEAN?

In addition to EFT, individuals who suffer from chronic addictions may need a structured environment, initially, to provide the necessary support for their recovery. Higher levels of care involve increasingly structured formats from intensive outpatient programs, where the addict is seen several hours a day for two or three weeks, to residential treatment programs lasting a month to a year.

It is not uncommon for an individual who has addictive disease to resist attending a higher level of care. It is very helpful to do EFT on their fears about attending a higher level of care, so that their decision is based on their best thinking rather than their worst fear. A setup and reminder phrase that may be used to deal with this resistance is:

38

Even though I don't think my problem with [specify] is bad enough to go to residential treatment, I accept myself deeply and profoundly.
Reminder phrase: Not bad enough

WHAT IS WITHDRAWAL?

Withdrawal is the body's reaction to the reduction and eventual elimination of the substance to which it has become accustomed or addicted. When it comes to addiction, it is very important to remember that EFT is not a substitute for appropriate medical care. An individual who has a substance-based addiction needs a medical evaluation to head off any medical crises that abstinence might bring with it.

For example, there are individuals who, upon the cessation of alcohol, can on the third or fourth day of abstinence experience a full-blown seizure (like a convulsion), referred to as an abstinence seizure. This type of seizure can be avoided with the proper medical care. That said, it is also important to note that EFT can be extremely helpful in dramatically reducing the discomfort of withdrawal and, in some instances, eliminate it entirely.

HOW DO YOU TREAT ADDICTION WITH EFT?

Briefly, EFT is most effective in treating addictions as part of an integrated system in which the medical and community support needs of the individual are met. EFT facilitates and supports recovery in a comprehensive approach that initially addresses cravings, urges, compulsions, stress and other psychological and neurological barriers to recovery.

As the addict stabilizes, he or she is evaluated for trauma work. When appropriate, EFT is used for treatment of trauma, losses and the psychological issues remaining regarding past injuries or illnesses. Additionally, the recovering addict may use EFT on an ongoing basis to deal with life stresses.

Joan called laughing with delight. A self-proclaimed candy monster and chocoholic, she had just experienced her first Halloween without being tempted, even slightly, to eat any chocolate or candy. She was very happy that there had been no feeling of deprivation or struggle in choosing not to eat candy. Using EFT on a daily basis had allowed her to deal with her negative emotions and stop escaping into the temporary pleasure that her candy compulsion offered. Because she isn't always in touch with her feelings, she uses EFT five or six times a day to address any stress she may accumulate.

WHAT IS THE MOST COMMON BLOCK TO TREATMENT?

Psychological Reversal (PR) is the most prevalent block to EFT's effectiveness. PR shows up in 40 percent of all issues being treated by EFT. However, PR occurs in more than 90 percent of all addictive behaviors. It is rarely present when addressing cravings and urges or withdrawal but is prevalent in all other aspects of treating addiction. That is why it is so hard to put addictive behavior into remission. PR causes an individual to act in opposition to their goal. This is so, even though the individual has the knowledge and ability to attain their goal.

For example, many veteran dieters have both a professed desire to lose weight and an impressive reservoir of information about how to achieve a healthy weight loss. Nevertheless, they fail repeatedly. Their repeated failures to lose or maintain weight loss are rooted in the individual's negative core beliefs about themselves, their life and their inability to make sustained positive changes in their life.

HOW DOES ONE DEAL WITH PSYCHOLOGICAL REVERSAL?

The EFT setup phrase or statement is a built-in correction for Psychological Reversal. However, the setup does not eliminate PR permanently. Psychologically reversed states exist on a continuum of severity from massive to minimal. Reversals may be specific to the problem being addressed, or they may be based on attitudes about releasing the specific problem. Treating the reversal disengages it, sometimes only temporarily, though hopefully long enough so that the problem can be treated effectively.

WHAT ARE SOME ADDICTION-RELATED PSYCHOLOGICAL REVERSALS?

The following is a list of commonly experienced reversals in treating addictions:

I accept myself deeply and profoundly, even if I don't believe I have an addiction to [specify].

I accept myself deeply and profoundly, even if I am not ready to eliminate this problem with [specify].

I accept myself deeply and profoundly, even if I feel it's not safe to get over this problem with [specify].

I accept myself deeply and profoundly, even if I will lose my identity if I get over this problem with [specify].

I accept myself deeply and profoundly, even if I am embarrassed that I have this addiction to [specify addiction].

I accept myself deeply and profoundly, even if I will never get over this addiction to [specify].

I accept myself deeply and profoundly, even if I'm not sure I want to get over this addiction to [specify].

I accept myself deeply and profoundly, even if I solve this addiction to [specify], I will feel deprived.

I accept myself deeply and profoundly, even if I don't have the strength to stop this addiction to [specify].

I accept myself deeply and profoundly, even if this addiction to [specify] can only be solved by someone else.

I accept myself deeply and profoundly, even if I will lose part of who I am if I ever solve this addiction to [specify].

"I actually finished my homework without pulling out any of my hair." Lynne has struggled with a number of self-damaging behaviors since adolescence. Trichotillomania (hair pulling) had been the latest one. While in her teens she would periodically show symptoms of other self injurious behaviors, mainly, scratching or sometimes making shallow cuts on her legs, as well as an eating disorder.

Lynne would relieve painful or hard to express feelings with self-injury. The relief, being temporary, is often repeated creating a self-destructive cycle. However, since she has been taught EFT, Lynne now has a tool she can easily use to deal with whatever urges she may have for self injury. But more importantly, Lynne has been able to address the underlying anger and sadness that has been pervasive since her childhood.

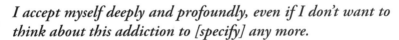

I accept myself deeply and profoundly, even if I don't want to think about this addiction to [specify] any more.

I accept myself deeply and profoundly, even if I want to solve this addiction to [specify], but I am too weak.

I accept myself deeply and profoundly, even if I can't stay focused on quitting this addiction to [specify].

I accept myself deeply and profoundly, even if I say I want to solve this addiction to [specify], but never do.

I accept myself deeply and profoundly, even if it could be a problem for others for me to get over this addiction to [specify].

I accept myself deeply and profoundly, even if I don't deserve to get over this addiction to [specify].

How would one correct the Psychological Reversals on this list?

To get the most out of this list, rate the above PR statements, regarding their relevance to your issues with an addictive substance or behavior, on a scale of zero (strongly disagree) to 10 (strongly agree). Do the EFT basic recipe on all PR issues rated above four. Address the other issues as appropriate. All PR fades and diminishes as anxiety and stress are significantly reduced and negative core issues are treated. It is essential to remember that initially, Psychological Reversals take time and diligence to be treated effectively. They need to be treated multiple times a day as part of your daily routine. It is recommended that PR be treated *15 to 25 times a day.*

ARE THERE ANY OTHER SIGNIFICANT BLOCKS TO TREATMENT?

Energy system disturbances that block EFT's effectiveness are caused by several factors. The one most often encountered is referred to as a neurological disturbance. Usually neurological disturbance is suspected when after several rounds of EFT there is no change in the individual's discomfort rating or it is going down very slowly, one point at a time. Additional common indicators of neurological disturbance are Attention Deficit Disorder, Dyslexia, stuttering, hyperactivity, panic attacks and anxiety disorders.

WHAT CORRECTS NEUROLOGICAL DISTURBANCES?

A breathing exercise referred to as Collarbone Breathing (CB) temporarily corrects neurological disturbances and allows the EFT treatment to work. If CB is needed, it should be done before every EFT treatment. Collarbone treatment points are located as follows: go to the base of the throat where the collarbone joins at the center. From that point feel for the notch in the center of the collarbone, go straight down about one inch and the points are on either side of the center of the sternum, just off the bone.

1. Place two *fingertips* of right hand on right collarbone point. Tap the Gamut point continuously, while doing the following breathing sequence:
    a. Breathe normally, for a minimum of five taps.
    b. Take a deep breath and hold it in for five taps.

    c. Let half that breath out and hold it for five taps.

    d. Let it all out and hold it for five taps.

    e. Take half a breath in and hold it for five taps.

    f. Exhale.

2. Bend the same *two fingertips* of *right hand* in half and touch the knuckles on the collarbone point, tap and breathe as above.

3. Place same *fingertips* on left collarbone point, tap gamut while doing breathing sequence.

4. Bend fingers in half and touch *knuckles* on the left collarbone point, tap and breathe as above.

5. Repeat steps one through four using *fingertips* and *knuckles* of left hand.

Can treatment blocks be caused by allergens?

Allergens and energy toxins, which include any substance, fume or fluid that is ingested, inhaled or experienced, cause a weakening of an individual's energy system. The major difference between allergens and energy toxins is the degree of disturbance that is caused. Allergies manifest physically, emotionally and energetically. Energy toxins manifest emotionally and energetically and, at times, only energetically.

There are three major treatment problems caused by allergens and energy toxins. They can block energy treatment from working and treatment failure is assumed. Or, a successful treatment can be undone when the client is again exposed to the allergen or toxins. Lastly, they can increase levels of stress and anxiety.

What can be done about allergens and energy toxins?

Primarily, avoidance is the best approach to dealing with these two energy blockers. Do not use scented products. Make sure your laundry products are perfume free. Air out all dry cleaning. If you can identify the toxin or allergen, use EFT to neutralize it. Use the following setup and reminder phrase:

> *Even though I have a sensitivity to [name of product or substance], I accept myself deeply and profoundly.*
> Reminder phrase: [Say the name of the product or substance]

CAN A PERSON'S FAMILY BE A BLOCK TO TREATMENT?

Typically, family members have a poor understanding of the dynamics of addiction and can become barriers to successful addiction treatment and recovery. A lot of family members are weary of the addict's problems. Too often they feel reluctant to use EFT for their issues that relate to the addict's problems (e.g., anger, shame, guilt, resentment or codependency) as well as problems related to their own life experience. They should be encouraged to identify these problems and treat them with EFT.

To contact Loretta Sparks, her e-mail address is LsparksMA@aol.com. Visit Loretta's Website at www.energypsychotherapy.com. Also, please see Loretta Sparks' biography at the back of the book.

ALLEVIATING ANXIETY
Erasing uneasy, apprehensive feelings

By Lindsay Kenny

"Nothing in life is to be feared. It is only to be understood."
Marie Curie

WHAT IS ANXIETY?

Anxiety has been experienced at one time or another by just about everyone on the planet. Anxiety can be a heart-pounding, stomach-churning, palm-sweating, or lump-in-the-throat event. More than any other emotion, anxiety is manifested in physical symptoms. For most of us anxiety is only a temporary feeling that passes once a situation is under control or the fear has been eliminated. For others, anxiety is a long-term, debilitating problem that often appears to have little or no cause, yet the physical symptoms persist. Anxiety is often the root cause of addictions, as well as a contributing factor for ulcers, high blood pressure, heart attacks, low self esteem, suicides and so much more.

WHAT CAUSES ANXIETY?

Most anxiety is fear-based, particularly the fear of not being in control. Having little or no control over any issue, situation, or person, causes high anxiety in some people. Similarly, we can experience anxiety if we're afraid of losing something: love, respect, dignity, security, etc. Being uncertain about an outcome (not being in control of it) can also cause anxiety: "What if this plane is hijacked?" "Will people talk behind my back at the party?" "What if I make a fool of myself during the concert?" These anxiety-driven thoughts are all founded in fear. It's not abnormal to experience anxiety occasionally, especially about an unknown. It's only when we obsess about it, or when anxiety interferes with living a *normal* life, that it becomes a serious problem.

Anxiety can also be caused by numerous other factors or nothing at all. We live in incredibly stressful times, especially those of us in the United States where terrorist warnings are a frequent occurrence. Worldwide, we have seen terrorist bombings in Spain, England, Bali and elsewhere, in otherwise peaceful nations. So the threat is always present that "it could happen at any time."

In the nightly news we hear daily updates on the war in Iraq, plus other violence. Every day we see or hear hundreds of images and sounds that can induce anxiety in even the calmest soul. Add to that the natural, uncontrollable disasters like hurricanes, floods, wild fires, tornadoes, mudslides, earthquakes and Tsunamis that dominate the news and its no wonder we feel more anxious than ever. In our neighborhoods we hear of "Amber Alerts" for children snatched from their homes and sexual predators living down the street. This can cause anxiety in any caring parent.

Additionally, there is much uncertainty about oil prices, the economy and our futures. Gone are the days we can leave our doors unlocked, even when we're home. Gone are the days when we can let kids watch television unsupervised. No longer can we trust someone with our children just because he or she is a teacher, priest, doctor, coach or other authority figure. All of these things compounded foster the makings for anxiety.

IF WE'RE ALL EXPOSED TO THE SAME BAD NEWS AND SIMILAR DAILY TRIALS AND TRIBULATIONS, WHY ARE SOME PEOPLE INCAPACITATED WITH ANXIETY AND OTHERS SEEM TO LET IT ROLL OFF THEIR BACKS?

By her own admission, Harriet was constantly anxious over "nothing and everything." She was pretty dysfunctional in that she lost her job, had broken up her marriage and had alienated most of her friends and family over her extreme anxiety. Although she couldn't remember any specific incidents in the past that might have started her anxiety, she did know it had been with her almost all of her life. I asked about her parents. She said her father, an alcoholic, was verbally and physically abusive to her and her mother.

As a result, they were always anxious about him coming home since they never knew what kind of mood he'd be in or what he'd do to them. They lived in an anxious state of terror 24 hours a day. Well, there was a clue! So we tapped on that core issue saying, "Even though I've always been anxious and sometimes it kept me safe, because I never knew what to expect from my dad."

At first we weren't getting any results so I suspected Harriet had a Psychological Reversal about getting over her anxiety. We did a Reversal neutralization saying three times, "Even though I don't really want to let go of this anxiety... I've had it so long I won't know how to function without it... It's kept me safe sometimes... I love and accept myself anyway." We then started the original setup again and went from a SUDS of 10 to a five, to a two and finally to a zero. Harriet came back for a couple of other sessions to work on some related issues. She has since reported that her life is working again, and she is completely free of her crippling anxiety.

After reading the reasons for all the anxiety-producing circumstances today, one might think everyone should be anxious. Yet millions of people function fine without letting anxiety get to them. Virtually everyone has experienced anxiety at one time or another in their lives. Whether it's being anxious over making a good impression with the in-laws or giving an important speech to a critical audience, we've all felt the temporary discomfort of being out-of-control or anxious.

Some people just get over it while others turn into chronic anxiety sufferers. Like anything else, it's not what happens to us that shapes who we are, but rather how we deal with what happens to us. Whether genetics, chemical make-up or learned behavior, the fact is some people deal with anxiety easily and for others it becomes a crippling, life-altering burden.

Some people try to ignore their symptoms and may eventually turn to illegal drugs or alcohol, while others seek professional help in the form of prescription drugs. Drugs may provide temporary relief from anxiety, but they only serve to mask the symptoms rather than dealing with the cause and elimination of this debilitating condition.

Those of us contributing to this book, as well as thousands of other EFT users around the world, know EFT can make a profound difference in the treatment of anxiety. Simply eliminating the negative emotion(s) fueling the anxiety — trauma, fear, uncertainty, feeling out of control, etc. — can often reduce or completely eliminate it. (More on how to do that is shown in the Question "How do I use EFT to alleviate anxiety?")

WHAT IS CHRONIC ANXIETY?

Chronic, as defined by Webster, is "being long-lasting and recurrent or characterized by long suffering." Those that experience chronic anxiety know it can range from terribly uncomfortable to completely incapacitating. According to the Mental Health Intervention Research Center, five percent of the U.S. population (about 12,500,000 people) suffers from chronic anxiety and millions more deal with frequent anxiety.

Chronic anxiety sufferers are anxious almost all the time with a sense of "waiting for the next disaster to happen." For some, their bodies actually develop a habit of feeling anxiety and so become "addicted" to it. That's not to say anyone would consciously *choose* to be anxious, but rather their body can start feeling more *accustomed* to being anxious than being calm and relaxed. Chronic anxiety sufferers often admit to "being anxious over being anxious." It's a horribly debilitating state of being in which to exist.

WHAT ARE THE LONG TERM EFFECTS OF ANXIETY?

Left untreated, chronic anxiety can lead to panic attacks, depression, high blood pressure, ulcers, insomnia, agoraphobia and more. Often anxiety greatly reduces a person's ability to function at work, in relationships and life in general. It's virtually impossible to be effective or enjoy life when you're suffering from chest pains, excessive sweating, a racing pulse and other symptoms of debilitating anxiety.

In severe cases people quit their jobs and live huddled in their homes experiencing their world through a constant veil of anxiety. Others manage to function only through the help of drugs. Neither option is ideal. Fortunately, EFT offers an excellent, safe and highly effective alternative.

HOW CAN EFT HELP ANXIETY SUFFERERS?

EFT can be a Godsend for those suffering from mild to severe anxiety. When in the state of anxiety, our bodies are out-of-sync, out of balance and off-center. We feel out-of-control and out of alignment. So by rebalancing ourselves and our body's energy system we can drastically affect the hold that anxiety has on us. Think of anxiety as a powerful magnet that has locked onto our body's nervous system, causing an electrical storm in our brains and nervous system. By tapping on the selected energy meridians and changing the polarity of those "anxiety magnets," we are neutralizing and releasing anxiety's hold in our body.

SO HOW DO I USE EFT TO ALLEVIATE ANXIETY?

First you need to determine, if possible, the cause of your anxiety. Are you worried about losing your job, anxious about your IRS audit, nervous about becoming a parent, taking a test, or performing in front of an audience? If you can identify a relatively simple source such as these then anxiety can often be resolved quickly and easily.

Note: Since the inside of the wrists are stress and anxiety points, and because so many people have anxiety issues, I always add the wrist points to my tapping locations for all issues. These points are located at the base of the palm on the inside of your wrists where a nurse would take your pulse. Simply bump your wrists together at that location.

WHAT ARE SOME EFFECTIVE SETUP PHRASES FOR SIMPLE ANXIETY ISSUES?

For simple anxiety issues (that is, ones where you pretty much know the reason for your anxiety) start with a simple setup statement like:

> *Even though I'm anxious about [whatever the issue is], I deeply and completely accept myself.*

Other simple examples are:

> *Even though I'm anxious about getting fired if they find out I went to the beach instead of staying home sick, I love and accept myself anyway.*
> *Reminder: This anxiety about being found out*
>
> *Even though I'm anxious that my boyfriend might find someone he likes better than me, I deeply and completely accept myself.*
> *Reminder: This anxiety over my boyfriend leaving me*
>
> *Even though my anxiety is over having to do a solo performance at the reunion, I love, accept and trust myself completely.*
> *Reminder: This anxiety about performing on stage*
>
> *Even though I'm anxious knowing I have to be in a closed-in room with lots of people at the dinner party and I might freak out, I completely accept who I am as a man.*
> *Reminder: This anxiety about being in small spaces. (Or use — my anxiety about freaking out.)*

Adam came to me with severe anxiety, panic attacks and nightmares that woke him up in a sweat. He had an alcoholic father whose abuse was verbal and emotional. His father never had anything good to say to Adam, nor could Adam do anything right. Even if Adam came home with straight "A"s, his father would say, "So, you think you're too big for your britches now?" When his father was drunk, which was most of the time, Adam's father would go into an uncontrollable rage, breaking and throwing things in the house, screaming at the kids, and taunting them with horrible threats.

When he was drunk, one of Adam's dad's favorite ways to terrorize the family was to sneak into the kids' bedroom and blow a loud athletic horn in their ears. The kids would wake up in terror, screaming and crying for hours. If they fell back to sleep, good old dad would come in again, blow the horn and laugh himself into a stupor. Who wouldn't be anxious with that kind of inexcusable behavior from someone who's supposed to love and protect you? We tapped on Adam's father being a "dooder-head" only we used more explicit words chosen by Adam, framing some of the incidents mentioned above.

Adam's intensity dropped from a 10 to a two in two rounds of EFT and we got stuck. So we switched over to tapping on, "Even though my father was a brute to me and my sister growing up, I'm now willing to start forgiving him." When that issue was collapsed, we checked in on his anxiety level and it was gone as well. It took additional tapping on Adam's part to clear out other anxiety-causing behavior. He did an excellent job in being persistent until he was finished. Adam now reports that he has even less anxiety than "normal" folks.

Even though I'm really anxious about having to go through airport security as an Arab-American, I totally accept myself as a good person and responsible citizen.
Reminder: My anxiety about being targeted as a terrorist

What about more complicated anxiety? Can EFT work on that?

Anxiety can often be a complex issue, especially when it's rooted in the past, or you've been experiencing anxiety for years. If it's not clear why you're anxious or you feel nervous for no particular reason, try to discover what's at the root of the anxiety by asking yourself, "When did I first start to experience anxiety?" "What else was happening in my life at the time?" "What did that teach me?" In other words look for the core cause of the problem.

For instance, I have a client named Joe who has been anxious all of his life, but had no idea why. By probing I discovered that his parents were holocaust survivors who were constantly anxious about *everything*. Finding a parking spot or standing in line to buy movie tickets produced anxiety attacks.

His parents worried about losing their jobs, neighbors thinking they were snooty for buying a new car, Joe's pending grades in school, etc. So for Joe, anxiety was a learned or even inherited "habit." Tapping on his parents' anxiety and forgiving them helped Joe get over his own anxiety.

Another client, Sue, found that the root of her anxiety about driving was that when she was a little girl her mother was killed in an auto accident, leaving her and her brothers orphans. She had to quit school and raise her four brothers. She found herself constantly worried about paying the rent, feeding them all and trying to keep the family together. Tapping on those specific events created instant relief from her anxiety issues.

 ### How do I phrase EFT setups for more complex anxiety?

When the reason for anxiety is unknown or rooted in the past, it's often (though not always) a more complex issue. The basic formula with EFT is still the same. However, the setup statements may be a little longer for more complex issues. With complex issues it's important to find the original cause for the anxiety.

Once you discover the core reason issue, simply tap specifically on that issue or incident. Also, with complex or chronic anxiety, there may be several aspects to a problem. Complex anxiety frequently needs to be taken care of with the help of an experienced EFT practitioner.

Here are some examples of more complex anxiety setup statements:

> *Even though my mother was anxious when my dad was late coming home on the night he was killed, so now I'm always anxious if my husband's late, I love and accept myself completely.*
> Reminder: *My mother's anxiety over dad's death*

> *Even though I inherited my dad's chronic anxiety over money and I'm always worried over not having enough, I accept who I am unconditionally.*
> Reminder: *Inheriting my dad's money anxiety* or *Always worried about money, like dad.*

> *Even though I grew up in a bad neighborhood with gunshots going off all night so now I'm anxious about loud noises, I love and accept who I am.*
> Reminder: *This anxiety over loud noises*

> *Even though I'm anxious about being able to provide for my wife and children should I die, the way my father died and left us destitute, I love and accept myself completely.*
> Reminder: *My anxiety about supporting my family*

> *Even though Frank was an alcoholic and beat me all the time and I could never predict his moods, so I lived in a constant state of fear and anxiety, I know I'm safe now and I want to love and accept the woman I can become.*
> Reminder: *The anxiety and uncertainty from Frank*

Just remember that the setup phrase needs to couch the negative issue (the root of the anxiety) with a positive love and/or acceptance statement.

WHAT DO I DO IF EFT ISN'T WORKING FOR MY ANXIETY?

This is one of my favorite questions, actually. There are several stumbling blocks that can keep an EFT procedure from working. It could be that you're not finding the *core issue*, you're not *being specific* enough about the issue, you're *shifting issues* and getting off course, you may be *dehydrated*, or something you've ingested or are wearing could be impeding your progress.

But in my opinion the biggest reason people don't get the expected results from EFT is because of a Reversal — either Psychological or Polarity. Especially if someone is having a difficult time getting over a "chronic" condition of any kind, I always consider some type of Reversal.

If someone has carried around an issue for a long time, whether it be extra weight, trauma, chronic pain, or anxiety it can become a part of his or her personality. It can literally get imbedded in the cells and can become part of his or her identity. The subconscious actually gets attached to the issue and becomes "comfortable" with it. I call this the Secondary Benefit Syndrome or SBS. To the non-rational, subconscious mind the consequences of eliminating a problem such as anxiety, could be very threatening.

For instance the subconscious, non-rational mind might be thinking that if I get over this anxiety:

- I may not be safe.
- I won't have an excuse anymore for my life not working.
- I may not know who I am anymore.
- I won't know how to act as a functional, non-victim or non-anxious person.
- I won't get the attention (or sympathy) I get now.
- I don't deserve an anxiety free existence.

I want to be very clear here. No one who suffers from chronic anxiety, trauma, phobias and countless other problems *deliberately chooses*

55

Casey was a junior in high school when she came to me. She was always anxious about her schoolwork, achieving good grades, getting admitted to a good college, being accepted by others and just doing well in general. Casey had an older sister, Rita, who was "perfect" and set a high standard for Casey. Rita had graduated at the top of her class in high school and college, excelling in athletics, school politics, and school plays. Although Casey's parents were supportive and never compared the two daughters, Casey always felt pressure to do as well as Rita or better. Casey's issue was self-imposed anxiety about her own abilities and accomplishments compared to her sister.

We tapped on the setup phrase, "Even though my sister is an exceptional person, I recognize that I have my own unique talents and strengths, and I really want to love and accept who I am." We tapped on that theme for a few minutes then switched to directly confronting Casey's anxiety. "Even though I make myself crazy being anxious about everything, I acknowledge that I'm exceptional and excellent in my own way." She had some resistance to this at first, so we worked around that until she was able to say without hesitation, "I am 100% free of anxiety about everything and I completely accept and love myself unconditionally."

to remain in that uncomfortable or non-functional state. Yet their subconscious can throw up a roadblock, over which their conscious mind has little or no awareness or control. This becomes a powerful impediment toward eliminating the issue.

Our subconscious is so powerful that, often when I start to work with someone with anxiety, their subconscious resistance actually causes them to become more anxious. Some get sick to their stomach or even break out into hives, so severe is their fear of losing this long-time companion of anxiety. Physical manifestations like that are a sure sign of a Reversal. To read more about this phenomena visit Gary Craig's web site www.emofree.com and enter the word "Reversals" into his search bar.

How do I overcome a barrier like Reversals or SBS (Secondary Benefit Syndrome) so EFT will work for me?

The good news is, once a Reversal is discovered, it is fairly easy to overcome. To fix a Reversal simply tap on the karate chop point saying one or all of these Reversal phrases three times:

Always end the statement with a positive acceptance statement such as, "I deeply and completely accept myself."

Even though I don't really want to get over this anxiety issue, I love and accept myself completely.

Even though it may not be safe to get over this anxiety, I love and accept myself completely.

Even though I won't know how to act if I'm not anxious, I love and accept myself completely.

Even though I won't have an excuse for my life not working if I let go of this anxiety, I love and accept myself completely.

Even though I don't want to forgive the people that ruined my life, I love and accept myself completely.

Even though I don't want to be normal, I love and accept myself completely.

Even though I'm afraid this EFT won't work and I'll never get over this anxiety, I love and accept myself completely.

Even though I don't deserve to get over this anxiety, I love and accept myself completely.

Even though I'm anxious about letting go of my anxiety, I love and accept myself completely.

Even though for whatever reason I don't want to let go of this anxiety, I love and accept myself completely.

It's important to note that you *don't* need to determine whether or not you have a Reversal or even what it might be in order to effectively treat it. If you get stumped doing EFT, then doing a Reversal neutralization process, as discussed, can only help your progress and cannot hurt if you're not reversed. Doing a Reversal neutralization only takes a few minutes and can be invaluable in your treatment.

How successful is EFT in overcoming anxiety?

Each person and each issue is different. Even people's motivation and determination to eliminate anxiety is different, so there's no definitive answer here. That said, it's my experience that with a qualified, competent practitioner anxiety can be relieved or completely eliminated for 90 percent or more of the sufferers. For people trying to alleviate anxiety on their own, it's reasonable even then to expect a 70 percent or greater success at alleviating anxiety.

The success rate is very much contingent on the skill of the person administering EFT, as well as the level of persistence applied. But even the worst case using EFT is far better than the weeks or months you could spend in talk therapy, taking drugs, or other methods and still not have the issue resolved. If you just can't resolve an anxiety problem on your own using EFT, consider consulting a qualified EFT practitioner. Even telephone consultations can be highly effective with anxiety challenges.

What are some of the factors that can help me be successful in dealing with anxiety?

Like using EFT for any other issue it's important that the user:

- *Be persistent.* Work on each issue until it's resolved.
- *Be specific about the issue.* For instance, use a setup statement that specifically names your problem, such as, "Even though I'm anxious about marrying Paul because he has children and I'm not good with kids…."
- *Be vigilant about finding the core issue.* Keep looking until you're sure you're at the root cause.

- *Be aware of Reversals.* They can impede your progress until the Reversal is neutralized.

- *Be gentle with yourself,* even if you don't get the results you want right away. Not all EFT 'cures' are one-minute-wonders.

- *Read as many of the case studies on anxiety and other issues as you can* to learn from others at www.emofree.com or elsewhere. Obstacles and different aspects of anxiety are creatively dealt with in real case histories.

Be patient and relief will come. For some there's almost instant release of anxiety and for others it may take hours. If you don't get the results you want and it's just not moving, read Gary's article on his website titled "When EFT appears not to work." EFT is so predictable, that if you do two or three rounds and your intensity level hasn't changed, then stop and reassess your tactics and specifically look for a Reversal. EFT does work if applied correctly. But as mentioned above there are things that can impede its effectiveness. Be persistent until you get relief.

In my opinion EFT is the most powerful tool for self help and transformation that's available today. And never has the world needed such a tool the way it does today. The only downside is you have to *use* EFT to benefit from it. If you're anxious about using EFT or afraid it won't work for you, then tap on those issues.

> *Even though I'm anxious about trying EFT for my anxiety, I accept myself completely and unconditionally.*
>
> *Even though I'm afraid EFT won't work for me and it's my last resort, I accept myself completely and unconditionally.*

Good luck and keep tapping!

To contact Lindsay Kenny, her e-mail address is LKcoaching-Linz@yahoo.com and her telephone number is 888-449-3030. Visit Lindsay's Website at www.LKCoaching.com. Also, please see Lindsay Kenny's biography at the back of the book.

BLOCKAGES & OBSTACLES
Breaking through to peak performance

By Maryam Webster

> *"Patience and perseverance have a magical effect before which difficulties disappear and obstacles vanish."*
> *John Quincy Adams*

WHAT ARE BLOCKAGES?

Blockages and personal obstacles are those things that keep us from completing goals, from standing up for ourselves and from fully living our lives. Blockages usually involve some sort of negative beliefs about our abilities, the "I can't" or "I shouldn't" type of repetitive endless loops that chatter incessantly in the backs of our minds and hold us down.

There's good news though: like diamonds in the rough, these obstacles and blockages actually contain little bits of your personal energy bound up in them, just waiting for you to retrieve them and put them to good use. And by retrieving these lost bits of our energy-self, we can regain tremendous resources, do things we thought we never could and more completely focus our lives for complete success.

Remember that when our energy systems become imbalanced we get a "zzzzzt" disruption or short circuit effect going on inside. EFT tapping can repair it. The "zzzzzt" is what's going on with personal blockages to success. That same energy disruption can be transformed by tapping into energy to help you not only get over the blockage, but also deal with the thing you have been blocked from accomplishing. You get a two-for-one power punch on clearing your issues and a nice fresh burst of energy into the bargain. We can, in short, begin living the beautiful life that we've always dreamed our lives can be.

How do personal emotional blockages begin?

Our limiting beliefs about ourselves are *very important* in the formation of blockages and obstacles to our perfect functioning. Limiting beliefs are what Gary Craig in his *Palace of Possibilities* video series calls the "writing on our walls." Do a search on *www.emofree.com* for "Palace of Possibilities." This "writing" consists of erroneous statements about your abilities which are imprinted deep in your mind when you are in a vulnerable state. One of those vulnerable states is when we are very young.

At some point, when we were between the ages of birth and seven years old, the major beliefs that run our lives were formed. These beliefs are both positive ("I'm a good kid") and negative ("I'm dumb in math"). When we're young and first learning how to do things in the world, incidents happen that cause us to doubt our abilities. Perhaps our parents yelled at us when we spilled a drink saying, "You're too clumsy to do anything right," or a teacher told us, in our first year or two of school, "You're not being very smart."

When we're so young, we trust authority figures. And, as we are not grown up enough to know differently, we believe what they tell us. These statements ("I'm always clumsy" and "I'm not very smart") imbed themselves deeply inside us, writing themselves on the walls of our mind and influencing events in our life from then on.

These put-downs, negative self-statements and limiting beliefs are the roots of our blockages. When we work directly on them with EFT, the blockages dissolve, great amounts of energy are released and we can do things we previously prevented ourselves from doing.

How do identify these Blockages?

To ensure the best success as you tap, you need to know some things about your blockage first. Below are some steps to help you identify

Here is a sample EFT "Blockage Profile" from a women's success group participant. Dana is internally blocked from asking for a raise, and is not able to afford a better living situation. Lacking the funds to move closer to her job in more expensive housing district, she spends two hours commuting each way. This reduces time Dana can spend with her family and on personal projects. Her social contacts have given up trying to see her.

Dana describes herself as "having no quality of life." She feels her stress as a mass of tension between their shoulder blades and around their chest, which feels like it is "in a vise."

Dana remembers feeling this way when her parents told the family they were out of money, and the father had to take a job in a town far away. Though Dana doesn't remember the circumstances at the time, she remembers her Mother saying "It's just our lot in life. We made the mistake of trying to rise above our station."

This stuck with Dana, becoming the blockage — "This is my lot in life. It is a dangerous and sad thing to rise above my station." This became the scene that Dana used EFT to eliminate, and the chief negative belief that she rooted out. With this belief gone, Dana was easily able to ask for and obtain a pay raise and to better her lifestyle.

blockages. First, identify one instance where you are stopped, stalled or scared to go on or where you are facing some sort of obstacle.

Next, take a look at the obstacle itself and do some writing about it. Writing things down is tremendously helpful. Describe the obstacle fully by noting the following as your "Blockage Profile":

- *How the blockage appears in your life.* It could appear as a bad situation that keeps happening, those little voices in your head that say "you can't/shouldn't/won't ever succeed if…. "You're dumb, clumsy, too fat, too skinny, too ugly to ever _____," etc. It could appear as fear, anger, sadness or any other emotion that is scary to think about. Be brave. This feeling is going to go away when you tap on it, but you need to know more about it before that can happen. Continue with the following steps.

- *How the blockage feels to you.* It could feel like a sourness in the pit of your stomach, tightness in your neck and shoulders or like a light airy space in your chest that feels frightening... these are all ways clients describe how their blockages have felt in their bodies. The way your body reacts to the stress of this blockage will be unique to you. Just think about the blockage, tune in on it and what it prevents you from *being, doing* or *having*. Note any feelings in your body that arise.

- *How the blockage affects you.* It might block you from asking for a raise, from saying something you need to, from getting out of a bad situation to a safe one, from being on time, or from having something you really want or in other ways. Those situations might in turn cause effects of their own. Note what you are prevented from being, doing or having by continuing to keep this blockage.

- *And what you are reminded of?* Look at the feelings you have surrounding your blockage. Maybe it makes you really angry, or scared or conflicted to think about. Figure out that feeling and write it down.

  Now ask yourself "When have I felt this way before?" Make a note of what comes up. If it's in the recent past you can go back further and even further. Keep asking yourself, as these scenes come up, what this feeling reminds you of that happened even earlier. You are looking for a reference that goes as far back in your childhood, in that crucial "birth to seven-years-old" period.

This is the root of your blockage. While you can get great results tapping on unformed feelings and uncertain scenes, the further back you can go with a memory when dealing with blockage, the more comprehensively effective your tapping will be. What beliefs limit and hold you back? How do they manifest, and where in your body? What do they prevent you from being, doing or having?

I had a client who used a "Blockage Profile" to great effect in crafting his setup statements. Jordan's memory of a broken relationship prevented him from dating. He traced this all the way back to an incident in childhood where an entire gang of other children snubbed him and did not include him in their play.

He tapped on this, using a setup phrase of, "Even though the B Street kids wouldn't play with me, and I was deeply humiliated, I deeply and completely love and accept myself." On the more recent relationship, Jordan used a series of three setup phrases:

"Even though she broke my heart and I'm afraid of getting my heart broken again, I deeply and completely love and accept myself."

"Even though I'm afraid that I'll end up with another woman who will only hurt me in the end and be broken beyond repair, I deeply and completely love and accept myself."

"Even though I feel humiliated and hate looking like a wuss because I got my heart broken over some dumb woman, I deeply and completely love and accept myself."

? **WHAT ARE SOME EFT SETUP PHRASES I COULD USE IN WORKING ON MY BLOCKAGES?**

Your setup phrases are going to be very specific to whatever blocks you. Fully flesh out your setup statements and give them as much life and color as possible! The more color they have, the deeper the healing will go. To increase that depth, add in the bodily feelings associated with the blockage. For example:

Even though she broke my heart and it feels like being suffocated with rocks on my chest, I deeply and completely love and accept myself.

64

Even though there's this sadness in my eyes that keeps spilling over ["this feeling like being crushed," "this sinking feeling in my chest," "my heartbeat pounding in my ears," etc.], I deeply and completely love and accept myself.

This approach addresses both physical symptoms as well as the fact of the incident. Keep going on physical symptoms until you have listed them all in the setup phrase.

To be even more thorough (thoroughness is essential to success with EFT), bring in the specific emotions now too:

Even though I am sad that my partner chose to end our relationship, and angry that she left me like this, I deeply and completely love and accept myself.

Keep on fleshing out the feelings involved, being sure to get very specific and work with specific scenes.

WHAT IF I'M REMINDED OF OTHER THINGS WHILE TAPPING ON MY SPECIFIC BLOCKAGE?

Those "other things" that we are reminded of are frequently other aspects of the problem. As you begin to tap these blockages away in your life, you will find things that you once only dreamed about not only possible, but actively happening in your life. With EFT, those fond hopes and dreams can become your everyday waking reality. Enjoy the extra energy and wonderful things that will begin to happen as you release those blocks and obstacles!

WHAT IS THE BEST WAY TO END AN EFT SESSION AFTER WORKING SUCCESSFULLY ON A BLOCKAGE?

I just love Dr. Patricia Carrington's "EFT Choices Technique" which you can find at the central EFT website *www.emofree.com*. This is an

As Surindar tapped on his sadness at an elder brother's put-downs, he was reminded of a teacher who never lost the opportunity to chastise him. This surprised Surindar as the teacher hadn't existed in his active memory for twenty years. Yet this caustic voice was now very obviously still there, continuing to chastise away. Once he focused on it, Surindar could hear the tone and inflection of the teacher's voice in addition to his words, and clearly remembered a dismissive wave of the teacher's hand that he had found so humiliating.

The teacher's voice of twenty years ago turned into an ongoing and ever-deeper hidden "endless loop" that told Surindar he was no good at anything he did. Indeed, a string of partial successes ending in failure had dogged Surindar throughout his life.

This aspect of his original difficulty all came back in a rush. As he was working on his relationship with his brother in particular, Surindar jotted down his memory of the "Chastising Teacher" briefly, and then returned to tapping on his relationship issue. When his SUDS number was down to a zero on this, he returned to the chastising teacher incident and proceeded to tap that down to zero.

Remembering his old teacher's voice provided Surindar the information he needed to go in and break up a blockage pattern that kept him from succeeding very long at anything he did. Freed from this blockage, Surindar went on to found a successful software startup company.

ideal way to end a session of tapping by putting something positive into the space you've just emptied out and by tapping the blockage away. You choose how you want to feel. What will you choose? Here are some things clients tend to choose:

- Hope
- Trust
- Peace
- Love

- Belief in myself
- Belief in my abilities
- To have knowledge come at just the right time
- Boundless abundance
- To know down deep that mom really loved me
- Joy and happiness
- Calm
- Equanimity

These are only a few possible Choices. What are yours?

 TELL ME SOME MORE ABOUT HOW I CAN MAKE THE RIGHT CHOICES. HOW DO I ATTRACT WHAT I WOULD REALLY RATHER HAVE IN MY LIFE?

A Choice example that a client, Jordan, made in the wake of his broken relationship was: "Even though I have all these emotions about the breakup with my girlfriend, I choose to trust that I can attract the right person and to feel peace in my heart."

Trust and peace are mighty strong medicine and are the exact opposite to what this person had been feeling. A heart filled with peace and trust is a beautiful, attractive thing. With trust and peace in there, radiating outward, an attractor field is set up to draw in others with the same characteristics, thus further ensuring the likelihood of attracting a suitable mate.

That's how the Law of Attraction works. If you have hate and anger in your heart, you will attract others who are hateful and angry. If you come from an attitude of peace and trust, you will attract others who are also trusting and peaceful-hearted, or at least striving in that direction.

If you are in a place of blockage and want a different response from others than you're getting, tap on the negatives and replace them with their exact opposite, using Choices. It's a no-brainer, and it works.

Let's look at an example of how to express a Choice statement. My client Meryl, a single mom in her mid-thirties had just lost her job. She had three children to feed, clothe and house. Once she tapped on things from her childhood that this situation reminded her of, Meryl chose to replace the negative emotions of fear and desperation she felt, with hope, optimism and a boundless belief in her own abilities.

From Gary Craig's *Palace of Possibilities* video series, we know that our consistent thoughts become our reality. Let those thoughts then be the best and highest qualities you can aspire to. Look at the opposite of what you're trying to get rid of and install those qualities deep inside yourself with the EFT Choices process.

With such powerful resources tapped into her energy system, Meryl's use of Choices set up a powerful attractor field that soon pulled the right job to her at a significant increase in salary. Making Choices focuses the mind sharply on those consistent thoughts, making them a reality.

And, if you're having a difficult time thinking of a suitable Choice to make, look to your role models in life. What qualities do they have that make you want to be like them? When modeling success, look at those who are successful. What is it they do, or have in their personality? What is the place that they come from in their hearts and minds that makes you admire them? Courage, truth, strength with numbers or words, personal integrity, caring or generosity? These would all be wonderful Choices.

I WANT TO MODEL SUCCESS! WHAT ARE THE KEY PERSONALITY TRAITS OF THOSE WHO ARE CONSISTENTLY ABLE TO REMOVE THEIR OWN BLOCKAGES AND OBSTACLES?

EFT expert, Steve Well's article series on "Peak Performance" (search at *www.emofree.com*) lists differences in those who consistently burst through their blockages and manage obstacles. He says that for those who have a commitment to peak performance it often represents a series of daily disciplines, an endless process of coming up against massive frustrations, and ongoing questioning and doubting, punctuated by periods of intense focus and inspiration.

Steve makes an excellent point in saying that being at your peak requires commitment to daily discipline. Completely working through the mental and emotional programs that have held you back from birth onward can be a daunting task. But with EFT, it is also an easy and pleasurable task.

You'll come to enjoy EFT so much that daily tapping will soon become a prized necessity, but one with a luxury feel to it. You'll find that you whiz through many of your obstacles and blockages in no time. And the rest are just a simple, relaxing tap or two away from resolution.

Sure, you might have bad days where nothing you do seems to matter, where your every effort is like pushing string uphill and doubts creep in. But those too, can become a thing of the past when you realize that you now have a choice about how to experience and, indeed, fully live your life. EFT puts that choice right into your hands.

When doubting your plan, take a firm grip on your resolve to see it through. Literally, reach out and grab it out of the air in front of you. Bring it back from wherever it journeyed off to and place it in your heart. Keep coming back to that charge you're going to get out of seeing your goal(s) through, as you tap a sequence from the top of your head down to the under breast point.

Visualize yourself winning the day in your mind, hear the congratulations on completing your goal and feel how good it feels to have it done. Then, when obstacles or other aspects of the problem come up, simply place your hand over your heart, remember your resolve to power through and tap on that determination and the fruit of your goal again. It works every time!

"Mostly," Steve Wells goes on to say, "the difference that makes the difference is that peak performers persist in going for their high goals despite these moments of doubt. They manage to keep themselves going despite the internal and external objections to their continuation on the path. They manage to stay committed to their goals even when all the outside evidence (and some of their inner voices) suggests it would be better for them to just quit."

EFT makes winners out of all of us. But it does take persistence and coming back to the problem again. Tapping when those "tail-ender" doubts and aspects appear is the key to long term success. Keep going. You're worth it. And EFT makes it easy.

 WHAT CAN I EXPECT WHEN MY BLOCKAGES START TO DISSOLVE THROUGH USING EFT?

Dissolving blockages is both easy and very rewarding. You'll notice abilities you never thought you had coming to the fore, and you'll be able to go forward on projects where you're stalled. Plus, you'll get what I refer to as that "EFT Bonus" of deep, delicious relaxation as trapped energies are freed up.

As you get free and clear of your blockages, you might find relationships changing as well. Those who were attracted to a person as a meek, shy, "say-nothing," may find it disconcerting when that same person uses EFT to get past their blockages and begins to assert themself and stand up for what they need.

Reflect that, as energy flows through your body, so does it flow through relationships. What served you when you were blocked and stuck, no longer serves you as a self-assured and successful person. Sometimes this means that, as your behavior and habits change, friends may leave you — or you might choose to leave them.

If people have a problem with you in a self-assured role, you don't need them in your life. But others will be attracted to the new, self-confident, successful you. And these will be people who are better for you, more nurturing and supportive. You will easily attract the kinds of people who will not only support and uphold your successful self, but will pull you forward towards greater things, even as you support them in your turn.

In short, as you tap away your blockages, your behaviors, your habits, your perceptions and feelings about yourself and even your relationships will "level up." You will begin to live the dream made into reality. And as other obstacles come up in life, you are easily able to tap on and resolve them even in the moment, as they occur.

The power is yours. Use it wisely!

To contact Maryam Webster, visit her Website at www.quantumflow.com. Also see Maryam Webster's biography at the back of the book.

CHILDREN & TEENS
Using magic fingers to energize youngsters

By Jan Yordy

> *"There are only two lasting bequests we can hope to give our children. One is roots; the other, wings."*
> *Hodding Carter*

 IS EFT A TECHNIQUE WHICH IS SAFE TO USE WITH CHILDREN OR TEENS?

Many therapists, teachers and parents have found EFT to be a wonderfully effective tool to use with children and teenagers. I personally have seen it shift emotionally overwhelmed and upset children/teens into calm and relaxed persons who could comfortably deal with their upsetting problems. When using EFT with children/teens, I have found that they either have very positive experiences or they may have trouble tuning into their problematic emotions and report it didn't work.

Some children are so fearful of re-experiencing their negative responses to upsetting past experiences that they block the process from working. These children often end up suppressing the uncomfortable feelings, creating more problems and issues for themselves in the long run. EFT, should they be willing to try it, could give them a safe way to work through whatever is upsetting them. EFT is one of those significant tools that every child should have available to them.

EFT is a natural for parents to use within the safety of the home. When whole families start to incorporate this amazing tool, the family dynamics shift as everyone learns better ways to express and process their own negative feelings. When parents model effective use of EFT for their own emotional management, their children will be more open to try the process and work on their own feelings.

WHY IS IT IMPORTANT FOR PARENTS TO TAP ON THEIR OWN ISSUES *BEFORE* APPROACHING THEIR CHILD TO DO EFT TAPPING?

Children often will mirror parents' issues and act out when they sense parents' vulnerability or negative feelings. When parents can examine their own feelings and reactions and release their negative feelings, often their way of reacting to their child will shift.

When parents work on their negative feelings first, the child's problem or issue begins to dissipate. One mother who contacted me about the stress and conflict between her and her 10 year-old daughter found that, when she tapped away her job stress and anger at her daughter, the relationship improved dramatically.

When the mother dealt with her own issues, her daughter began to talk more easily about her fears for her mother's long-term health because of smoking. Together they were able to change their communication patterns and work at their unresolved feelings using EFT, which created a more harmonious relationship.

As parents of children or teens, you can easily come across in critical or judgmental ways unless you have properly dealt with the uncomfortable feelings stirred up by your kids. Many issues that first appear to be related to your children, after closer inspection and some EFT tapping, are revealed to be your own stuff. Spending time identifying your issues, then resolving them using EFT, will pay off in more positive relationships within the whole family.

 WHAT ARE SOME PARENTAL EFT SETUP PHRASES TO HELP WORK ON OR PROCESS PARENTAL ISSUES?

Use the following reminder phrases, or others appropriate to your situation, and end each one with "I deeply and completely love and accept myself."

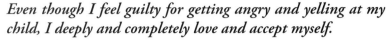

Even though I feel guilty for getting angry and yelling at my child, I deeply and completely love and accept myself.

Even though I feel like the world's worst parent when my child [whatever the issue is], I deeply and completely love and accept myself.

Even though I am tired and don't have enough time to deal with a fussy, whiney child, I deeply and completely love and accept myself.

Even though I am embarrassed by my child's temper outburst, I deeply and completely love and accept myself.

Even though I am worried about my child's [whatever the issue is], I deeply and completely love and accept myself.

Even though I feel guilty for leaving my child at daycare or with a babysitter, I deeply and completely love and accept myself.

Even though my child knows exactly how to push my anger buttons, I deeply and completely love and accept myself.

Even though I want to control my child and make [him/her] listen to me, I deeply and completely love and accept myself.

Even though I don't have time to be a good enough parent, I deeply and completely love and accept myself.

Even though other relatives, teachers or friends like to tell me how to parent my child, I deeply and completely love and accept myself.

Even though I feel overwhelmed by this [baby/child/teenager], I deeply and completely love and accept myself.

Even though I resent my child for [whatever the issue is], I deeply and completely love and accept myself.

These are just some suggestions that I hope will help you begin to examine your parenting issues. Feel free to create your own personal EFT setup phrases.

WHAT ARE SOME WAYS OF INTRODUCING EFT TO A CHILD?

Start with a simple explanation that includes the idea of emotions being energy, which can either feel good or yucky inside his/her body. Remember to use language and concepts your child already understands. When I explain EFT to a child, I may have him recall a time when he was angry, scared or sad, and I ask him if he noticed how that energy felt in his body.

If the child can connect to a physical sensation such as a tight/nervous stomach, heaviness in his chest, lump in the throat or tingling/hotness in hands or face, I explain that these sensations were energy vibrations.

Unless we work to release this energy, the uncomfortable feelings can stay stuck in his body. I ask him to tune into that emotion again and picture what was happening in his mind. When he is tuned in to the negative energy, he can release it from his mind and body by a simple tapping process called EFT.

I describe and show how he has *magic fingers* he can use for tapping at key energy points to release and move that energy out of his body. Then I ask if he would like to try this technique called Emotional Freedom Techniques (EFT) and see if he can make it work for him. Most children respond with "yes," but hesitant children need more time to feel safe.

If the child agrees to try it, I give him several choices on how to proceed. I show him the special tapping spots and ask if he would like to tap these spots using his *magic fingers* or if he would like me or his parent to tap these spots for him. If the child seems especially hesitant, I have the parent demonstrate how they can tap away some of their own negative feelings.

The child will also have some choices about what feeling he would like to shrink first. If the child has trouble thinking of what to work on first, I either ask the parent for suggestions or quickly think up some from what I know about the child and his issues.

If the child decides not to use the EFT tapping process this time, I give her options about other techniques that may help her express or process her feelings. I also like to tell her what some other children have processed using EFT — nightmares, fear of riding a bicycle, issues with a bully or feeling anxious about taking a test. Until the child feels safe enough to try EFT, I help her develop lots of positive ways of coping with her uncomfortable feelings.

Parents can help their child by occasionally modeling appropriate uses of EFT. If your child sees and feels your anger dissipate about being stuck in traffic, the dog's muddy feet on the couch or a burned dinner, she will be more open to trying it too. Please note, I wouldn't recommend processing negative feelings *about the child* in front of them. These issues are your own issues and need to be processed privately first.

When is the best time to use EFT with a child or teen?

The best time to use EFT with a child is when you are in an emotionally balanced space. You are less likely to get resistance from the child when you are calm and supportive rather than stressed and demanding.

After the child has had an introduction to the EFT method, any intense emotional issue can be an opportunity for releasing negative energy using EFT. It is a tool that can quickly help the child calm down, release his/her negative feelings and feel better. To start with, utilize EFT for the child within the privacy of the home or office. When he has had some success using it, it may be appropriate to use it more extensively.

Remember, any negative issue can be improved by tapping at key acupressure points. When a child is emotionally upset may be an excellent time to employ EFT. However, how you approach the child to engage them in using EFT is important. Be respectful of his heightened emotions, provide choices about doing the EFT, and make sure your energy is calm and accepting.

Assist him in the process only if he finds it helpful. If your child is resistant to the process, don't try to force it because it won't work. Just wait until a better time or check to see if you can do some surrogate tapping (explanation follows).

The first thing in the morning, or as part of bedtime, may be helpful times to build in an EFT routine. If your child has experienced a negative dream or nightmare, the morning may be a good time to decrease the frightening emotions. If your child is anxious or worried about anything that is coming up during the day, tapping first thing in the morning may be an excellent time to shrink that worry.

Bedtime also provides a wonderful opportunity for connecting with your child about the upsetting events of the day. What was the most challenging part of her day? What uncomfortable feelings did she have to deal with? Are there any leftover feelings that could be released right now with EFT? Daily supporting your child to find healthy ways of processing negative feelings will increase her self confidence and create resiliency for coping with life's inevitable problems.

 WHAT DOES THE BASIC SETUP PHRASE FOR A CHILD LOOK LIKE?

The basic setup for children is similar to adults except everything is simplified. First, simplify the setup phrase. Children need words and concepts to express upset feelings as well as for accepting themselves. Be creative about creating phrases that acknowledge the child's feelings in the situation.

Learning to accept himself, even though he has these big feelings, is an important step toward emotional maturity. Help the child fine tune the statements so they really feel they address her feelings. "Even though I am angry with my sister, I like myself and I'm okay," is a phrase simple enough for most children to understand and use.

Another setup adaptation is to have a child gently tap the Karate Chop points of each hand against each other to help clear energetic reversals.

Having the child say the setup phrase and then take a deep breath releases energetic toxins stored at the bottom of the lungs and helps the EFT tapping work more efficiently. Most children will feel a positive energy shift in their stomach and chest area just by doing this Karate Chop setup process.

You should also simplify the rating scale. If the child is still quite young, she may not understand how to rate her problem/feeling with a number. Using your hands, demonstrate a more helpful scale. Use hands touching to mean zero and hands wide apart to mean 10. Sometimes I use numbers along with the hand scale for added clarity. That seems to work well for most children who are six or older.

Here are the steps I go through when utilizing EFT with children:

1. Think of a problem or feeling you would like to shrink. How does that make you feel?

2. Using your hands, show how big the problem is. You can also pick a number from zero to 10 to represent the size of the problem.

3. Do the Karate Chop by tapping one hand against the other in a gentle chopping motion. While tapping say the setup phrase out loud three times. "Even though I have this [whatever the problem is], I still am a super kid." (Change the words to fit the situation/child.) Take a deep breath following each repetition of the phrase.

4. Tap at the special spots with your *magic fingers* to let go of the yucky feelings. If you like, you can say while tapping, "I am letting go of my anger" or other appropriate words.

5. For children we often use fewer tapping points. I recommend the following:
   a. Eyebrow point
   b. Side of eye point
   c. Under eye point
   d. Under nose point

    e. Chin point

    f. Collarbone point

    g. Under arm point

    h. Below nipple point

6. Check to see how big the problem or feeling is now. Can you give it a number?

7. Tap the Karate Chop point again if there are still some yucky feelings left. You might want to change the reminder phrase to say something like "Even though I still have some of this [whatever the problem or yucky feeling is], I like myself and I'm a terrific kid." Remember to repeat it three times and to take a deep breath following each repetition.

8. Do another round of tapping to continue releasing the blocked emotional energy.

9. Keep tapping the Karate Chop point with the phrase, continuing until it appears the child is at a zero. Don't forget to check if other aspects of the problem are coming up and need to be tapped on as well.

10. Use this tapping process whenever you or your child needs to process some yucky feelings. If you make it a regular part of your child's life, such as in the morning, after school or before going to bed, he/she will improve even faster.

WHAT KINDS OF ISSUES ARE MOST EFFECTIVE TO PROCESS WITH CHILDREN USING EFT?

Anything and everything can be issues to process with children. Notice what triggers their strongest negative feelings. It may be a conflict within the family, a bully at school, fears about trying something new or being afraid to go to sleep at night because of nightmares. The following topics contain some setup phrases to help you think about the kind of issues your child may want to process using EFT.

For feelings, end each phrase with "I like myself and I'm okay."

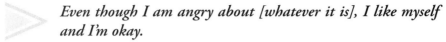

> *Even though I am angry about [whatever it is], I like myself and I'm okay.*
>
> *Even though I am scared of [whatever it is], I like myself and I'm okay.*
>
> *Even though I am sad about [whatever it is], I like myself and I'm okay.*
>
> *Even though I resent or am jealous of [whatever it is], I like myself and I'm okay.*

For sickness or physical pain, end with "I like myself and I am still a great kid."

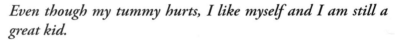

> *Even though my tummy hurts, I like myself and I am still a great kid.*
>
> *Even though I feel like I am going to throw up, I like myself and I am still a great kid.*
>
> *Even though I have this pain in my [wherever it is], I like myself and I am still a great kid.*
>
> *Even though I believe I am going to have an asthma attack, I like myself and I am still a great kid.*
>
> *Even though I am embarrassed because I was car sick, I like myself and I am still a great kid.*

Although EFT often brings a significant reduction in physical symptoms, don't hesitate to seek appropriate medical care when needed.

For nighttime issues tap using one of these setup phrases:

> *Even though I am scared of the monsters in my dreams, I like myself and I'm okay.*
>
> *Even though I feel scared and need to have a light on when I go to sleep, I like myself and I'm okay.*
>
> *Even though I pee my bed when I go to sleep, I like myself and I'm okay.*

Even though I don't feel tired and want to stay up as late as my brother or sister, I like myself and I'm okay.

Even though I am scared of what I see in my bedroom at night and don't want to sleep alone, I like myself and I'm okay.

For school issues, end with "I like myself and I'm still okay."

Even though I feel stupid and hate going to school, I like myself and I'm still okay.

Even though I am afraid of my teacher and the way she yells at kids at school, I like myself and I'm still okay.

Even though I feel anxious about taking this test, I like myself and I'm still okay.

Even though I am embarrassed about getting in trouble at school, I like myself and I'm still okay.

Even though the teacher blames me for something I didn't do, I like myself and I'm still okay.

For teasing and bullying, end with "I like myself and I am a super kid."

Even though I am scared of the mean kids at school, I like myself and I am a super kid.

Even though the neighbor boy calls me names and makes fun of me, I like myself and I am a super kid.

Even though a girl who I thought was a friend is spreading rumors behind my back, I like myself and I am a super kid.

Even though I don't feel safe at school, I like myself and I am a super kid.

For conflicts within the family, end with "I like myself and I am a super kid."

Even though I feel like everyone in the family is upset at me, I like myself and I am a super kid.

Even though I have to do chores that I don't want to do, I like myself and I am a super kid.

Even though I am lonely and no one has time to spend with me, I like myself and I am a super kid.

Even though I had a fight with [name], I like myself and I am a super kid.

Even though I am bored and have nothing to do, I like myself and I am a super kid.

For grief and loss issues use:

Even though I can't believe [person or thing] is gone, I like myself and I am a super kid.

Even though I am angry about my parents moving us to a new home, I like myself and I am a super kid.

Even though I am angry at the person who [whatever they did], I like myself and I am a super kid.

Even though I miss my [person or thing], I like myself and I am a super kid.

For self-esteem issues, end with "I like myself and I choose to see my good qualities."

Even though I feel like nobody likes me or wants to be my friend, I like myself and I choose to see my good qualities.

Even though I feel too [fat, skinny, tall, short, clumsy, shy, stupid, bored, lonely, etc.], I like myself and I choose to see my good qualities.

Even though I feel nervous about giving a speech in class, I like myself and I choose to see my good qualities.

Even though I feel different from everyone around me, I like myself and I choose to see my good qualities.

For music or sports performance, end with "I am a super terrific kid and I choose to play my best."

> *Even if I am nervous about playing in the next game, I am a super terrific kid and I choose to play my best.*
>
> *Even though I am worried that I may get hurt again playing the game, I am a super terrific kid and I choose to play my best.*
>
> *Even though there are others who play much better than me, I am a super terrific kid and I choose to play my best.*
>
> *Even though I hate to practice things that are hard for me, I am a super terrific kid and I choose to play my best.*

WHAT IS MEANT BY SURROGATE TAPPING AND HOW IS IT DONE?

There are many times when children will not cooperate to use EFT for parents, teachers or a therapist. They may be energetically reversed, sense your need to have them do it or they are scared to be in touch with their unpredictable feelings. Attempting or forcing a child to do EFT is really counterproductive to helping them feel safe enough to release these troublesome feelings. Another option when children will not cooperate to do EFT is to do *Surrogate Tapping*.

Surrogate tapping means that, for a short period of time you take on your child's energy to help them release some of their problematic feelings. The process is quite simple, effective to carry out and often helps your child feel better. Here are the steps to carry out this process.

1. Resolve your own issues about your child and what she is dealing with using EFT.

2. Tune in to your child and his emotional issues. Silently ask his permission to do this process for him. Wait for a positive or negative internal response before continuing.

3. If the response is positive, then focus energetically on your child and say, "I am no longer [your name]. I am now [child's name]."

4. Focusing on your child's feelings, establish the level of upset and the appropriate setup phrase to start with. Begin tapping through the acupressure points using a reminder phrase if it is helpful.

5. Continue focusing on your child's feelings and tapping until it feels resolved.

6. When finished say, "I am no longer [child's name]. I am myself again."

7. If the problem is a long standing problem, you may need to repeat this process several times to make a shift in the energetic pattern. I know parents who have gone into their child's bedroom to tap nightly while their child is sleeping. They reported very positive results.

AT WHAT AGE DO YOU RECOMMEND INTRODUCING CHILDREN TO EFT? DO YOU HAVE ANY HELPFUL STRATEGIES FOR SHOWING EFT TO YOUNGER CHILDREN?

Most children who are four or five years old can pick up EFT tapping. Make sure the language you use is developmentally appropriate and that you pick a time when your child is open and receptive. One idea for introducing younger children to EFT is to show the tapping to them using a favorite doll or teddy bear.

When they're familiar with the process, they may want to tap on their doll or teddy bear's negative feelings, which will be similar to theirs. A gentle exploration of their feelings with some validation that it is okay to have those feelings is reassuring for a young child.

ARE THERE TIMES WHEN A PARENT SHOULD SEEK PROFESSIONAL HELP FOR AN ISSUE WITH THEIR CHILD?

Yes, if your child/teen experiences significant trauma, such as a serious accident or sexual or physical abuse, it is advisable to seek support and help. During these times parents often have their own emotional baggage about what has happened, which may preclude them from being there in a positive way for their child. When looking for a caring therapist to assist your child, a feeling of safety and trust is a key ingredient for the healing process.

 DO YOU HAVE SOME TIPS FOR MAKING EFT MORE SUCCESSFUL FOR CHILDREN?

- Tap along with the child.
- Be creative about your approach. Keep it lighthearted and fun.
- Problems are like puzzles with many pieces. The more pieces the child and parent work on, the better they feel.
- Try it on everything! It can't hurt.
- Be persistent. The more EFT is used, the better the child feels.
- Make EFT a routine part of the day. Bedtime rituals or morning clearings are great.
- Ask children if they want to be the "Boss of their Feelings." With EFT they can choose when they want be upset and when they want to feel better!

To contact Jan Yordy, her e-mail address is
yordy@energyconnectiontherapies.com and her telephone number is
519-664-3568. Visit Jan's Website at
www.energyconnectiontherapies.com.
Also, please see Jan Yordy's biography at the back of the book.

FEARS & PHOBIAS
Taming our overpowering fears

By Mary Stafford

"Love is what we were born with. Fear is what we learned here."

Anonymous

WHAT IS FEAR?

Fear is a normal human emotional reaction. It is a built-in survival mechanism with which we are all equipped. Even as babies, we possess the survival instincts necessary to respond when we sense danger. Fear is a reaction to danger that involves the mind and body. Fear serves a protective purpose as it signals us and prepares us to deal with danger.

A fear reaction happens whenever we sense danger or when we are confronted with something new that seems potentially dangerous. It can be brief, as when you are surprised by something you did not expect. The sudden fear response is what triggers the body's survival mechanism known as *fight or flight*. That is exactly what the body is preparing itself to do — to fight off the danger or to run like crazy to get away.

WHAT IS HAPPENING IN THE BODY WHEN YOU EXPERIENCE THIS REACTION?

The brain triggers a response that causes the heart rate to increase. Blood is pumped to large muscle groups to prepare them for fight or flight. Blood pressure increases. Skin starts to sweat to keep the body cool. The body stays this way until the brain signals that it is safe to relax.

WHAT IS THE DIFFERENCE BETWEEN NORMAL, SELF-PROTECTIVE FEARS AND PHOBIAS?

Phobias are excessive, irrational fears that keep people from doing ordinary things. Without phobias, people easily do such everyday things as riding in elevators, climbing up ladders or being in water. Normal fears protect people from taking excessive risks. Phobias prevent people from doing the normal everyday things that are not really dangerous.

WHAT CAUSES PHOBIAS?

Some people are born with a natural tendency to be more cautious and inhibited. Others have an inborn tendency to be more bold and uninhibited. Having a cautious style may make it more likely for a phobia to develop.

Learning plays a part in helping phobias develop and linger. Children learn by watching how their parents react to the world around them. If parents are over cautious or over emphatic toward danger, children may learn to see the world this way, too.

Some people develop phobias as the result of a traumatic, life-threatening experience. An example is a person who is unable to get back behind the wheel after a severe car accident. Sometimes people do not remember the situation that started their phobia, especially if it began in childhood.

WHAT ARE SOME PHOBIAS THAT EFT HAS TREATED SUCCESSFULLY?

EFT has successfully treated the majority of phobias for which it has been used. Some successful examples are phobias of flying, elevators,

Some phobias are very easily treated with one or two rounds of EFT. The first person I treated for a heights phobia was a 6'5" man, Tom. He could not get up on a chair to change a light bulb without great difficulty. He was totally unable to climb a ladder to get onto his roof to service his evaporative cooler. Tom said all he could do was stand on the hood of his car, hold on to the edge of the roof, and look at the cooler.

I asked him to stand on a chair to assess his difficulty before we tapped. The color in his face drained away, and he was shaking. Tom got down from the chair. We did two rounds of tapping focusing on his fear. He was then able to easily get back onto the chair and was smiling as he did it. There were some empty chairs in the room, and he asked for them to be put into a circle. Tom hopped from one chair to another laughing loudly as he did it. In one month, Tom called me to rejoice in the fact that he had easily been able to climb a ladder and service the cooler on the roof of his house.

cockroaches, spiders, snakes, heights, driving, water and public speaking. The list goes on to include small enclosed spaces (claustrophobia), small rodents (such as rats and mice), agoraphobia (the fear of leaving your home), needles, using public restrooms, dentists and hospitals. Also on the success list is the fear of strangers and of being touched or looked at by others. By using EFT, many people have begun to like or enjoy what they once dreaded.

How can I use EFT to treat my phobia, when it is so overwhelming that I can not even think about it?

Some peoples' phobias are overwhelming. They have trouble even thinking about them. For those cases it would be advisable to do some preliminary tapping on that additional problem before tapping on the specific phobia. Some appropriate setup phrases would be:

Even though I have these fears that I cannot control, I deeply and completely love and accept myself.

Even though there are things that terrify me, I deeply and completely love and accept myself.

Even though I don't want to think about this, I deeply and completely love and accept myself.

There is no need to get terribly upset when thinking about the problem. You can sneak up on it by first tapping on those issues.

HOW DO I USE EFT TO TREAT MY PHOBIA, AFTER I HAVE GOTTEN TO WHERE I CAN THINK ABOUT IT?

You pick a specific phobia, such as the fear of getting back behind the steering wheel of a car. Focus your thoughts on a particular traumatic memory that you have about driving a car. Gauge your intensity on a scale of 0-10. Ask yourself if you feel this fear anywhere in your body. You may have a queasy feeling in your stomach, sweaty palms, a pounding heart, shortness of breath or a lump in your throat when you focus on the fear. Begin by tapping on the Karate Chop point on the side of the hand, above the little finger, while saying:

Even though I am terrified by this car accident, I love and accept myself.

Repeat the statement, while tapping, three times. Then, focus on the terror of the car accident while tapping all of the points. Your intensity will usually decrease with each round of tapping until it is down to a SUDS of two or less. Your physical feelings associated with the fear should also decrease as the fear decreases.

SHOULD I FOCUS ONLY ON THE FEAR WHILE I AM TAPPING, OR ARE THERE OTHER ISSUES ON WHICH I SHOULD FOCUS?

It is very important to treat all of the aspects of the experience, such as

> At one of the first EFT trainings I did, I demonstrated EFT with Susan, who had a severe phobia of cockroaches. When she would see a roach, she would scream and run from the room. In the training we were sitting on tall three-legged stools at the front of the room. Susan first applied EFT to her fear of roaches, and the intensity went from 10 to zero. I asked her imagine that roaches were crawling up the legs of the stool toward her. Her intensity increased to eight. She did more tapping on that image, and her intensity again went down to zero.
>
> I brought out a live roach I had found in the shower that morning. Susan's intensity went back to four. After another round of EFT, she was back to zero. She was able to hold the glass bottle, with the roach in it, with no difficulty. Six months later, Susan called me to say she had noticed a roach on her wall at home. She had calmly taken a fly swatter and dispatched the roach with no emotion. Before using EFT, Susan would have run screaming out of the house.

what you saw, what you heard and what you felt. Some setup phrases you could use, in the case of the driving phobia, would be:

> *Even though I was terrified at the sight of the car coming toward me, I deeply and completely love and accept myself.*
>
> *Even though the sound of the car hitting my car still terrifies me when I think about it, I deeply and completely love and accept myself.*
>
> *Even though my head hurt when it hit the windshield, I deeply and completely love and accept myself.*

In addition, it is important to treat the different feelings associated with the experience that come into your awareness as you tap. These feelings might be guilt, embarrassment, anger or shame. Possible setup phrases are:

> *Even though I am so angry at this jerk for running into my car, I deeply and completely love and accept myself.*

Even though I am so embarrassed that I was not paying more attention to that car, I deeply and completely love and accept myself.

You should also process with tapping any memories of past experiences that come into your awareness as you are tapping. Treating a traumatic situation that led to a phobia is like peeling the layers off an onion. There may be many layers to your phobia that you need to peel away before you come to the core of peace and relaxation.

WHEN YOU TREAT A SPECIFIC PHOBIA WITH EFT, DO YOU NEED TO TREAT IT AGAIN THE NEXT TIME YOU ENCOUNTER THE SITUATION?

No, not if you have done a thorough job of treating all of the different aspects of the phobia the first time. If you neglected to treat all of the different aspects, then some fear may come up later. You will be able to tap that away in the same way you did initially. Your assistance will be available at your fingertips!

HOW DO YOU KNOW WHEN YOU HAVE COMPLETELY TREATED A PHOBIA?

You will not know for sure until you are in the experience that previously was a problem. You can test your results by trying to bring your intensity back by focusing in on the issue, but you really will not know unless you do something that is similar to the original experience. In the case of the driving phobia, for example, you would try to get back behind the steering wheel of a car and then try to drive on the same street where the accident happened.

WILL TREATING A PHOBIA OF HEIGHTS, DRIVING OR SNAKES CAUSE YOU TO LOSE YOUR NORMAL SELF-PROTECTIVE FEARS THAT KEEP YOU FROM DOING THINGS THAT ARE UNSAFE?

A more recent case was a woman who had a phobia of snakes. She had no memory of being scared by a snake as a child. She did two rounds of tapping, and her intensity decreased from 10 to zero. To test her treatment, I brought out a fake plastic snake I have in my office. Looking at the fake snake, her intensity increased to eight. She again tapped while looking at the snake.

As she was tapping, a childhood memory, of having a male babysitter expose himself to her, came into her awareness. She tapped on that experience, and her intensity on that, as well as the snake, went to zero. This case demonstrates that sometimes phobias are the result of a traumatic experience that occurred in childhood. You may not remember it until you do the tapping on the phobia.

No, EFT only treats the excessive, irrational fear of a phobia. It does not change your normal self-protective fears. You will not lose your common sense and endanger yourself.

WHAT DO YOU DO IF A PHOBIA COMES BACK AND DOES NOT RESPOND TO TAPPING?

Occasionally a phobia is successfully treated, tested and found to be gone, but returns later and does not respond to tapping. This most likely means that an energy toxin is involved. An energy toxin is a substance that is being breathed in or eaten that weakens the energy system and prevents EFT from working.

If you play detective and pay attention to the clues, you can frequently discover what substance is the energy toxin. Whenever the symptoms return and are not able to be treated with EFT, ask yourself what you just did. Did you just eat something, put something on your body or smell something? It is helpful to keep a journal and to note what you eat and do and what happens to your symptoms.

A good question to ask yourself is, "What food or substance is it that I crave?" The answer to that question is likely to be the energy toxin. The most common energy toxins are wheat, corn and sugar, but just about anything can function as an energy toxin. I had a client one time whose energy toxin was black pepper. She craved it, and, as she phrased it, "I like a little salad with my black pepper."

If you are unsuccessful when you try to detect what substance is acting as an energy toxin, you should consult an EFT practitioner who uses muscle testing for this purpose. Energy toxins are easy to detect with muscle testing.

What if EFT does not work on my fear or phobia?

If EFT does not appear to work on your fear issue, it would be important to contact an EFT practitioner. They know additional tapping points and techniques to help in the more difficult cases. They will be able to see what you are missing and help you understand where you are going wrong. Do not assume EFT will not work on your issue, without consulting an EFT practitioner.

Can you treat the fear of dying with EFT?

Yes, the fear of dying is treatable with EFT. It has been used in hospices and was found to help terminally ill people. After tapping on this fear, they then can relax and have a much easier transition.

Does EFT treat the common fears that keep people stuck, such as the fear of failure?

Yes, many people have used EFT to recover from the common fears that prevent them from achieving their goals. As a group, these are called *fear of failure*. You will never be successful if you never try because you are afraid of failing. An example of the fear of failing is commonly called *writer's block*. When an author is afraid that what he writes will not be good enough, he finds it impossible to get started.

If the author taps on this fear, he will later find it easy to begin writing. This happened to a writer who attended one of my EFT trainings. The following day she called to tell me she found herself writing the first chapter of her book the previous evening. She had been trying to get started for a month before the training.

No matter what fear or phobia you'd like to overcome, you'll find that EFT is a safe, gentle way to get emotional relief.

To contact Mary Stafford, her e-mail address is mstafford@mindbodytherapy.com and her telephone number is 520-575-1497. Visit Mary's Website at www.mindbodytherapy.com. Also, please see Mary Stafford's biography at the back of the book.

HAPPINESS
The ultimate success

By Brad Yates

"Success is not the key to happiness. Happiness is the key to success. If you love what you are doing, you will be successful."

Albert Schweitzer

WHAT IS HAPPINESS?

That could start off quite a philosophical debate, as the exact definition of happiness varies from person to person. In general, it is defined as a state of well-being, the experience of which may range from simple contentment to intense joy. It's the experience of feeling good. It might also be considered the absence of negative feelings, if one was inclined to look at it from that standpoint. Even though there may be unpleasant circumstances in one's life, he or she may still feel happy by refusing to harbor negative feelings about the circumstances.

Happiness is the ultimate goal. The Dalai Lama has said that the very purpose of life is to seek happiness. If you ask someone what they want in life, they will often give you a laundry list of material items — the sports car, the mansion, the diamond watch, etc. — or other external conditions such as great friendships or a great job. Not that there is anything wrong with any of these, mind you.

Abundance just is — there is plenty to go around — and I am all in favor of folks enjoying all the perks and goodies life has to offer. However, if you were to really dig deeper and ask why they want those things, I believe the ultimate reason will be, "Because it would make me feel good. I'd feel happy."

The funny thing is, when someone simply answers the question "What do you want?" with "I just want to be happy," they are often scoffed at. It may be that they are perceived as trying to be evolved, or naïve or that they just aren't asking for enough. There's this inclination towards complicating the issue — and in doing so, we sometimes miss the mark. What we really want is to be happy. Granted, that's a belief on my part. But it's my story, and I'm sticking to it.

? IS HAPPINESS REALLY AVAILABLE TO ANYONE?

Absolutely. In the United States Declaration of Independence, happiness is listed as one of our unalienable rights. It has also been suggested that our Forefathers did us a disservice by listing it as the "pursuit" of happiness — as though it were something we had to go after, something based in external circumstances, rather than something we could simply choose to experience. Barry Kaufman, founder of the Options Institute, put it very simply in the title of one of his books: *Happiness is a Choice.*

Actually, I believe that happiness is our birthright and our natural state of being. If you observe babies for any length of time, they appear to be happy most of the time, unless there is some condition that is causing them discomfort, such as hunger or a wet diaper. While loving attention is critical to the development of a healthy child, a baby can manage to be quite content in its absence. Infants are also delightfully unattached to what adults perceive as material value. It can be quite amusing — if not a little frustrating — to see a child more fascinated with the wrapping paper and box than with the expensive gift inside.

Obviously, some children are born into unfavorable circumstances, and they experience happiness on a more infrequent basis. Again, though, it seems that happiness is the norm as we enter this world, and we move away from it depending on the level of discomfort. Unfortunately for them, infants are incapable of doing much in terms of regulating their circumstance. As we grow older, we have much more control. And, what we have ultimate control over is how we feel about things. As Viktor Frankl observed in his book, *Man's Search for Meaning*:

> *"Everything can be taken from a man but... the last of the human freedoms — to choose one's attitude in any given set of circumstances, to choose one's own way."*

Dr. Frankl managed to maintain a positive attitude in spite of the horrific conditions he faced in a Nazi concentration camp.

WHY WOULD ANYONE BLOCK HAPPINESS?

We don't really know any better. We are all doing the best we can given our particular model of the world. Most of that is learned from our parents, though it isn't fair to completely blame them. First, they are only one source of information — few of us are around our parents 24 hours a day, seven days a week, during our formative years.

Second, they are simply the recipients of the same misinformation that has been handed down through generations of folks who believe it is their duty to "honor thy mother and thy father," even if that means buying into their limiting beliefs.

Abraham Lincoln is quoted as saying that "most folks are about as happy as they make up their minds to be." Much of our mind is made up very early on, based on those beliefs we have adopted from other people — the "comedies" or "writing on our walls," as Gary Craig puts it. It isn't that we make a conscious decision to block happiness, but rather that we unconsciously create so many rules about when we are allowed to experience happiness.

Where did these beliefs come from? Perhaps from a need to justify an absence of happiness experienced by an ancestor. Great-great-great grand pappy Albert got upset about a misunderstanding with an Italian immigrant and decided that the upset was a necessary consequence of dealing with Italians. He taught this "lesson" to his kids, who taught it to theirs, and so on.

Along the way, different associations may have been made to the original situation, such that the upset is now the anticipated result of dealing with a variety of nationalities. It isn't even logical — the original reasons being long buried with Albert. But darned if we don't keep such family traditions alive and unwell. The excuse for being unhappy becomes like a family heirloom — "It's been in our family for years."

Basically, we have learned to make happiness conditional. We say that people and things "make us" either happy or unhappy, as if our emotions were at the mercy of external forces. We have rules about when we can be happy. In fact, many folks have rules that make it easier to be unhappy than happy.

I can only be happy if:

- I am in a perfect relationship.
- I am driving a car worth over $45,000.
- Everyone I know (even those I don't like) sing my praises.

I must be unhappy if:

- Someone cuts me off on the road.
- My magazine doesn't arrive on time.
- It's Monday.

I often ask people, "How long should you be upset about anything?" It would be helpful if there were a book that listed the necessary lifespan of an upset: breaking a nail — five hours; breaking up with a significant other — the number of months you've been together times three… But there is no such book. It is subjective. You get to choose. Why not choose "not at all?"

Have you ever been confronted with (or, God forbid, confronted someone else with), "Why are you smiling?" or "What are you so happy about?" As if we need a reason! As if there were something wrong with simply being happy. But it is a matter of being raised in a world — at least for most of us — where happiness is something to be pursued and therefore conditional.

> Janet is 60 years old, and has been struggling since her divorce 20 years ago. She had been enjoying increasing success until then, which had lead to difficulties in her marriage. Her husband served her with divorce papers on her 40th birthday. After agreeing that she had suffered enough, we applied EFT to the various feelings that were still as painful as they were 20 years earlier.
>
> Some humorous reframing was used when we tapped on, "Even though my ex-husband had terrible taste in birthday presents…" After several rounds of tapping on this and other phrases during the hour, she felt the weight had been lifted. During subsequent communications, Janet reported that the whole thing still seems a little funny now, with none of the previous pain. She finds herself much freer to successfully pursue both personal and professional opportunities.

The interesting thing about life that too few are aware of is that we create our reality. We are waiting for more favorable conditions on the outside to make us feel better, when in fact it is allowing ourselves to feel better that, by the Law of Attraction, creates the more favorable circumstances. The happier you are, the more abundance shows up. In other words, being happy is a condition for attracting joyful abundance, rather than the other way around.

Can **EFT** make me happy?

Yes and no. Technically, as described above, nothing can make you happy. Happiness is something you allow. However, EFT is just about the best way there is to break your rules about when you can allow yourself to be happy.

You may be thinking, "It's about time he started talking about EFT." However, everything up to this point has been designed to clearly mark the targets at which to aim EFT. The *need* to be unhappy is not a tangible truth. Unhappiness — and any of the related feelings — is the experience of uncomfortable emotions or, more clinically, a disruption in the energy system. This can be cleared. Clinically speaking, one might call happiness the experience of a balanced energy system.

Again, it is our natural state. In fact, all the other chapters in this book are, ultimately, ways at clearing the path for greater happiness in your life. You will quite likely feel happier when you have less stress, more abundance and you are free from a fears or phobic limitations. Rather than using any of these conditions as an excuse for being unhappy, choose happiness, and clear whatever is causing the limiting disruptions.

What are some EFT setup phrases I might start with?

The best way to form setup phrases for EFT is to look at what is bothering you. If you can name it — and, even better, rate your feelings about it — you've got a great place to start. As mentioned in the instructions on how to do EFT, you want to try to rate the upset on a SUDS scale of 1-10. This isn't necessary for EFT to work, but it certainly helps both to see the improvement and to let you know if you are on the right track or need to adjust your setup.

I'll often ask clients to close their eyes, take a deep breath, and ask themselves, "What is bothering me the most right now?" What comes up may not be the core issue. The subconscious mind is protective of its issues, believing them to be necessary to our safety, and will offer up lesser entities, but it will be a gateway.

So, what are you experiencing that does not feel like happiness? Add an "Even though…" to the beginning, and you are in business.

For example:

> *Even though I am angry at Bob, I deeply and completely love and accept myself.*

With a statement like this, you may also ask yourself, "What does this anger remind me of?" There may be an anger from years ago that is still haunting you, and Bob simply triggered it. You can go directly to tapping on this, and the Bob issue will likely be resolved as well. However, tapping through the Bob issue can also help to clear related issues, so it is a good place to start.

> *Even though my family isn't being supportive of me, I deeply and completely love and forgive myself and them.*

This, again, is just a starting point. There are likely to be old family issues involved in this. There will also be issues unique to each family member, so you will want to doing clearing work on each separately as needed.

> *Even though I don't have everything I want, I deeply and completely accept myself.*

An extremely general opening line — but isn't that sometimes how we want to answer the question about why we aren't happy? A similar one would be to simply start with:

> *Even though I'm unhappy, I deeply and completely love and accept myself.*

Definitely rate that one on the scale of 1-10. Tapping on that phrase may not bring it down much, but it will be a great benchmark to look back on after you have tapped on more specific issues. You will want to use more specific phrases for truly effective clearing, but as you tap through these, the layers of the onion will be peeled, and you will become clearer about exactly what to focus on. You will be able to identify those rules that you will want to break.

> *Even though I don't feel worthy of happiness, I deeply and completely accept myself.*

The issue of not feeling worthy and deserving comes up more than any other in my work with clients. I think this is one of the greatest tragedies

Although he had participated in several EFT teleclasses, Ted was feeling that things were not improving financially — and maybe getting worse. Working one-on-one, he declared a sense that the Universe had it in for him. We tapped on this feeling using some rather colorful phrasing. Ted came to see that the Universe was pulling for him, but was allowing him free will.

Part of his subconscious was choosing for it to be difficult, and life was complying. With this new insight, he became free to choose more wisely. He called recently to tell me that, in the same week, he moved into a new apartment which was much nicer and yet less expensive than his previous one, and he got a new job which paid twice his previous salary.

of the human experience. Joy and abundance are our birthright. They are right there in front of us, waiting to be experienced to the full with nothing asked of us more than a simple yet sincere, "Yes, I accept."

But most of us feel we aren't good enough, haven't done enough, aren't this enough or that enough. This is all learned from past experiences and opens the door for a number of other EFT setup phrases. Look for the various mental "mini-movies" that served as negative learning experiences regarding your worthiness:

Even though Dad said I didn't deserve to win the spelling bee, I deeply and completely accept myself.

Even though I overheard Aunt Meg tell Mom that I'd never be pretty enough, I deeply and completely accept myself.

Even though Todd got a better grade than I did, I deeply and completely accept myself.

Even though the coach wouldn't play me in the last game, I deeply and completely accept myself.

Even though I stole that stick of gum, and the storekeeper said I was a bad person, I deeply and completely accept myself.

Even though I played that note off key in the third grade recital, I deeply and completely accept myself.

Too trivial, you say? You'd be amazed at how even the simplest incidents get lodged in there as reasons for denying ourselves happiness. Very often, a client will say, "I just remembered something, but it's too insignificant to mention. It's nothing." My take on it is this: if it's nothing, then why is it coming up? Even if it is a red herring, you might as well clear it.

I also get, "We don't need to work on that. I cleared that up with years of therapy." Again, why is it still coming up? Very often when I ask them to tell me a little more about it, the tears start coming. Here is a wonderful opportunity to do some clearing to open one up to a far greater level of happiness — and it was almost skipped over.

Since EFT is such a quick process, it is better to be safe than sorry. Go ahead and tap on everything that comes up. The worst that can happen is you give up a few minutes of time tapping on something that might actually be of little consequence. However, even then you'll be balancing your energy system. And, it is likely to lead to greater clarity on what is more important.

Gary Craig developed what he calls the Personal Peace Procedure. Visit his Website at www.emofree.com. Basically, you write down everything you can think of that bothers you — particularly every incident in your life that you wish you had not experienced. For most of us, this list may be fairly extensive, and you might be surprised at what comes up when you put in a little conscious effort. Then, you get tapping, focusing on three or so items a day. Don't be surprised if, as you clear these, other items get added to your list. But it won't be long before you are noticing a greater level of happiness.

Admittedly, this may involve a little more pain than most folks are willing to face. We would almost rather deal with a limited amount of happiness than go through the fires that could lead to a much greater level of joy. Make the decision to be as happy as you can and then perhaps do some preparatory tapping:

> *Even though I'm afraid to face the past, I deeply and completely accept myself.*
>
> *Even though I'm afraid it will be too painful, I deeply and completely accept myself.*
>
> *Even though I'm afraid I can't handle it, I deeply and completely accept myself.*

Of course, there are some places you don't want to go alone, and tapping with a professional — or even a trusted friend — is a very good idea.

You might also write down your rules for happiness. On a sheet of paper, write down what your criteria are for being happy. Start with, "I can allow myself to be happy when… " Then tap on those rules:

> *Even though I think I need to have an expensive car to be happy, I deeply and completely accept myself.*

In tapping on these rules, you are likely to uncover their roots. For instance, if you had the hypothetical rule above, you might remember your father watching television commercials for expensive cars, and saying, "Man, if only I had one of those babies, then I could be happy." You may never know why he had that as one of his happiness rules, but it isn't necessary for you to keep carrying it.

> *Even though Dad taught me that I need an expensive car to be happy, I deeply and completely accept myself.*

Again, there is nothing wrong with having a nice car — by all means, get one. Here's the thing. The best means to getting one is to let go of any negative energy around having one, especially the idea that you can't be happy without one.

This brings up an important point about happiness and financial abundance — money does not buy happiness. Otherwise, how would

The most challenging crowd I work with is at Sacramento County Drug Court. Rather than having chosen EFT as a means of recovery, the participants are court ordered to be in my class. This crowd looks at the tapping process with a certain amount of skepticism if not outright ridicule, and most engage in the work half-heartedly, if at all.

Doug was no exception. He was a pretty hardcore addict from the mean streets, and had been at Level One for sometime. One particular morning, he came in very distressed over his dissolving relationship with his "old lady," who was still using drugs. He was ready to be open. We worked one-on-one, with the rest of the class "borrowing benefits." Within a couple of short rounds, we brought his intense feelings from a 10+ to a zero.

He looked at me with astonishment and said, "This s**t works!" After that, there was a very noticeable change in his demeanor, and he shortly moved up to the next level in the program. He still has a long way to go, but has a powerful new tool to help free him from his troubling emotions.

we explain all the rich people who are seemingly miserable? Money may make you more comfortable, but it won't automatically break the rules you have. It's been said that money just makes you more of what you already are.

So, if you have a tendency towards being unhappy, money will likely give you plenty more to be unhappy about. I am a big proponent of enjoying wealth. I am a bigger proponent of clearing your way to happiness first.

Continuing the exercise for discovering setup phrases, also write down your rules for when you must be unhappy:

> *Even though I must be upset when someone cuts me off on the road, I deeply and completely accept myself.*

The truth is that these are not hard and fast rules. Plenty of people are allowing themselves a certain amount of bliss despite not meeting your criteria. If they aren't letting it upset them, why should you?

Also look for the deeper meaning in the things you let upset you. What do you say it means about you when these things happen? For instance, when someone cuts you off:

> *Even though other people take advantage of me, I deeply and completely accept myself.*

You can then trace the origins of that belief. Yes, this process can lead to a multitude of issues, one that is seemingly endless. Eventually though, you will hit upon the core issues that will lead to a freedom beyond belief. You are welcome to settle at any point along the way, but I hope you will decide that you deserve more than you already have.

Tapping in affirmations is a great use of EFT. After you have written down and tapped on your old rules for happiness, you can create new ones and tap them in — ones that make it much easier for you to allow happiness:

> *I can only be happy on days whose names end in day.*

Why not set yourself up to win? You are welcome to argue with me if you like, but I hold this truth to be self evident: *You have a right to be happy!*

ANYTHING ELSE I SHOULD KNOW?

Yes. It's been said so much that it has become a cultural truth: Misery loves company. Don't expect those around you to suddenly be happy for you that you are choosing to be happy — especially when you are breaking rules that they also subscribe to.

> *Even though others don't want me to be happier, I deeply and completely love and accept myself.*

And, because of this:

 Even though it doesn't feel safe for me to be happier, I deeply and completely accept myself.

But you can either be stuck in the muck with the masses or be a trailblazer to joy. Choose wisely. I believe we ultimately want to be happy — and for others to be happy as well. The higher self of those around you is rooting for you. If someone seems unenthusiastic about you becoming happier, it likely comes from a fear on their part that such increased joy is not possible for them.

You can't be miserable enough to make them happier, but you can be happy enough to be a positive example. So, being happier is far from a selfish act, it is a gift to those around you. And because we are all connected on an energetic level, the happier you allow yourself to be, the more your energy is balanced and the higher the level at which you vibrate, the more that is felt by humanity as a whole. So, thank you for tapping.

To contact Brad Yates, his e-mail address is brad@bradyates.net and his telephone number is 916-729-0347. Visit Brad's Websites at www.bradyates.net and www.golfbeyondbelief.com. Also, please see Brad Yates' biography at the back of the book.

HEALTH
Exploring the mind/body connection

Dr. Alexander R. Lees

"He who sings frightens away his ills."

Cervantes

WHY IS IT BENEFICIAL AND VALUABLE FOR ALL OF US TO LEARN SOMETHING ABOUT THE MIND/BODY CONNECTION?

I'd like to take a moment to tell you a little bit about myself. Maybe hearing my story will help you to understand why I feel it is important for everyone to have some knowledge about the Mind/Body Connection and health.

I didn't have a burning desire to learn about this stuff, when I was young. Forty years ago I was a single male driving a sports car across the country and having a great time. The next thing I knew, I woke up in a hospital and three weeks had gone by. "What happened?" was the first question I asked when I came out of the coma.

The doctor proceeded to tell me I'd had a horrific car accident, and I would never walk again. The world as I knew it no longer existed. In one way I was fortunate as I was in the Air Force at the time, and the best medical care would be provided. But, the words kept ringing in my ears, "You'll never walk again."

What could I do? Maybe it was my age. I was only 20. Or, maybe it was my character. I am strong willed. Some people call me stubborn. But, I knew, on a very deep level that the doctors were wrong, and I could do something to prove it.

I began my healing journey by reaching out to anyone, and everything I could find to help myself. Thus began my journey on the road to discovering the Mind/Body Connection. Way back then there wasn't much information, but what there was, I found. It was a long journey and painful at times, but I'm happy to report that after a bit of time I was out of the wheelchair and walking.

My life took many interesting twists and turns before I knew what I wanted to do with it. One day I realized that I wanted to help others. Help them the way I had helped myself. And, one way I could do that was by learning as much as I could about the Mind/Body Connection, and then spreading the word.

Now, many of you may think science is something only for geeks. Not so. Allow me to introduce you to some fascinating science, and do me a favor. When you think of the word *science*, at least during this discussion, realize we are simply referring to facts as we know them. Hopefully, I will provide some insights, and a better understanding of an amazing subject by doing so.

WHICH CAME FIRST... THE CHICKEN OR THE EGG?

Another way of asking the same question is, "What came first? Was it mind, or was it matter?" Did an animal somehow learn to think, or did thinking (mind) somehow become a physical form? Interesting question. Before we get right into the science of all of this, I'd like to share a little history first, just to set the stage.

Descartes was a 16th century philosopher, among other things. One of the things he wanted to do was to study the human body. He wanted to delve inside and have a look. In order to do that, he had to make a deal with the Church. The Church would deal with the departed mind, spirit and soul, and Descartes would be allowed to delve further into the human, physical body left behind.

The significance of this agreement is that from this point on in history the concept of Mind/Body became the mind *and* body. In other words, they became two separate entities. To this day, there still exists a division in the two subjects, mind (psychological) and body (physical).

Well, the fact is, they are still *one*.

Thanks to some brave pioneers of our time, the facts are beginning to emerge from the laboratory as to how it all works. The following is a brief summary of the efforts and dedication of many different researchers, and is my version of connecting the dots.

How does it all work?

Until recently, the popular belief was that a human could feel or experience severe emotional states and the immune system was immune to these states. In other words, it is taught that the immune system operates on its own, and is therefore unaffected by outside influences. We now know the immune system is directly affected by our emotional states.

We now know that how a patient *perceives* a situation can have an effect on how the immune system operates. Now let me ask you a question. Have you noticed when you are stressed that this is the time you are most likely to get a cold?

The immune system has a memory. So does the mind/brain. They talk to each other and share information. For the first time in our history, we are beginning to discover the actual link between mind (thought) and body (matter) used for exchanging this information.

Do we know what the mind and body are talking about?

If we were to eavesdrop a little, we might hear things like, "Make a little more of this protein," or "A little less of that one." The message might be, "Cells, stop dividing, we have enough for now." Or, "There is danger out there. Forget healing. Use your energy for fighting."

Now, before some of you begin to think all this is too far outside your understanding, too far outside your reality, I would suggest you recall the term biofeedback. Biofeedback is used to effect all sorts of changes in the body, including blood pressure, headaches and anxiety, just to name a few. Biofeedback equipment has been with us for some 30 years, and confirms that changing your state of mind causes changes in the body that are measurable.

Now, I would like to draw your attention to one of the really important parts.

 WHAT IS THE DIFFERENCE BETWEEN MIND AND BRAIN?

Great question. Let's clarify. To begin with, Mind is an abstract that is no molecular movement, no occupation of space, and no mass. Brain, on the other hand, is physical because it does satisfy all three of the above rules. We think, which is a mental process somewhere within the realm of the Mindfield. I'll explain what I mean by Mindfield a little later. Right now, I'd like you focus on thinking and thoughts.

Our thoughts have fuel to run them, and that fuel is an emotion. As the brain processes the thought/emotion, it translates it into a language the body can understand and act upon. That language is — chemistry.

The thought/emotion is now physical — from nothingness to somethingness. One moment it's not there (a thought is non-physical), the next moment, it is there, in physical form (chemistry). We cannot see a thought, but we can see the resulting chemistry.

Dr. Candace Pert, a Research Professor at the Department of Physiology and Biophysics, Georgetown University Medical Center, Washington, DC, has 15 years of research behind her statement: *"The biochemical equivalent of an emotion is called a neuropeptide."*

Thank you for hanging in there and following all the science so far. I'm going to ask you to stay with me a little longer. I promise you, it will be worth your time.

Ryan sat down in my office and announced, "I have been an insane, crazed lunatic for eight years. Something has happened to me and my life, and I've managed to end up in the gutter. I'm going to lose my family, my wife, my home, and my career if I don't do something." I asked him, "So what's the problem?" Ryan began to rattle off a list of general self-diagnosed problems. When he was finished I asked him to picture a feeling that he would like to dismiss forever. Then I walked over to him and started tapping.

Ryan seemed a bit amazed at what I was doing because I hadn't explained anything about EFT or what I was going to do. I just tapped on him as he was focused on the feeling. A moment went by. He released a huge sigh. "The tapping felt like a veil of heaviness being lifted from my brow," Ryan said. Then very quietly he added, "This is one of the most profound experiences I have ever had in my life."

We had several more sessions in the following two weeks, tapping every possible negative emotion Ryan could access. At the last session, Ryan announced, "It's all gone. Don't ask me where. What I do know is that it is gone, and that's all that matters. Currently I feel, work, and play better than I ever remember. What a feeling. What a gift. Thank you, Alex." I said, "Thank EFT, not me. I was just the facilitator."

WHAT IS A NEUROPEPTIDE AND WHAT DOES IT DO?

A neuropeptide is like a train, with amino acids linked together like railway cars. The neuropeptide is binary coded information. This information is now available to all the cells in our body. Once the coded information reaches the cell, the cell needs to read it. Microscopic antennae, attached to the surface of every cell, do the reading of this information.

This next part is really fascinating. The antennae on the cell now pick up information coming into the cell, the *environmental* information, and the cell acts upon it. The DNA in the cell now has instructions and, like a highly sophisticated and willing team, goes to work in the manufacturing business, filling orders for what the body needs, i.e., producing proteins, making insulin, etc.

The cell/DNA not only processes environmental information, but also *inherited* information, which is based on previously learned and stored information about growth, survival and evolvement.

So, the cell/DNA contains inherited information and the antennae on the cell pick up or receive new environmental information. This new environmental information can be considered the upgrade information and is filtered through our perceptions and colored by our emotional responses to that information.

The information coming through the antennae into the cell can then be classified in two ways. One is positive, that is, conducive to growth and health, and the other is negative, or non-conducive to growth and health, depending on how it affects the individual.

 DOES THIS UPGRADING OF INFORMATION AFFECT OUR EMOTIONS?

Yes! Let's take it one step further. Once a person's antennae are tuned through experience to the negative, then the processed thoughts evoke a negative emotional charge, producing a negative message within the neuropeptide. Given a sufficient intensity, this will produce a certain malaise, or discomfort all the way down to the cellular level.

If this happens long enough, and the emotion is intense enough, these emotional charges will eventually change the cell, and it will function on a dysfunctional level. The result is a dis-ease, based on a fearful response to that environment. Another way of saying this is: *Unresolved negative emotions are a precursor to disease.*

ARE YOU SAYING THAT IF WE HAVE UNRESOLVED NEGATIVE EMOTIONS WE CAN GET SICK?

Yes, it's highly possible, and probably likely. It has been estimated that a human mind processes some 60,000 thoughts a day. The rules governing this phenomenon belong more to the concept of a field, an energy field. I like to call this energy field the *Mindfield*. One of the useful aspects of this Mindfield is the following. By repeating many of these thoughts daily, the world remains the same.

We therefore have a certain knowing, and the world is somewhat predictable. In other words, each of us follows certain pathways, or repetitive lines of thought, within this field. Because of this, our world remains the same, and so do the problems.

DOES THIS MEAN **I** SHOULD PAY MORE ATTENTION TO MY THOUGHTS?

Yes. You see, the mind is an equal opportunity device. It will process limiting thoughts just as easily as life-expanding, self-empowering ones. If you wish to make changes in your life, then the first step is to begin to pay attention to the thoughts. Start with a subject. Notice how your mind begins to think about that subject.

Notice the beliefs that must be there in order to think those particular thoughts. Then ask yourself, "Is it useful for me to think in that particular way? Is there another way to think about 'X' subject that would serve me better?" To borrow a famous quote, *"We are not victims of the world we see. We are victims of the way we see it."* When we decide to change (I prefer the word expand) the way we think, there are certain new pathways we can learn to follow in order to do a more effective job.

All right, you've learned how thoughts are formed and why it's important to pay attention to your emotions. The next step is to find out what you can do to change some of your less than helpful, or less beneficial, thoughts. There is a pathway you can follow.

The client seated in my office was a middle aged, no nonsense female, and had made it very clear from the beginning that "We have some serious work ahead." Just to set a frame of reference for this case, when Barb first arrived, she insisted on reading me a list of issues she had, many of them going back to her childhood. She said that this list contined to grow each year. We spent fifty-two minutes of our first session going through Barb's list.

The list included, multiple issues from childhood, including a lifelong fear of rodents, low self esteem and feelings of inadequacy. The items on this list had continued to expand yearly. Other items included the following: insomnia/sleep interrupt, panic/anxiety attacks, social phobia, bathroom phobia, fear of being alone, male proximity, stomach pains, neck pain, throbbing in the head, dizziness, vertigo, tinnitus, fear of driving, fear of being in a moving vehicle, flashbacks on car accidents, and flashbacks regarding her ex-husband — especially the apparent murder attempt.

"Where would you like to start?" I inquired. "I don't really know," she replied. I said, "Okay, let me ask you another question. If you could live your life over again, but were allowed to skip one thing, and only one thing, what would that be?" "All of it," Barb replied. "I'm overwhelmed by how much there is to fix," she added.

I said, "Supposing you were in a boat and somehow all of your life's burdens were right there with you. Now then, further suppose that if you were to throw the right one overboard, the boat would remain afloat, and take you to shore. Now, you can only throw away one of them, so which is the heaviest?" "Life," she replied. I reached over and grabbed her hand and started tapping the Karate Chop (Psychological Reversal) point and saying, "Even though I'm overwhelmed with all there is to fix, and even though I've spent time, money and effort to do so, then I come to see this guy because someone said I should, and all I get is some bearded old dude slapping the side of my hand."

That broke the ice, and Barb's color returned. She laughed and cried for a few minutes. This began our fifteen sessions together. During these hours, we cleared the issues mentioned above. I would like to say not one iota of any of her issues exists today.

WHAT ARE THE PATHWAYS WE CAN FOLLOW?

Before you know what path to take it may be helpful to learn which ones NOT to take. There are several pathways our thoughts can follow. Some will lead us to where we want to go, like a map through the Mindfield. Other pathways can lead us to where we don't want to go. First, let's examine one that doesn't work. Most people can talk about the problem quite well. This is the *What's Wrong* Path. It's a circular route, a form of self-hypnosis, and tends to lead to why is this so? A more useful path is *How Do I Change It?*

HOW DO OUR EMOTIONAL STATES OF MIND AFFECT OUR PROGRESS, AND/OR OUR HEALTH?

We now know that the emotional state of an individual plays a major role in health. When we think, we use nerve cells in the brain to do so. Imagine these brain cells as a wheat field — each neuron ready to lean over and communicate with another. The emotions are like the breeze blowing through that field, causing patterns. These patterns are what we refer to as beliefs, attitudes and values. Eventually, if these emotions continue over time, the results of their influence will appear in the body.

HOW EXACTLY DO WE GET OURSELVES INTO THESE STATES THAT AFFECT OUR HEALTH?

The simple answer is *experience*. Given enough negative experiences, the perception becomes biased toward negativity accordingly. The key to remember is that we are being programmed by the negative emotional charge accumulating in the system. Let me remind you once again: *"We are not victims of the world we see. We are victims of the way we see it."*

At this time I'd like to tell you another personal story. I believe in the information I have written above and put my beliefs into action every day. All this information wasn't available when I had my car accident, but at that time I learned enough to get me out of a wheelchair. Now, I'd like to fast forward in my life to about ten years ago. I had a routine physical. I generally get one every five years or so, and I came home one day to a message on my telephone answering machine. It sounded ominous. I'd never had a request to call my doctor and book an appointment to see him (probably because the only illness I'd had was the car accident). "I'm a fairly healthy guy." Or so I thought.

I go in and see the doctor. And, I hear the worst possible words. The doctor said, "You have cancer — an aggressive form of Leukemia." My mind froze. I have what? Before I could ask, he proceeds to tell me that this is very serious. They don't know the cause, and there is no cure. If I choose to take the available treatments which are chemotherapy and/ or radiation, it *might* help. There were no guarantees. Maybe in a few years there will be a course of treatment that can provide more hope, but we don't have one at the present time. I should go home and put my affairs in order.

My mind is screaming, "Put my affairs in order… what, and how, am I going to tell Berit (my wife)?" It's truly amazing how our minds work. On the way home I made a decision. This bit of news, this issue, this cancer, was not going to win. I needed to be 100 percent congruent regarding this. Otherwise I couldn't tell Berit without both of us breaking down.

I got home and told Berit. I also told her not to worry, and I'd take care of it. You're probably asking yourself I mean by "*take care of it.*" So did Berit. I reminded her of my car accident and how my life turned out. I said I'd do the same thing again. I would apply my knowledge of the Mind/Body connection and I would be okay. She cried.

I hate to see a woman cry, so I hugged her and said, "Trust me." I realize that "Trust me," could also be a question and I told her that I meant it as both a statement and a question. Berit said, "Yes."

Then I went about doing what it is I do, talking to my self, visualizing, and practicing all the stuff I've learned over the years. Three years into the

Erin was devastated. Her cancer had been in remission for 14 months and now she'd had a relapse. Erin had been told that if a bone marrow match was not found, the best the doctors could give her was seven months to live. "You cannot begin to imagine the degree of resentment I have to this betrayal. I'm angry, resentful and scared. I don't want any psychotherapy or analysis. I want a quick fix," she announced. I briefly explained the mind/body connection and then segued into a brief explanation of EFT. "Show me," she said.

For the next three sessions, Erin and I worked on her attitude, resentments and fears. The grip the cancer had on her life began to loosen and she was able to pull away and look at all the other aspects of her life. Soon after, her blood levels returned to a level which would allow a transplant. When a bone marrow donor was found, the match was not ideal so we tapped on "Even though this isn't a perfect match, I trust my body to make the appropriate adjustments, and I deeply and completely trust myself, and believe in the body's innate wisdom."

The mismatched bone marrow was accepted by Erin's body. And, to the doctor's astonishment, the transplant had caused only minimal, therefore controllable, side effects. The critical time frame for Erin was set at 100 days. If she made it through that time period, she was told that she'd probably make it. On day 124, Erin dropped by my office to say hello, thank me for introducing her to EFT and ask, "So, what are you going to teach me next?" In Erin's words, "There is an old Chinese saying that when the student is ready, the teacher will appear. It sure took me a while!"

diagnosis I was still okay. The white blood count had not changed. It was at this time I discovered EFT. What a blessing. Now I felt like I had a full battalion to fight the war, and I gave all my soldiers their new orders.

It's been ten years since the diagnosis, and my white blood cell count has not increased. Not one bit. I have the same white blood cell count as the day I was diagnosed, as if it became frozen in time. I have not had any medical intervention or treatment.

My doctor thinks I'm a walking miracle. "You're certainly outside the text books," was one statement uttered. I know that the information I have about the Mind/Body connection and using EFT has done the job. I am fully confident that I'll live a lot longer and not become ill.

Thank you for allowing me to share my story with you. Now, I'd like to summarize what you can do to help yourself.

WHAT CAN YOU DO TO HELP YOURSELF?

Deal with the emotional issues first. Learn a technique that can adjust the map in your head, and adjust it in such a way that you can aid and abet healing yourself, be it physically or emotionally.

To begin with, you have an experience. You perceive that experience, that sensory-based data. You then must interpret and decide what that experience *means to you*. The meaning, the interpretation of that experience is then filed as a memory. The emotion I'm talking about is primarily derived from this interpretation, and the constant retelling reinforces the interpretation, downloading the emotional response over and over.

How many times have you experienced the following? You are telling a story (stimuli) and the listener says, "Oh, that reminds me of" and launches into a story of his or her own (response). The retelling then, the re-accessing of the memory, also becomes a memory.

Suppose that the story is negative. Each time it is re-activated, a new negative emotional charge floods the antennae of the cells. Once you are introduced to these facts, would you like to learn *a relatively simple procedure to remove the negative charge* with its potential for damage? Enter EFT.

HOW CAN EFT BE USED FOR IMPROVING YOUR HEALTH?

EFT is one of the simplest and most efficient techniques to come along in a long time for dealing directly with unwanted emotional responses. Perhaps EFT can be explained best in the following way. Did you know that tapping, with a finger, on certain acupressure points, while focusing on an unpleasant or unwanted memory or circumstance, removes the negative emotion?

Please, take a moment to realize the significance of this. By learning and applying EFT, you have found a way to stop the negative code (neuropeptide) from being formed in the first place. I like the concept for two reasons. Anyone with a desire to feel better can learn the technique and begin to remove the negative emotions stored in the Mind/Body whenever they want to. And second, think of the money and time saved by skipping extensive analysis.

 SO THE ENVIRONMENT IS CONSTANTLY UPGRADING OUR SOFTWARE, AS IT WERE?

Yes. Now, it's time to tie this all together.

Something happens. An event, situation or circumstance occurs. Instantaneously, your mind translates, assigns meaning and interprets the event a certain way. If the translation is positive, all is well and good. Happy neuropeptides flood the cells with messages akin to "Hey, it's safe out there. Build proteins. Self repair. Reproduce."

If, on the other hand, the experience is deemed negative, then unhappy, nervous neuropeptides rush to the cells with a message akin to "Danger, the sky is falling. We're all doomed. We're in trouble. We're gonna die." Either way, *the cells willingly adapt to the message.*

So, now let's say you've had a negative experience — or many of them. The negative emotional response attached is where the real concern is. Remember, it's the emotion that converts to a set of instructions (neuropeptides).

Another way of saying this is that EFT removes the glitch caused in an otherwise magical, happy and self-repairing system.

WHAT HAPPENS IF I USE EFT ENOUGH?

You feel better, and by extension, will perform even better than you did before. I thank you for reading this far. I trust that you have a better understanding of the Mind/Body connection and how your perception and interpretation of experiences can positively or negatively affect your health.

EFT provides you with an effective tool for erasing the charge of a negative emotion, thereby stopping the negative code (neuropeptide) from being formed in the first place. If what I've shared encourages and motivates you to learn and use EFT, then my mission is accomplished.

To contact Dr. Alexander R. Lees, his e-mail address is lees@dralexlees.com and his telephone number is 604-542-6277. Visit Alex's Website at www.DrAlexLees.com. Also, please see Dr. Alexander Lees' biography at the back of the book.

Pain Management
Relieving physical and emotional pain

By Gwenn Bonnell

> *"Pain is no evil unless it conquers us."*
>
> *George Eliot*

How did you get involved with EFT?

I endured chronic burning, throbbing leg pain for 12 years until I found someone who turned me on to EFT. For about an hour or so, we tapped on some spots on my face, torso and hands while I repeated some statements and affirmations. EFT seemed weird to me, but my pain went away and stayed away. As the days went on, I really tested my leg, doing all sorts of things that previously would cause burning and throbbing. A few weeks passed, and I went on vacation. For a minute or so while traveling I felt the pain beginning to sneak back. But as I began to tap it went away.

Since then, I have witnessed dramatic results using EFT for all sorts of chronic and traumatic pain. Some pains disappear in minutes. Others require time, patience, persistence and some detective work to get results. I've seen relief from headaches and migraines, neck and back pain, joint pain and fibromyalgia. I've seen EFT alleviate discomfort due to mechanical reasons such as rotator cuff problems and reactions to medications such as those for neuropathy.

Nobody should have to live in pain. EFT is such a great tool. Once you learn it, you can use it anytime to get freedom from any kind of pain you have in your life. This is the gift of EFT.

How does EFT take away pain?

If we expand on Gary Craig's "Discovery Statement," the theory is that the cause of all emotional and physical discomfort is a disruption in the body's energy system.

Traditional Chinese Medicine (TCM) explains that pain is often a symptom of "stuck" energy. Could it be that EFT gets that energy flowing again and releases the pain?

The response I get most often from people experiencing EFT is that they feel more "relaxed." We have all had the experience of getting stressed and having that stress show up in our body as pain. Doesn't it make sense then that, as EFT relaxes the body, the energy flow (and blood flow) is restored to those stressed areas in our body, allowing our muscles to relax and release any pain?

Do you have an energetic Achilles heel, somewhere physically in your body that is affected by traumatic or constant stress? You may be holding your stress (or unresolved emotions) at the weak point in your body. In fact, that part of your body may be acting as a barometer for various unresolved negative emotions.

Although specifically addressing the physical pain with EFT often brings relief, neutralizing the underlying emotional stress behind the pain will also bring relief.

Using EFT not only balances your energies in the moment, it also teaches the body that the next time you are in that same stressful environment or you come across that same trigger, you don't go into an unbalanced state that causes stress or pain. Using EFT teaches your energy system to stay balanced, and your body to stay relaxed and pain-free.

How do I know EFT will work for my pain?

If you have chronic or recurring pain, and you have been thoroughly treated by your doctor or physician, you owe it to yourself to try EFT. The best case scenario is that within a few minutes you will feel the pain release. Even if it takes more persistence with EFT to release the physical pain, EFT will often help relieve any emotional pain and stress you have about your condition.

How do I address the pain with EFT?

First, treat the physical symptoms. Be as *specific* as possible when describing the physical symptom(s). Meet the pain at its level, recognizing when and where it hurts.

- Where exactly is the most intense pain located?
- What does the pain feel like? Describe the most uncomfortable physical symptom — sharp, dull, burning, stabbing, slicing, pinching, throbbing, pressure, tight, achy, tender, uncomfortable, intense, unbearable, tolerable, etc.
- When does it hurt? Is there a certain time of day or a situation that causes more intense pain? Is there a movement that causes pain, or makes the pain worse, such as pressing on a certain area, standing, sitting, bending, walking, moving up or down or forward or backward, running, stretching, swinging, sleeping, deep breathing, etc.?

Incorporate your answers into an EFT setup statement:

> *Even though I have this stabbing pain in my lower back, especially when I bend over, I deeply and completely love and accept myself and my body.*
>
> *Even though I have this throbbing pain in my right hip, especially when I jog or run, I deeply and completely accept myself.*

Eileen's roller-blading was put on hold when she fell and fractured her elbow in four places. After her cast was removed, physical therapy was unendurable. Trying to straighten her elbow was impossible. It hurt so much that she invented "new ways of swearing." This excessive pain inhibited her recovery until our EFT session.

Afterwards, though the elbow was still sore, the extreme pain while stretching the arm was gone. In fact, her physical therapist kept asking her, "Aren't I hurting you?" Eileen continued therapy without the intense pain, recovered full motion in her arm, and now is enjoying roller-blading again.

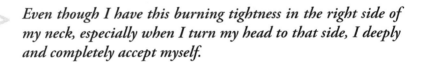

Even though I have this burning tightness in the right side of my neck, especially when I turn my head to that side, I deeply and completely accept myself.

WHAT IF ADDRESSING THE PHYSICAL SYMPTOMS DOESN'T WORK FOR ME?

This is a good time to bring emotions into the equation. To quote Gary Craig, "Sometimes our physical ailments are contributed to by angers, fears and other emotions." I don't know if that is true for you, and maybe you don't either, but it is worth a try.

What is the first thought that comes to mind when you ask yourself, "What is the emotion behind this pain?" You might have anger, fear, guilt or who knows what emotion. Or, you might even feel ready to "lose it."

Even though I may have anger, fear, guilt or who knows whatever emotion, I deeply and completely love and accept myself.

Even though I feel like I'm going to lose it right now, I deeply and completely love, accept and forgive myself. I know I always do the best I can.

How do you feel about having this pain? You might feel like crying, or being angry, sad, overwhelmed, helpless, scared, hopeless or frustrated.

> *Even though I'm really frustrated because I can't do the things I want to because of this pain and I don't know how to get rid of the pain, I deeply and completely love and accept myself.*

Combine the emotions with the pain:

> *Even though I have this anger in my arms, I deeply and completely love and accept myself.*
>
> *Even though I have this sadness, and I feel it as a tightness in my chest and heart, I deeply and completely love and accept myself.*
>
> *Even though I have this anxiety churning in my stomach, I deeply and completely love and accept myself.*

Usually, combining the emotional issue and the physical sensation will quickly lower the intensity level of the pain.

WHAT IF I TAPPED FOR THE EMOTION AND THE PHYSICAL SYMPTOMS BUT STILL HAVE THE PAIN?

After you tap for a round or so on those emotions, go a little deeper. Which emotions might be a little more current for you? What situation in your life holds those same emotions? What is the stressor causing those emotions?

Sometimes I get very literal. For pain in the neck I'll ask, "Who or what in your life is a pain in your neck?" Depending on the type of back pain, I might ask, "Who in your life is a pain in your butt," or "Have you ever felt as if someone was stabbing you in the back?"

Incorporate your answers into one tapping sequence:

> *Even though my boss is a pain in the neck, especially when he looks over my shoulder when I am working on the computer, I deeply and completely love and accept myself. I forgive him for being such a pain.*
>
> *Even though I'm mad at my husband and I feel that anger burning in my lower back, and sometimes he is a real pain in the butt, I deeply and completely love and accept myself and my body.*

Forgiving someone who we feel has wronged us is often the most beneficial thing we can do for ourselves to relieve pain, and it can be important to include in the EFT statement. If you find it difficult to say, or even consider, use EFT to address any resistance you have about forgiving someone. You will be glad you did.

WHAT CAN I DO IF I CAN'T SEEM TO FIND ANY EMOTION TIED TO THIS PAIN?

Look for a relationship between your pain and stress. Notice what stressful events increase your pain and discomfort. Do you have any painful events in your past that still intensely affect you?

I was working with a gentleman who had intense neuropathy, and had been going to therapy for many years, but he could not get in touch with his emotions.

What I had him do was recall his favorite movie, specifically the most moving scene of the movie. We related the emotions he felt about that movie to certain events in his life. Over and over, we were able to bring up and relieve those emotions with EFT. Can you remember watching a movie where you cried or otherwise got emotional?

While doing the tapping, note if you have any flashbacks or thoughts of specific events. If you do, they are probably related to the pain even if you don't feel a related emotion.

Walking, jogging, and playing tennis contribute to Mary's fitness. She holds the Senior Olympic Gold Medal for tennis in her age group. Unfortunately, she developed a burning pain in her hip while jogging. It would especially hurt after exercise. It was intense enough that she visited her doctor. To relieve the pain, Mary had to quit exercising for at least two weeks. Even after the layoff, the same burning hip pain returned when she began playing tennis and jogging again.

During our EFT session, the pain completely disappeared. Even when emulating the same motion that would cause the discomfort, the pain did not return. Mary was able to jog with no pain. She stayed pain free after playing in a tennis tournament — both singles and doubles — the very next weekend. Her real test was facing the cold winter weather. She was afraid the hip pain would return even when she walked her dog. That was not the case. It's been almost three years now, and she continues to walk her dog, jog and play tennis pain free.

Use EFT to address that event with "The Movie Technique" even if you don't feel an emotional intensity. Visit www.emofree.com to learn this technique.

Sometimes it is not things from the past that are holding you back, but fears about how your life would change once you release the pain. Ask yourself who or what you would lose from your life once you release this pain. What is this pain holding you back from accomplishing in your life? Do you have any fears about being successful? List your answers to these questions and address each with EFT.

SHOULD I STOP TAPPING IF THE PAIN STARTS GETTING WORSE?

There might be layers of emotions, memories and pain. When addressing emotions with EFT, more intense emotions might pop up as you peel away the "protective layers" from the core emotion. Similarly, this can happen with pain. Usually, however, if you keep tapping the points over and over and stay focused on the pain, the intensity will begin to subside quickly.

You probably don't need the EFT setup statement at this point since you are already focused on the pain. Just keep tapping the points until you feel the pain become more manageable.

Many people new to EFT get scared when pain (or emotions) start getting more intense. Certainly use your common sense. You may need a qualified healthcare professional to help you through some issues. Still, this could be the perfect opportunity to tap away intense pains or emotions.

If you get scared you can tap for any fear that you feel.

 WHAT DO I DO WHEN THE PAIN STARTS IN ONE SPOT AND THEN MOVES?

You are having what we call "chasing the pain." After you address the most intense pain with EFT and that pain subsides, you notice pain somewhere else in your body.

For example, you might have the most intense pain in your neck, and, after a few rounds of EFT, the pain might move to your shoulder. If the sensation is more intense in your shoulder, address that area with EFT. Then an emotion, or another feeling of discomfort, might arise somewhere else in the body. Keep chasing the pain, addressing what is most intense to you at the time, until all the symptoms clear up.

 The following is an example of how we started with neck pain, and finally found relief after chasing the pain:

(Pain started in the neck as a *knot*.)

"Even though I have this pain in my neck in my life, and it's a hard knot to untie…"

(Changed to a stabbing pain in the shoulder.)

"Even though I have this deceit movie in my life, I got stabbed in the back and I'm angry and I'm afraid and I'm feeling that in stabbing pain my shoulder, I accept myself, I love myself, I forgive myself for always being stabbed in the back and I forgive all these other people, these actors in my movie, and I choose to have this movie end honestly."

(Pain shifted to a *dull jabbing*.)

"Even though I still have some of this dull jabbing pain I choose to completely let it go. I've played out deceit enough in my life, and I choose to play out honesty from now on. No matter how painful or scary or angry I might get, those are just emotional energy, and I choose to let that energy flow through me instead of having it stab me in the back."

"Even though I sometimes feel anger, I can be honest about it, and others can be honest with me. I love feeling honest and happy, and having an honest happy back, and having happy honest people in my life, and if my back is my barometer to my honesty and the honesty of others I accept that too."

(Shoulder and back pain at a zero. Remembering the original "deceit" incident brought up anger and feeling sick in the stomach).

"Even though I have this sick in my stomach feeling when I replay that deceit movie, I love myself and I accept myself and I forgive myself, and choose to throw up all this deceit, regurgitate all of this deception and throw away all the deceit of other people. I can't swallow deceit, but I can stomach honestly, and I love having honesty in my life."

(The stomach, shoulder and neck were fine, and she felt tears of relief. To finish…)

"Even though I feel these relief tears that's okay, these are good tears and I choose to release them all now."

Debbie came to the second session of my EFT training series on the recommendation of her friend. Since she missed the introductory class, I spent a few minutes with her before the class teaching the mechanics of EFT by tapping for her neck and shoulder pain. She seemed totally amazed when her pain subsided. During the class, she kept raising her arm with a puzzled look on her face, checking for the pain that wasn't there. However, the pain returned after a few days. It turns out that she's had this pain for over eight years after falling down some stairs. She had visited many doctors and therapists and spent thousands of dollars, but nobody had been able to alleviate her pain. After our personal EFT session, Debbie experienced total relief from the pain. I talked with her a year later, and she was still pain free.

THE PAIN STARTED DIMINISHING BUT THERE IS STILL SOME LEFT, AND IT'S STUCK ON THE **0-10** LEVEL. HOW CAN I BREAK THROUGH THIS PLATEAU?

First, you can include the pain algorithm, which involves tapping on the Gamut point and the collarbone point. To find the Gamut point, make a fist with one hand, then draw a "V" on the back of your hand from your little finger knuckle and your ring finger knuckle. In the middle of that V there is a depression and it's that depression you want to tap on. Tap the Gamut point on the back of the hand 50 times, then tap on the Collarbone point five times.

Perform the Floor-to-Ceiling Eye Roll: Hold your head level and move your eyes down, looking at the floor. Then begin tapping the Gamut point as you move your eyes upward in a straight line until you are looking at the ceiling.

Rate the pain again on the 0-10 scale. If you are not at a zero, tap the Gamut Point 50 times again, tap the Collarbone Point five times again, and re-rate the intensity. Repeat this until you are at a zero, then cement in the progress with another Floor-To-Ceiling Eye Roll.

Secondly, you can add some affirmations into your setup statement and tapping sequence to connect yourself with feeling better, moving away from suffering and distress towards peace and hopefulness. How would you like to feel instead? Tap and program that in.

Sample affirmations include:

It doesn't matter how this pain started, because it is reversing its course right now.

I choose to relax through this.

Well-being is natural to me.

I am relaxing more and more and breathing out all this pain.

Third, you can use affirmations in the setup statement:

Even though I am completely over this pain I deeply and completely love and accept myself and my new pain-free life.

SHOULD I STOP TAPPING WHEN THE PAIN DISAPPEARS?

To make sure that you have successfully addressed all the aspects related to the pain, test your results by performing movements or positions that would usually cause the pain.

For example, I used EFT to eliminate sore throat pain. Except for the next two weeks, every time I yawned I could still feel the soreness in my throat because I didn't address the "yawning pain" aspect.

Often even when the pain is released, the muscles surrounding the painful area have been so tense for so long that there is some soreness or tightness. The more you address and eliminate every aspect, including aspects such as soreness and tightness, the more you increase the odds that the pain is gone for good. You might also have thoughts that the pain is going to return, or doubts that it is gone for good. Try this:

> *Even though I doubt this pain is gone for good, and it always comes back, I deeply and completely accept myself and accept that the pain is gone for good.*

STILL NOTHING IS HAPPENING… HOW LONG DO I TAP?

When dealing with any chronic, and medically "incurable" situation, you may need long-term, persistent application of EFT.

I also recommend the "Personal Peace Procedure," using EFT for lifetime events you wish never happened. For information on the PPP, visit www.emofree.com. Practice the Personal Peace Procedure every day for at least a month, being sure to note your physical condition before you start so you can compare your progress at the end of the month.

You also have the option of consulting with an experienced EFT practitioner. Many are available for phone sessions. Or, find an EFT buddy and work together. Sometimes having a partner to guide you and witness your healing is the catalyst that releases your pain.

If you are using EFT persistently throughout the day, and you are not getting results, you are probably feeling some frustration. Tap for the following:

> *Even though I have this frustration because this should be working and it's not, and I don't know why, I accept myself anyway.*
>
> *Even though I don't know why I need this pain or where this pain came from, it doesn't matter. I easily, quickly and completely release this pain and give up the reason to know why.*
>
> *Even though I don't understand the cause of this pain, my body knows what to do to heal this pain. I accept my body and this pain. I allow my body to completely release all of this pain.*

What if the pain is from an accident or an emotionally traumatic event?

If you are aware of a significant event in your life around the time this pain began, definitely address that event with the Movie Technique. Certainly the trauma you went through disrupted your energy flow.

Do you have any residual emotional response about the event? Are you still punishing yourself or feel any guilt, anger or resentment because of what happened? Address these feelings with EFT.

Will EFT still be effective if there is a physical cause for the pain?

First, realize that EFT is not always a substitute for medical care. Do not rely on EFT when common sense tells you otherwise. A broken bone needs setting and appendicitis needs medical attention. Still EFT will help take the edge off, if not eliminate, many pains that have a physical cause and can facilitate healing.

What if the pain comes back?

Note that even when you get completely pain free, at first this might last only a few hours, or a few minutes. This is where consistency and persistence come in. Over and over again, you have to get the energies balanced and teach the body how to be pain free.

If the pain returns, it doesn't mean that your EFT session didn't work. It means there are more aspects to deal with and different triggers that still disrupt the energy system that you still need to address.

Notice any pattern to your recurring pain. Does it return every hour, every few hours, in the morning or at night? Are there certain events that cause the pain?

Do EFT systematically throughout the day, making sure you tap before the pain is scheduled to return. Put that wording in your setup statement:

Even though this back pain returns every two hours or so, I deeply and completely accept myself and my body.

Even though I get this pain in my legs every night when I lay in bed, I deeply and completely accept myself. I choose to release all the stress out of my body and my legs so I can fall asleep peacefully, sleep soundly and wake up pain-free.

Even though just thinking about [whatever the issue is] gives me a headache, I deeply and completely love and accept myself. I choose to stay relaxed and at ease.

Even though having dinner with my relatives usually makes me sick to my stomach, I deeply and completely love and accept myself. I choose to enjoy myself anyway.

Even though I get this nagging hip pain every time I play tennis, I accept my body, and choose to stay flexible and pain free on the tennis court.

To contact Gwenn Bonnell, her e-mail address is gwenn@tapintoheaven.com and her telephone number is 954-370-1552. Visit Gwenn's Websites at www.tapintoheaven.com, www.tapawaypain.com, www.tapawaystress.com, and www.Chakrativity.com. Also, please see Gwenn Bonnell's biography at the back of the book.

PERSONAL DEVELOPMENT
Developing a more positive relationship with your Self

By Carol Tuttle

"Things do not change, we change."
Henry David Thoreau

HOW WOULD YOU DESCRIBE PERSONAL DEVELOPMENT?

Personal development is a relationship with yourself; your self esteem, your feelings of self worth, your confidence to go out and achieve success and get the results that you're hoping to get, to continue to advance your ability to think well of yourself, to pursue your dreams and goals and to create success in your life. Furthermore, it consists of your experience — spiritually, mentally, emotionally, and even physically. It involves the process of fine-tuning and advancing one's Self.

HOW HAVE YOU USED **EFT** FOR YOUR OWN PERSONAL DEVELOPMENT?

After practicing EFT for many years myself, I began to see that I could assist other people, thereby helping them advance in their own personal development. In my private practice, I've worked with numerous clients, teaching them to use EFT as a treatment process in a therapeutic setting, as well as how to use it in their daily lives. Over time, the amazing power of EFT became evident to me, not only in my own life, but in the lives of others.

I've used EFT to reach a variety of goals, as I advance my own sense of who I am and build my own esteem. Here is an example. About five years ago, I challenged myself to run a marathon. For me, this presented an almost overwhelming challenge. The apparent impossibility of running 26.2 miles raised fear and resistance in me, and revealed doubts that I could ever achieve that goal. Yet, deep down within my being, I felt inspired to take on the challenge.

My husband and I began an eight-month process of training and preparation for our first marathon. Throughout my whole training process, as I became aware of my limiting beliefs and fears about running, I used EFT. As the miles increased, more issues and limiting beliefs came up. I would use EFT to collapse those beliefs, "reframing" to instill within myself a sense of confidence and capability.

My self-esteem improved, and my sense of achievement started to grow. Although I still felt a bit "iffy" on the day of the marathon, I used EFT throughout the race to handle any limitations or fears I experienced.

Only eight months earlier, I had never run more than five miles at a time, and had believed running a marathon was next to impossible for me. Crossing the finish line of that first marathon, having run 26.2 miles, was one of the most spiritual epiphanies I've ever had. I realized then that I was able to show up and achieve a goal, and that I had developed the ability to succeed.

EFT, used consistently, truly has the power to advance one's level of achievement, to reach even goals that are set high, and certainly to overcome day-to-day challenges.

 YOU HAVE FIVE CHILDREN. HOW HAVE YOU USED EFT IN YOUR ROLE AS A MOTHER TO HELP YOUR CHILDREN TO ADVANCE IN THEIR OWN PERSONAL DEVELOPMENT?

Using EFT, I've helped my children overcome significant challenges and trials that definitely would have impaired their personal development. I've used it to help them conquer difficult issues, eliminate dysfunctional patterns, and release their fears of not being able to achieve their desired

As the author of this chapter, Carol Tuttle, I'd like to share a personal story. Our adopted son joined our family when he was 15 years old. Understand that he came with a lot of emotional baggage, very limiting thinking, and very low self esteem. He deeply needed to acquire the benefits provided by a tool like EFT. From the very beginning when he joined our family, we taught him about the resource of EFT and that it would help him. We really encouraged him to put it to use himself, assisting him while we taught, guided and facilitated a lot of EFT sessions.

In just a two-year period, an amazing life transformation occurred as he started to increase his level of confidence, gained a sense of himself and recognized his ability to go after his life goals and vision. At the time he became part of our family, he had a profound belief that he was worthless and incapable. He believed that he might never have a good job or achieve success. He felt that he'd never have any chance for getting ahead in life or making a difference. His life, in every facet, was riddled with a complete sense of inadequacy.

Gradually, we started to see improvements that quickened in pace and momentum. By his senior year, two years into being part of our family, we saw a definite stability and a true foundation of self-worth emerge, along with a new knowledge of his personal value and a deep, abiding sense of the dignity that every human being is meant to experience and feel.

Our son no longer had to keep trying to focus, or to consciously think of his goals and force his feelings. Rather, a healthy sense of value and personal worth developed in him. He realized that he has a right to success. He successfully achieved this through using EFT, at first in formal sessions with assistance, then later on his own. It's been nothing short of a miracle. We've seen EFT help him overcome some life-damaging beliefs and feelings that could have diminished his full potential.

goals. EFT has helped them clear their limiting beliefs and the typical feelings of low self-worth that commonly burden young people during their junior high and high school years.

Now that my children are older — they range in age from 18 to 24 — I can look back and see how EFT successfully assisted them as teenagers and young adults. Having used EFT together with each of them during their teenage years, we've all become more proficient at it. Although I was the one to initiate their practice of EFT, and engage them in it, I've seen how they have embraced it in their own right, implementing the process without needing my constant participation.

For example, one of my younger sons is 18, and a senior in high school. He has a little note thumb-tacked to the ceiling over his bed. When he wakes up in the morning, and as he is going to sleep at night, he sees it. It is one little word: TAP. One night as we were talking, I happened to lie down on his bed next to him and looked up at the ceiling. It amused me to see that little square piece of paper with that short reminder on it. Because I didn't tell him to put it there, I thought it was really cool.

As a parent, I've learned not to draw too much attention to things like that because my kids still think EFT is kind of weird and funky. But they're willing to use EFT because they've seen the results. They know firsthand that it improves their feelings of self worth, lifts their mood, and increases their overall sense of well being. They're encouraged by that, and motivated to implement EFT based on results, regardless of how out-of-the-ordinary EFT might be.

As another example, I can point to my daughter who is now 20 years old. She was a junior in high school when she decided to run for senior class president. That was a big goal because, in her very large school, competition was keen. As in competitive sports, school politics is another arena in which EFT can be a valuable resource. While you're developing yourself as an athlete or player, you realize that only one team or one person gets to win, and this can bring up fears and limiting beliefs.

I knew EFT would release her fear of failure, raise her spirits and build her courage. At my suggestion, she first listed her fears on paper. I taught her to use EFT a few times each day during the campaign, to "tap out" her fears on particular points along her energy meridians. This helped her clear any negative programming she had accumulated. Next, she used EFT to firmly anchor positive energy, "tapping in" what are referred to as "reframes." By reframing her fear statements, she was able to focus on the desired outcome.

Some of her positive statements included:

"I am getting my name out there."
"I am known by my peers and the students of my school and am held in high regard."
"I am winning the election."
"I am doing this for the right reasons."

As she made reframing a part of her campaign experience, it was really exciting for me to see how — win or lose — she was increasingly able to work with herself, developing more confidence in pursuit of something with an unpredictable outcome. Although she did not win the election, she enjoyed the campaign tremendously. And she developed her confidence in a way that otherwise would not have been possible.

 WHAT WOULD YOU SUGGEST TO THOSE WHO WOULD LIKE TO START USING EFT TO FURTHER THEIR OWN PERSONAL DEVELOPMENT?

First, I'd say to use EFT to support yourself. It's a useful tool to start implementing several days a week in the beginning, eventually increasing to daily use. I teach my clients to think of using EFT in the same way that they think of brushing their teeth, as a habit that becomes second nature. In our culture, most people have been raised to have a certain level of hygiene, and it has become a habit for them to brush their teeth. They want good oral hygiene and good dental health. In order to have those conditions, tooth brushing is essential.

To have good self esteem and continually develop yourself, use EFT on a daily basis. It is one of the most magnificent tools you can add to your lifestyle. Negative thoughts, fears, emotional patterns, and defeatist feelings are disruptive to our progress, and can become roadblocks to pursuing goals and dreams with grace and ease.

Using EFT consistently gives you hands-on practice in becoming the manager of your thoughts and feelings. You learn to intervene with EFT, positively influencing the way you think and feel, with almost immediate results. The more you do EFT, the more beneficial your results. By tapping acupressure points on the meridians along which energy flows, your energy patterns come to respond more readily.

Start to see EFT as a support tool, something that will help you achieve a better life and realize more of your full potential, rather than as a treatment tool to subjugate an issue, condition or problem in your life. EFT becomes a resource to support growth and increase strength. If you were preparing for a marathon, you'd start running, training to become more physically prepared, gaining strength and endurance, ready to run the race. In the same way, EFT can be considered a personal development training tool.

Perhaps the best way to explain it is to ask you to think of a goal, something you've wanted to achieve, and show you a way to explore what's keeping you from achieving it. Start working with something familiar. Maybe you've set the goal already. Maybe you've tried and were unable to achieve it. Maybe you've never done more than think about it. First of all, determine what your goal is.

Next, give yourself a week to notice — just as my daughter did — the thoughts, feelings and behavior patterns you start to recognize that are blocking or interfering with your ability to pursue your goal. Every day, write down what you notice, and you'll start seeing some recurring themes and identifying common denominators. Once you have that information in hand, you have the data you need.

You've got what's keeping you from achieving success, and now you are going to use it to create a script. Using EFT with a script is so helpful

Recently, I've been working with a client I'll call Tim, helping him develop a stronger self esteem. Interestingly, Tim came to me after achieving great success in his work and financial life. He's the owner of several successful businesses. Yet what he lacked was the feeling within his own being that matched what he had created in his external world.

His situation is less common than those I'm accustomed to seeing. More often, I'll see people who are wounded on the inside that have outer lives that reflect their wounded state. Most wounded people don't achieve a high level of success. Tim's situation has an interesting dynamic.

He's a client who has created great outcomes and reached many of his goals. Yet, he has had no inner sense of value to balance his external life. In fact, he harbored a lot of guilt, and a feeling that he didn't deserve what he had or what he had developed.

I felt it was important for Tim to work with EFT in the weekly sessions and also to use it on a daily basis. What worked most effectively for Tim was to take command of his life and of his thoughts. Following my recommendation, he tapped when he started to feel bad, sorry for himself, or worthless. This was a cyclical pattern that Tim experienced on a weekly basis. He'd descend through guilt, worthlessness, and depression, to the point of real despair.

I taught Tim to start to notice the pattern when it was coming on, as it was just starting to form and engage. I sensed that if we could step in during the beginning of the sequence, EFT would probably diminish it and he'd have the power to stop it from advancing, if not completely, then at least to the extent of weakening the pattern before it became overpowering.

I met with Tim earlier this week, and he said that he had been actively using EFT, not allowing the negative emotions and thoughts to take over. He had a couple of instances during the week in which the negatives had truly shown up, ready to run their course and take him down into his big slump.

I asked him, "What are you doing and saying?"

He answered, "I'm not always sure where to tap or what to say," and showed me where he was tapping on a couple of the points. He continued, "But I'll just say out loud, 'I'm feeling better. I'm not letting these feelings take me down. I deserve to feel better. I'm choosing to feel better right now'." Using EFT, he had taken command of his feelings, recognizing his right to feel better and that he didn't have to let those negative feelings take him down.

When I asked him how it was working, he replied that he was noticing a difference. He wasn't able to eliminate the problem completely, but said, "I'm still going there, although it's not as heavy. It's not as deep, and I'm noticing that I cycle through it faster, and don't stay there as long. I'm able to pull myself out." I asked him how he felt about that and if he felt as though it was working. He surely did, and said, "I'm really encouraged."

In his church, Tim and his wife serve as counselors of young, single adults. He was so encouraged by the results he was getting with EFT that he had started to teach how to tap in some of his counseling and advisory sessions. Again, he said, "I'm not sure if I'm doing it right. But I just know it can make a difference. I believe that the people I'm counseling need to start working with EFT and learn that they have the power to work with themselves."

This is a very positive outcome. I know as he continues to use it, Tim will see better and better results. Eventually, he will be able to look back and say, "I remember when I had those bad feelings and how hard that was," and will be able own his success. Much of his progress is the result of his willingness to use EFT, to be persistent with it, and his continued commitment to its use for the advancement of who Tim is.

because you have your own words right in front of you. I've done this myself, with my children, and with clients. Let me give you an example of what I mean by "writing a script."

For instance, let's assume that you want to learn to play the guitar. You've thought about it for years, but you never have taken the first steps. From your notes, you start to notice what's keeping you from really starting the process of playing the guitar. Maybe your script would include:

"I don't have time."
"I don't have enough money to take the lessons."
"I'm not capable of learning this. It's too hard."
"I'm too old."
"What's the point? I should have learned it earlier in my life. Then, it would have been meaningful. Why bother now?"

Your script will look like a list of phrases. Also, you will have written down related thoughts and feelings. Some of the feelings might be sadness that you didn't pursue it earlier, feeling frustrated, angry at yourself, hopeless, discouraged, bothered. These words will now become part of your script, and you will use the tapping sequences while repeating these statements, developing your own phrasing. As you do, you'll notice yourself starting to collapse your fears, blocks and limiting beliefs, because that's what EFT does. It releases the energy that's holding all that negativity in place.

Once you've released that, I always like to throw in a forgiveness step. That's a big part of my EFT protocol. To be able to generate more healing and more resolve by going through the forgiveness step, you might include such phrases as:

I forgive myself for creating these blocks and this resistance to something I really want to do.

I'm doing the best I know how.

I forgive myself for putting this off for so long. I'm ready now. I'm going to do this now.

I love and accept myself even though I've not done so earlier in my life.

I forgive my mom and dad that they didn't provide guitar lessons when I was young.

It's never too late. I'm ready now.

Then, take these statements and rewrite them as positives. Every one of those negative statements can be turned into positive statements. Be sure to write them out. It's helpful to have a written tapping script to guide you. Positive rewrites of your statements might look like:

I'm experiencing that it's never too late to start something new.

I'm ready now. I'm ready to learn to start playing the guitar.

I'm free to change my mind and to learn something else if I find I feel differently about it later.

As you're tapping, your positive "I am" statements will activate those positive feelings and thoughts within your own being. You can eventually get to a point where you can focus primarily on the positive and what you want, on the goal that you're striving to achieve, phrasing it in "I am" statements in the present, as if you've already achieved it, and just tap on that continually. Taking a goal you've not yet achieved and labeling it a present experience, acting as if you've already achieved it, is a great and powerful way to use EFT to help move you toward that outcome, creating a momentum that will support you.

In the scenario of the goal of learning to play guitar, you might consider statements such as:

I'm grateful for how much fun I have playing the guitar.

I'm grateful that I always find time in my life to practice, to learn new songs, and enjoy this experience.

I'm grateful for the people I have to share it with in my life.

I love playing the guitar.

I'm having fun playing the guitar.

I'm grateful that I've been able to pursue and achieve this goal and continue to grow in it.

This is an awesome way to use EFT in pursuit of developing new skills, talents and visions in your life.

YOU'VE MENTIONED THAT IT'S GOOD TO USE **EFT** ON A DAILY BASIS. HOW OFTEN WOULD YOU SUGGEST IT BE PRACTICED?

As with anything else, it is possible to overdo EFT, which can actually lead to honoring your fears and causing you to feel overwhelmed. I would suggest practicing EFT only a few times a day. It's most helpful to use it as soon as you notice things coming up.

Set aside some time every day. Even once a day would be really helpful. Use your script, work with it, add to it, embellish it, and employ scripting when you create new goals. As you create new scripts, you will continue to expand your vision of what you want in your life.

If you're not free to do it every day, a minimum of two or three times a week will allow you to really focus on clearing whatever interferes with reaching your goals. If you're not feeling interference, take the time to deeply anchor in, tap in, the positive reframes that will propel you toward your desired outcomes.

WHAT IF YOU'RE IN A SITUATION IN WHICH IT WOULD NOT BE COMFORTABLE TO TAP? FOR EXAMPLE, YOU MAY BE WITH OTHER PEOPLE OR IN SURROUNDINGS IN WHICH IT WOULDN'T BE APPROPRIATE.

There may very well be times when you're in this situation. The beauty of EFT is that you're working with energy. Emotion is energy. It's energy in motion. This tool, EFT, is an acronym which stands for Emotional Freedom Techniques. You're actually working with thoughts and feelings as emotion, energy in motion. The awesome thing about energy is that it will respond to your thoughts and your imagination. The body likes the tapping and enjoys the interaction. It's enlivening and refreshing to the body, and energy will respond to your thoughts.

If you find that you are in a situation where you're not able to actively practice the tapping process, just mentally imagine yourself applying EFT. This will create a shift, and it still will be quite effective. Your imagination is powerful. Energy responds to what you think, what you're focusing on. EFT can be practiced internally, in a discreet manner. Even in a public setting, you'll find you can comfortably apply this inconspicuous form of EFT.

 WHAT ARE SOME OTHER CREATIVE WAYS TO USE EFT IN THE PURSUIT OF PERSONAL DEVELOPMENT?

Well, you really have the resource right in your hands, because everything in this book refers to development of the Self, for personally advancing your capacity to live a fuller and a more successful life. Take the time to thoroughly read the information in this book, because in every section there's a beneficial EFT reference. It will give you the support for personally developing into a more fully-actualized, successful human being.

There are some great resources on the Internet. As others have mentioned in this book, the best resource is the Website of Gary Craig, the founder of EFT. Visit www.emofree.com. The site is full of valuable tools and volumes of information on using EFT for self-help. I'd recommend you do some research and notice the myriad of topics, categories and issues for which EFT can be applied. There's really no limit to the benefits of EFT.

 IF EFT IS SO EFFECTIVE FOR HELPING PEOPLE ACHIEVE A MORE SUCCESSFUL LIFE AND IN ASSISTING THEM WITH PERSONAL DEVELOPMENT, WHY AREN'T MORE PEOPLE USING IT?

New things take time to be integrated into our culture and our consciousness. It's happening fairly quickly though. As the number of people learning about EFT grows, more people are willing to avail themselves of this valuable resource.

The dynamic of EFT is a bit different from the usual intervention techniques. Anyone has to develop a rapport with something so new before they can begin to create a comfort level with it. One of the dynamics that inhibits this process is that we have a tendency to need to fit in with society and do what others do.

When we're doing something most of our neighborhood is not doing, we tend to be a little self conscious or hesitant to embrace it, let alone weave it into our personal, day-to-day experience. If you're bold enough, and willing to use a tool like EFT, you will facilitate great changes in your life. Be open to being different and unique, to think outside the box in a sense.

Just be wise about those with whom you share EFT, how much you share, and how you share it. Get a sense of those who might be open and supportive, versus those who would be critical or who might approach EFT with putdowns, making fun of you for what you're doing. Be mindful of that, be wise and supportive of yourself, and only share EFT with those who are interested, open, and supportive.

In fact, this particular challenge would be a good place to start. If you have fears about using this tool and making EFT a part of your own self-development, (what I referred to earlier as a "personal development training tool"), I'd suggest you start by writing down your fears, your concerns, your negative thoughts about why this wouldn't work or what you believe others might think. Essentially, uncover whatever is keeping you from using EFT to better your life and enhance your daily experience.

I've personally found EFT to be one of the most valuable resources I have. One of the greatest things about it is its ready availability. All it takes is me. I've got it all in one package right here. The process itself can be applied, engaged in just by being present with yourself. You have a set of hands. You have a face and torso. You've got the acupressure points.

You don't need to have any special equipment or someone with years of experience to professionally guide you through it. What can happen when you incorporate EFT as a process, when you make it a part of your lifestyle, is so simple, yet so profound. It's truly one of the most affordable, accessible resources we could ever have.

WHAT DO YOU SAY TO PEOPLE WITH CONCERNS OR ISSUES AROUND EFT IN RELATION TO THEIR BELIEF IN GOD, SPECIFICALLY THAT EFT MIGHT SOMEHOW USURP OR REPLACE THEIR BELIEF IN GOD? HOW DO YOU HELP PEOPLE RECONCILE THE USE OF EFT WITH THEIR BELIEF THAT GOD IS THE ONLY POWER THAT CAN CHANGE US?

That is a very valid question. I am frequently presented with this question, as I am very active in my religion. My spiritual foundation is Christian, and I have considered the purpose of EFT and where it fits in my life. I feel that my responses to these concerns are sound, and that answers which have helped me certainly can help many others put EFT into the right perspective in life.

First and foremost, I think it's important to recognize that, in my belief system, EFT is not a healing power. Healing can only come from God. EFT is a tool that facilitates a change. As humans, we are masters of keeping ourselves stuck and actually preventing God from being able to bless us and, in a lot of cases, heal us. What we're doing with the EFT process is facilitating a clearing, an opening, a shift in our energy, to allow God's healing power to have an effect on us.

Keep in mind that EFT has its place. It's not meant to be a spiritual practice. It's not meant to be a spiritual dogma or doctrine. It's a tool, and as such it helps you. Much like a toothbrush, it's a tool. A toothbrush helps you keep your teeth clean and healthy and, in much the same way, EFT helps keep your thoughts and feelings clean and healthy. So use it as a tool, one which is anchored in the foundation of your own spiritual path.

Whatever you believe is the source of all healing, just connect it with that. Truly, that is the source of power. As you align the use of EFT with the power greater than yourself, big things and miraculous things can happen for you.

To contact Carol Tuttle, her e-mail address is carol@caroltuttle.com. Visit Carol's Websites at www.caroltuttle.com and www.YourEmotionalHealing.com. Also, please see Carol Tuttle's biography at the back of the book.

PROCRASTINATION
Moving beyond excuses and smoke screens

By Gloria Arenson

"Procrastination is the thief of time."

Edward Young

HOW DO YOU DEFINE PROCRASTINATION?

Putting things off and not finishing tasks are ways to avoid the pain of guilt, shame, anxiety and fear. Procrastinators are people who do this habitually and hate themselves for it. The worst part is that they believe they have no power to stop it. Procrastinators come in all sizes and shapes, young and old, all colors, denominations, from all walks of life and many cultures.

CAN I RECOVER FROM THIS PROBLEM?

Procrastination is not a disease, although procrastinators rarely seem to be able to recover from it. I used Google to search *procrastination* and discovered that we view procrastination as a "horrendous condition," "impossible to conquer." It is so daunting that we should: avoid it, trick it, manage it, get around it, learn to live with it, structure it, control it, reduce it or push past it.

It's not what you do that seems to matter, it's what you tell yourself about what you do that counts. In psychotherapy we call this a "self-fulfilling prophecy." That means that you unconsciously make it come true. Procrastinators label themselves with this embarrassing trait, but

154

it is not genetic. The good news is that you can put an end to chronic procrastination with EFT.

How can I tell if it's just a bad habit or a real problem?

You have a problem if you have experienced painful consequences by putting things off or not finishing projects. Arthur delayed so long handing in a term paper that he was given an incomplete and had to pay a hefty sum to repeat the class. If you don't pay your credit card statements on time you will be penalized and your credit rating may be impaired. If these kinds of things keep happening to you, you have a problem.

If you are sick of the negative outcomes of your delaying actions, you have a problem. If you are sick and tired of being late with deadlines, you have a problem. If your friends, co-workers or loved ones get upset with you because you don't follow through with promises or projects, you have a problem.

Why can't they accept my good reasons?

An excuse is a way to condone putting things off and avoid guilt or shame for not living up to the expectations of others. These explanations are smoke screens that keep procrastinators from understanding what their behavior is really all about. Choose a specific goal you have been putting off. Write all your reasons for delaying. Most likely they will fall in one of the following categories.

Excuses about time are: "I'll do it later;" "I can do it another time," "I don't have enough time to do it all," "I still have time before the deadline," or its cousin, "Ninety percent is done. It can wait a little longer." A variation is "I'll do it now… but first I'll make dinner, watch the World Series baseball, take a nap etc." Don't forget the dieter's put-off, "I'll start on Monday."

Biological justifications are: "I'm tired." "I've been working hard, and I deserve a break." "I'll stay up too late and miss my sleep." One man

Often the primary problem has nothing to do with what the procrastinator is putting off. That is what happened with Carla. Carla wanted to reorganize her clothes closet because she had too many clothes that she wasn't wearing anymore. She wanted more space. Carla looked forward to having a neat closet and couldn't figure out why she kept putting it off. When she used EFT she discovered that one reason she delayed was that in the past when she put old clothes in a box to give away, her husband would go through the box.

As she tapped, Carla realized that she felt violated when he did this. More tapping revealed that there was not enough privacy in her family when she was growing up. The worst memory was when her mother and sister read her diary and taunted her. After Carla uncovered and tapped away the trauma about her privacy being invaded by others, she immediately set to work on her closet project.

maintained that his doctor ordered him to exercise instead. A New Age procrastinator explained, "My horoscope shows it's not auspicious because Saturn is transiting my Moon."

Another ploy is *blame*. "I would have completed the task last week if only I had the right equipment." "I had to wait for a sale so I could get the parts cheaper." When in doubt, a seasoned procrastinator can come up with generic reasons, "It's too hot, too cold, too early, too late, too boring or too costly."

Excuses that ring of compassion may get you sympathy. During a drought one homeowner who let his gardening chores go announced, "I'm saving water." Another frugal procrastinator felt righteous because putting off a project would save energy costs. A college student whined, "I've got a new girlfriend and I have to give her time." My favorite excuse was offered by a young man who may have been studying Buddhism, someone who is truly living in the now, "I'm young — there's time."

Cross out your excuses. They are worthless and won't get you off the hook anymore. Forgive yourself for all your excuses by tapping:

> *Even though I have used lots of rationalizations for putting things off like [whatever the issue is], I now choose to leave excuses behind and move forward successfully.*
>
> *Even though I have tricked myself and others with my excuses, I deeply and completely forgive myself.*

Tap until you really mean it.

You can now turn to the actual core issues of anxiety and fear that lie beneath your delay tactics, and free yourself by using EFT.

WHY IS IT SO HARD TO STOP PROCRASTINATING?

Procrastination is more than a bad habit. It is a way to cope with underlying issues that you are avoiding. Disorganized desks, missed deadlines, and unfinished projects are often symbols of deeper issues. Sometimes sad or frightening concerns lie at the heart of procrastination.

Very few people want to experience emotional pain and early in life discover ways to distract themselves. This becomes habitual, yet the pain is always below the surface. When a procrastinator removes the distraction, the fear or anxiety may surface, and, if it is too uncomfortable to face, it gets covered up again. EFT can stop this cycle. Once the excuses are thrown aside it is possible to look for the original problem and tap to resolve it once and for all.

WHAT CAUSES PROCRASTINATION?

Procrastinators aren't lazy, stupid or weak. At the core of procrastination is *fear*. Some of the fears that lead to procrastination are:

- Fear of failure
- Fear of judgment by others
- Fear of success
- Fear of authority
- Fear of the future

These fears pervade the lives of people who put things off or don't finish what they start. EFT will transform the negative feelings that trigger procrastination into positive action.

Aren't most people afraid to fail?

People tell me their fear of failure is good because it encourages them to do better, but this is rarely the case. Fear of failure usually leads to chronic anxiety and low self-esteem. The worst-case scenario is: fear of failure leads to perfectionism that leads to paralysis and procrastination. If you are afraid you will fail because you aren't good enough, you may not begin a project at all.

How can I stop worrying about being judged?

Procrastination is not genetic. Little children are like puppies and kittens. They play happily without a care about who is richer, smarter, or prettier. Then one day they become *self*-conscious. That is the day someone gives them a command or commandment that makes them feel imperfect and judged.

One of the most harmful commandments is: *People won't like you if....* People won't like you if you are fat. People won't like you if you talk back. People won't like you if you are too smart. People won't like you if you look different.

"You'll never amount to much" is a both a criticism and a command to not succeed. Hidden within it is the implied commandment. "People won't like you unless you are successful." These unloving comments

This is a personal story about me, the author of this chapter, Gloria Arenson. Fear of not being perfect changed my life. Growing up, I believed an "A" grade represented perfection. I thrived on scholastic competition the way an athlete enjoys challenges in an exciting game against well-matched opponents. My motto was, "Difficult things are easy for me." This idea backfired when I went to graduate school.

After majoring in archeology in college, I was accepted at Columbia University graduate school. I felt as if I was finally on the "A" team. Then I signed up for the seminar, "Art of the Russian Steppes." When I entered the classroom on the first day, I saw chalkboards filled with notations written in Chinese and Russian languages, since Russian and Chinese archeologists had done the excavating. Inside my head I heard my voice screaming, "How can I get an A? I've got to get an A!" I panicked.

I became worried, sleepless and had nightmares. I couldn't figure out how to get through the course, let alone get an A grade. I finally dropped the course and took a leave of absence from graduate school. I never went back. For the first time in my life I had met my match and collapsed under the pressure to achieve perfection.

Many years later I taught classes about procrastination and perfection in which I told this story as an example of how powerfully fear can affect our lives. I noticed that I was still upset by that memory and decided to use EFT. When I tapped I realized that the other students who stayed in school had passed. Suddenly I understood that their lives weren't based on the belief that if you aren't perfect you're a failure. I felt a sudden shift as my tension left and was replaced by a feeling of peace and forgiveness.

might cause someone to give up trying or to procrastinate to delay the negative prediction from coming true.

What happens when someone tells you, "You're just like so-and-so?" When mom tells you that you are just like your father, does it mean that you are a good athlete or a slob who never puts things away? If you were named after someone in the family, must you take on their characteristics?

Bill was named after a beloved uncle, but Bill procrastinated about getting married. EFT helped him discard the belief that because his uncle had tragically died in his thirties Bill was going to follow in his uncle's footsteps, so why start a family?

Procrastinators and perfectionists are created when you hold yourself back for fear of being judged because you believe people won't like you if: you speak up, are too good, break the rules, aren't good enough, aren't perfect, etc. A deity did not proclaim these commandments. They are simply the opinions of a bunch of people, many of whom are dead and gone.

Use EFT to talk back. Make a list of the commandments that instill fear in you. Choose one of the people whose commands have led to great pain in your life. Tap:

> *Dad, even though you told me I had to do/be/have [whatever the issue is], and it led to great unhappiness in my life, I choose to free myself now.*

As you tap each point, talk out loud to the person. Say something different at each new tapping point. It is okay to be angry. Keep going around and around until you feel finished with the issue. Then complete this sentence and tap one round saying it aloud.

> *I now choose to [whatever your choice is], even if you disapprove.*

It may take a number of tapping sessions to complete your entire list, but you will feel light and free when you are finished.

WHY BE AFRAID OF SUCCESS?

Fear of success may be buried in your unconscious. Lots of people fantasize about winning the lottery or writing a best seller, yet they have a hidden belief that they aren't worthy of having good things happen to them. Sometimes these negative thoughts begin early in life when you decide that it's not okay to make more money than your father or be prettier than your sister. If you feel guilty about out-doing someone else, use EFT to get to the heart of that sabotaging thought. Tap:

> *Even though it is not okay for me to have more [thing you want] than [person] or be better than [person], I deeply and completely accept myself.*

Keep tapping until you shift into a new attitude.

If you know how young you were when you first decided that you were unworthy, tap about that memory.

> *Even though I decided that I was bad/stupid/undeserving/a sinner when I was [age] years old, I choose to be free of that self-imposed curse.*

Perhaps you remember the circumstance that led to your decision about yourself. Treat yourself for what happened. Tap:

> *Releasing what happened when I was [age] years old.*
> *Releasing what happened when my father caught me stealing coins from his pocket.*
> *[Or whatever the incident was]*

Another activity to overcome the fear of success is to make a list of the successes you want to have in your life and tap away your fear of manifesting them. Do you want $500,000, a new home, a new car, a wonderful job, a successful relationship, or new friends? Tap:

> *Even though I don't deserve a new car, I am treating myself for this self defeating belief.*
> Reminder: Fear of new car

Continue tapping while reminding yourself "fear of new car" until you have reached zero and your fear is gone.

HOW CAN I TELL IF I FEAR AUTHORITY?

Procrastinators are not born; they are created. One of the causes of procrastination is rebellion. *I don't wanna and you can't make me!* This starts in childhood. Did you love doing homework or studying for a spelling test? Would you rather have stayed outside playing ball, skating, bike riding or home watching TV? If you weren't prepared for the test or didn't like studying geography or math you might have dragged your feet when it was time to go home to hit the books. By the time you were out of school this habit had taken hold and spread to different areas of your life.

Who are *They?* *They* are the people in charge of you when you were growing up and learning how to be a civilized person. *They* include parents, teachers, relatives, clergy, police, the government, and God as interpreted by *them.* Who were your *Theys?* What rules did they hand down to you, and are you still putting off following them? I feel sad when I see an adult whose misery is created by living a life led under the critical gaze of someone who is long gone but still lives inside the procrastinator's head.

I maintain that *there is no such thing as lazy.* Lazy is what *they* called you when you weren't doing what *they* wanted you to do — pick up your clothes, put your toys away, write thank you notes, practice the piano.

How old do you have to be to be able to decide how to live your life? A wise man said, "What other people think about you is none of your business." Think of the rules you accepted from *them.* Make your own "I don't wanna and you can't make me" list. Think of what you keep putting off because it feels like a chore such as cleaning out the garage, paying bills or going to the dentist.

Take time daily to tap away some of these feelings of rebellion. Some of the "have to's" will turn into "choose to's" when you decide that you agree with some of what they asked of you. However, you may still disagree and decide to do it your way. After you tap you may be surprised that the anger, guilt or shame is gone for good.

WHAT DOES FEAR OF THE FUTURE MEAN?

One of my clients kept putting off clearing off her desk. She couldn't bring herself to get started until EFT showed her she was afraid that if she cleared off her desk she would have to begin to clean out her garage and sort through boxes of her mother's belongings. She didn't want to face her feelings of grief and loss about her mother's death. As long as her desk was still messy she could stay in denial.

Another man kept putting off taking the exam to get into graduate school. He learned that his fear was that in grad school he would find many fascinating people that shared his interests and he would break up with his girlfriend.

These people realized they were not really fearful about doing the job they were putting off. They were fearful about what they would face once they were free to move on. One way to find out if you are procrastinating because you have a fear of the future is to tap and talk to yourself out loud.

 Even though I am putting off [whatever the issue is], I am wondering if I am afraid of what will happen when that is done and over with, and I accept myself because I am doing the best I can at this moment.

As you tap say, "I am afraid of what will happen next" or "Once I am finished with this, what am I afraid I will have to face next?"

HOW CAN I STOP FEELING GUILTY FOR PUTTING THINGS OFF?

I should get my car washed. I should eat less. I shouldn't sleep so late on the weekend. Our lives are filled with *shoulds*. *Shoulds* keep us on the straight and narrow path. What are *shoulds* and where did they come from? We can trace them back to the original holy set, the Ten Commandments, but I think *shoulds* existed before that.

A *should* is created when a group of people agree about how the world is or might be. But this may differ from culture to culture and century to century. Democrats have different *shoulds* about the world than Republicans. Believers and non-believers differ about the *shoulds* that label us good or bad.

Shoulds lead to procrastination. Putting things off is often the result of your conflict with a *should* because shoulds are inflicted on us from the outside. From our earliest years we are told what a good boy or girl *should* or *should not* do to gain approval from parent, teacher, family and community. We are not allowed to challenge these instructions. When we do we may march to our own drummer, but we may also carry a load of guilt or shame about breaking away from what is expected.

Whose voice do you hear when you say, "I should wash my car, pay my bills, eat less?" You may say it is yours, but where did the original rule come from and who gave it to you? Take a moment to think about some of the things you are procrastinating doing right now? Pick one.

Pretend you are standing in front of an ATM about to make a withdrawal. This time you are going to withdraw some information. Imagine typing in this question instead of your pin number: "How young was I when I decided that I would be a bad person if I didn't [fill in the thing you are putting off]. Take a deep breath and as you let it out a number will pop onto the screen.

As you know your age you may automatically know what was happening at that moment. Acknowledge all the guilt or shame you have felt throughout your life as a result of this experience. Tap on the memory or just tap:

> *Whatever happened when I was [age].*

Please don't think I am telling you to drop all *shoulds* and rebel against everything. The result would be chaos and harm. Children need *shoulds* to help them conform to the expectations of their culture and to keep them safe. But once we are grownups we can assess the rules and decide which ones fit our beliefs and which don't.

Grownups can choose which expectations they want to follow. Try this. Go back to the *should* you chose above. Tap as you say it out loud:

> *I should do my laundry.*

Notice how you feel. Is there tension in your stomach or throat? Do you feel ashamed of yourself for being lazy? Keep tapping until you reach a decision or gain insight. People find that when they trade in their *shoulds* they get rid of guilt and shame. Eliminate the words *should, shouldn't, must* and *have to* from your life this week by using EFT.

Procrastination doesn't have to slow you down. Use EFT to eradicate all the roadblocks of doubt and fear that keep you from moving forward.

To contact Gloria Arenson, her e-mail address is glotao@cox.net and her telephone number is 805-563-1140. Visit Gloria's Websites at www.GloriaArenson.com and www.meridiantherapy.net. Also, please see Gloria Arenson's biography at the back of the book.

RELATIONSHIPS
Crossing the feelings barrier to successful personal and business relationships

By Paul & Layne Cutright

> *"There really isn't an ideal relationship. It's how you deal with the imperfections of the relationship that makes it ideal."*
>
> *Unknown*

HOW DID YOU LEARN ABOUT EFT?

We learned about EFT around 1998 when we were going through a period of professional burnout. An energy worker in Arizona used EFT with us on the phone with spectacular results — so much so that we decided to travel from San Diego, where we lived at that time, to spend a weekend with her enrolled in a private intensive. She worked with us on rapidly overcoming the burnout we were experiencing, and EFT was a big part of what she did with us. Our personal experience with EFT showed us the huge potential for it in our own work.

HOW DID YOU RECOGNIZE IT WOULD APPLY TO RELATIONSHIPS?

When someone sees us for help, there's unwanted emotional pain. That's what we had been experiencing, too: difficult, seemingly overwhelming emotions. We were having trouble letting go of and processing our feelings. We've been energy psychologists since 1989, and we're adept with many other energy repatterning tools — none of which were working very quickly for us right then. We recognized immediately that EFT is just a more advanced technique, but very similar in a lot of the principles to what we'd already been using to help people in their relationships.

We specialize in crisis intervention for romantic couples and business partners, so usually people have some pretty big problems by the time they're ready to reach out, which is unfortunate. We often wish they would have called a year before, but this just tends to be the way human beings are with relationships at this stage of our evolution. They wait and wait and wait until it gets really, really painful, and then they reach out for help.

By the time people call us, they're flooded with a lot of confusion and conflict, and so we help them sort that out. It may sound too good to be true, but we have found that for any difficulty that shows up in relationships, if there's an emotional component to it, EFT helps.

And since there is invariably an emotional component in difficult relationships, EFT is the single most powerful and efficient tool or intervention we have found for helping people, whether it's with big grief or raging anger or feelings of abandonment or feeling misunderstood — whatever the feeling is. Literally in a matter of minutes, they can "clear" those negative feelings. Quickly, they can be restored to a state of emotional equilibrium, clarity, and balance, thus becoming more resourceful for addressing whatever problem triggered those feelings to begin with.

 WHAT DO YOU MEAN BY *TRIGGERED*?

A trigger is something that occurs when you're going along in life, and everything is fine, and somebody says or does something or fails to say or do something that you want, or you see something on television or something happens and you get upset. You have unwanted, negative emotions or reactions. It can be something as simple as frustration over balancing your checkbook, as seemingly impersonal as getting upset with world events, or as intimately dramatic as a romance disrupted by a serious breach of trust.

Layne Cutright had been working with Stephanie for several months when something incredibly disruptive to their coaching relationship happened: transference. Stephanie started imagining and acting as if Layne was her mother. She perceived that Layne, as her coach, had begun behaving just as the mother had which was always taking Stephanie's father's side instead of supporting her daughter.

Stephanie felt betrayed and began speaking to Layne as if they were enemies which was in sharp contrast to what the relationship had been up until that point. Layne pointed out that this was a classic case of transference, something that happens not only in therapeutic settings, but in many kinds of intimate pairings, from husband-wife to employer-employee relationships. Aware that this kind of dynamic can be terminally destructive to any bond, she suggested they begin EFT treatments immediately.

After just two rounds and about five minutes, Stephanie completely shifted. She became trusting, coachable and grateful again. What's more, she could see how she might have set up other people in her life this way and walked away with a tool for disassembling those old transferences too.

We call all of these situations triggers. You can feel like you're out of control. EFT is a technique people can learn to use to manage and clear these types of unwanted feelings, to defuse the triggering event and the resulting rampant emotions.

CAN YOU TALK ABOUT HOW SPECIFICALLY YOU USE IT IN YOUR COACHING PRACTICE?

Some examples might be that a boyfriend has said something or not said the right thing, or someone's been fired, or there's been an argument, or someone's jealous, or someone's afraid of losing somebody — it's the whole spectrum of emotions that show up in human relationships.

When people call, upset and triggered, one of the first things we do is use EFT so they can get back to a sense of calm and a greater state of resourcefulness. Often, when people are triggered, their limbic brain is running the show. They're on automatic. Their instinctive brain is running things. They're afraid.

They think they need to protect themselves, and they're not able to access their prefrontal cortex, their ability to reason and to think through things. So, as soon as we do five to ten minutes of EFT with people, they feel calmer, more resourceful, and they're able to access their own solutions better. They're also able to take our coaching.

YOU SAID "WHEN PEOPLE CALL"… DOES THAT MEAN THAT YOU DO THIS WITH PEOPLE OVER THE PHONE?

Yes, most of the work we do is over the telephone. We work with people all over North America and other parts of the world, so that's another reason EFT is so attractive to us. Unlike some of the other tools that we use in relationship energy repatterning, which require our being face-to-face with people, EFT is just as effective over the phone as in person. We use EFT in just about every single coaching session we do with anyone.

Plus there are parts of EFT that we can teach our clients to do on their own, so it becomes a self-help tool for them to use in between their sessions with us.

WHAT DO YOU MEAN BY THAT — USING IT AS A SELF-HELP TOOL?

It's something clients can use on their own, and it's fairly easy to learn so they can give themselves a treatment. When something comes up in everyday life, clients can figure out what needs to be done then practice EFT.

We frequently give EFT work as an assignment to use between sessions to accelerate progress, to address whatever specific issue we're addressing in our ongoing coaching with clients, or, as we just mentioned, to deal with the stresses of everyday life. We maintain an extensive online audio and video training for our clients, as well, so they can learn more if they want.

Many of our clients go on to use this in their own professional practices, just as we did after we experienced EFT with the practitioner in Arizona. So we train therapists and coaches and lay people in how to use EFT in professional settings and in everyday life.

Does EFT ever fail to work?

In our experience, 95 percent of the time it works immediately and dramatically. Some of the most powerful feelings that show up in romantic relationships are jealousy and betrayal, and we've seen it work wonders in even these intense situations. But when it doesn't work, there are a few possible reasons. You could sum it up as lack of willingness to let go of the unwanted emotion. Some people attach to pain even though they think they don't want it. Somewhere, somehow, there's a payoff.

They get something out of feeling that way, especially with grief. When you've suffered the loss of a loved one, grief is something that allows you to stay connected to your friend, your family member or your pet, so to let go of the grief feels like you're letting go of the one you love. So we've watched people where we've helped them reduce the level of grief so they don't feel it, and they want it back, because the grief helps them feel connected.

In traditional psychological terms, that would be called secondary gains, and in energy psychology and in EFT in particular, it would be called Psychological Reversal or counter-intention. And there's a piece in the dynamics of EFT that specifically addresses the psychological reversal so that people can let go of it, which we believe is one of the reasons that EFT is as effective as it is.

When Carol found out about Bob's infidelity, they flew in from different parts of the country to attend a crisis-intervention session. They'd only spoken on the phone about it and hadn't seen one another in person until they arrived at our home office in Santa Fe, New Mexico.

When they stepped across our threshold, it was immediately clear we had some intense feelings to help them get through before we could even begin to talk about what had happened or guide them to a place of personal responsibility, problem solving, or reconciliation. As you might imagine, there were explosive emotions. Carol was so angry she wanted to "rip his face off," and Bob felt like he deserved her wrath, so he came in feeling bad and guilty.

Neither of them could think straight so we worked with them separately for an hour using EFT. When they came together after that hour of individual work, they chose to sit close to one another on the couch. They were holding one another's hands and gazing at each other. You could tell that their hearts had opened even though they still had some hurt, confusion and guilt going on. They were present to one another, willing and ready to roll up their sleeves and recreate their marriage.

Ultimately, we worked with them a total of three to four hours that afternoon, but it was that first hour of EFT that made the rest of the work we did possible. Today, they're still together. They're deeply in love, and they've learned from the experience.

It takes a bit of training and a deep understanding of the human psyche, however, to be able to ferret out these counter-intentions, and, though we teach our clients how to use EFT with themselves, usually it's pretty difficult for people to see their own blind spots. This is where a coach becomes instrumental. So when our clients are using EFT and it seems like it's not working for them, they'll call us. Almost always, it comes down to not focusing on the right thing. They weren't in touch with the counter-intention, so we help them clear that and then the treatments that they do on their own are more effective.

ARE THERE EVER ANY NEGATIVE SIDE EFFECTS FOR PEOPLE?

That's a great question, and the answer is no. The very worst thing that can happen with EFT is that nothing happens, that it's not effective, but there are no known reported bad reactions or negative side effects at all.

One of the challenges is that usually the results are so fast and so dramatic — we're talking five minutes or less — that people start to develop an expectation that it should always work quickly. There are some issues in relationships that people need to work on using this technique every day for several weeks, and sometimes several months. If they've been used to these five-minute miracles, sometimes they misjudge the level of focus that they have to have to use the technique.

YOU MENTIONED TEACHING CLIENTS TO DO THIS ON THEIR OWN AND THEN ALSO COACHING THEM ALONG AS THEY NEED IT. DO YOU EVER TEACH COUPLES OR BUSINESS PARTNERS OR COLLEAGUES TO USE EFT TOGETHER?

We teach couples to do it together, especially if there's been some sort of sexual dysfunction, such as they're not feeling as passionate with one another. We'll have them use the treatment while they're looking at one another, which is incredibly effective and builds intimacy. And we guide them through certain statements to say that will help clear the issue. But with professional colleagues, usually they use the technique privately, and then that allows them to have better conversations, specifically problem-solving conversations.

WHAT CAN YOU SAY ABOUT SURROGATE EFT? DO YOU TEACH THIS METHOD TO PARENTS OF PRE-VERBAL CHILDREN?

Sure. This is another one of the more remarkable aspects of EFT: You can use EFT on your own body or on a friend's body on behalf of a child or an animal, whether the child or pet is present or not. We're aware of some remarkable stories of using surrogate EFT for animals. In fact, there was one lady we trained in California, who works exclusively with horses, trainers and riders.

She had an EFT session with a trainer in physical contact with a horse, doing the work on the trainer on the horse's behalf. And the horse had a lame right rear leg, and there was no apparent physical reason. The vet couldn't find any physical reason why the horse would be limping, and then after the EFT treatment, the horse was just fine and he wasn't limping anymore.

So surrogate work with non-verbal living creatures is a very powerful and wonderful thing to be able to do.

 WHEN YOU DO AN EFT SESSION, I KNOW YOU UTILIZE CERTAIN SETUP PHRASES. ARE THERE SOME THAT YOU CAN SHARE THAT ARE COMMON FOR PEOPLE WHO ARE FOCUSING ON RELATIONSHIPS?

It is useful to understand that there are four components to an EFT treatment. For classic EFT, the first part is the setup, the second part is the sequence, and then the third part is the nine-gamut procedure, and then there's a repeat of the sequence. Our sessions include some combination of those four elements.

The first part, the setup, is where psychological reversal or counter-intentions are addressed, and so a setup statement would sound something like this:

 Even though I have this deep feeling of sadness, I completely love and accept myself.

That's the structure of a setup statement. We do have a number of setup statements we use with predictable challenges that people have in their relationships.

We worked with Alice who came to us because of anxiety. We used EFT to drop her level to what we call a zero, which means she had no anxiety at all, no symptoms and no subjective experience of anxiety. Yet when it was over, she let us know she didn't like the feeling of no anxiety. She didn't want to let go of her "edge" because she didn't feel safe without it.

So this is a case where the client felt that EFT actually worked too well. We continued with a series of treatments to deal with the underlying need for her anxiety which were her feelings that she needed it to be safe in her relationships. This was a classic presentation of the unconscious counter-intention to letting go of pain. In time, she became ready to relieve herself of the pain. After that, EFT was an effective tool for the second and final round with her anxiety.

There are categories, such as issues around receiving love or giving love, issues around communication and trust, intimacy, fear of commitment, and sexuality. Some of the setup phrases might be like these:

> *Even though I'm afraid of losing love, I completely love and accept myself.*
>
> *Even though I'm afraid of losing love, I choose to know that I can experience love and feel safe.*
>
> *Even though I'm afraid to let go and trust John, I choose to love and accept myself.*
>
> *Even though I'm afraid to let go and trust John, I choose to know he's a trustworthy person and he deserves to be trusted.*

When we work with clients, we ask them a few questions to really get a sense of what's truly going on, and they give us all the clues we need to help create these setup statements. So they're usually personalized and customized to whatever unique situation the client is facing, although many situations fall into certain categories, and being able to see those patterns helps us come up with the phrasing quickly.

One of the reasons many other mental and emotional health procedures are ineffective is that there's not a means for addressing this unconscious part. So what we're doing is acknowledging that that part exists:

> *Even though I'm afraid to trust, I completely love and accept myself.*
>
> *Even though I don't think I can trust, I completely love and accept myself.*
>
> *Even though I don't think I deserve love, I completely love and accept myself.*

Whatever the issue is, you state one of the following:

> *Even though I have this [whatever the issue is], I completely love and accept myself.*
>
> *Even though I have this [whatever the issue is], I choose [whatever you want in place of that].*

What you're doing is acknowledging the truth about how things are and at the same time accepting what is. So it's not denying that this particular condition exists. In fact, it embraces the condition with love. So it brings in the power of love, which in our experience is the most powerful healing, transforming force in the universe. Simply invoking the power of love next to this thing that has been problematic or unconscious can, by itself, produce a powerful result for people.

HOW DO YOU SEE YOUR WORK EVOLVING FROM THIS POINT FORWARD WITH EFT, AND WHAT IS YOUR VISION FOR THE FUTURE OF EFT ITSELF?

A few years ago, we did EFT with a room of between eight hundred and a thousand people who knew nothing about it, and we didn't know what their issues were. We just taught them the basic procedure, told them to think of an issue that was present for them, and walked them through the EFT procedure a couple of times. We should say that, when working with EFT, you ask the person to rate the intensity level of the emotional pain or the discomfort of the issue on a 0-10 scale (SUDS), 10 being the highest and zero being nothing.

So we had them rate whatever their issue was and to make a note of it, and then after the procedure to notice, to tune in and see: Had that number changed? Had the intensity level changed? And then we asked people to share their experiences, and easily 85 percent of the room reported a significant shift from a high level of intensity of pain and discomfort to either next to nothing or a very small number.

So when we look at disasters like Hurricane Katrina or the tsunami last year, and there are large numbers of people who have been traumatized and affected by this sort of thing, we would like to see a way of working with these masses of people to help reduce the emotional and psychological trauma that they feel.

We're very excited about moving beyond the realm of personal relationships, even though it's great to be able to help people heal the emotional pain that causes them to feel disconnected from their family members, to be more resourceful in asking for what they want, to be able to create new levels of communication. But we like to think about how it could be applied to society as a whole.

We see that there are definite applications for EFT in overcoming so many of the cultural problems we're experiencing right now, such as prejudice. It's about overcoming fear of "the other," whether the other lives down the block or across the ocean. EFT is a highly effective tool for letting go of fear of any kind, and fear is the biggest troublemaker in all of our relationships: personal, business and social.

As the word gets out, people will learn that EFT is a life skill that they can use — an everyday life skill like bathing, brushing your teeth, eating, driving a car, using the telephone or getting on the Internet. When most everyone can manage their emotions, reducing stress and fear, this will mean that all of us can evolve to be better human beings.

What we see as the growing edge, the evolutionary edge for humanity is in the domain of our relationships: personal, social, global, political and cultural. Reducing and eliminating the fear that people have of one another, increasing our capacity to be connected — these things are going to allow humanity to evolve and begin to create a world that truly does work on every level for every living being on the planet. And, unless we learn how to do that in our relationships, we're assured of more of the same kind of discord that we've been seeing so much of in the last few years and decades.

So, in a nutshell, what EFT can do, in our vision of it, is to help people overcome their barriers to cooperating at higher and higher levels. And if human beings can dig down deep and bring forth the best in themselves, we believe we can consistently create miracles and turn situations around that seem like they were at an impasse. We can turn those situations around and turn defeat into victory, so much so that miracles will become ordinary.

To contact Paul & Layne Cutright, their e-mail address is partners@paulandlayne.com and their telephone number is 505-474-6018. Visit their Websites at www.IntegralRelationships.com, www.EFTTrainingOnline.com, www.enlightenedpartners.com, and www.PaulandLayne.com. Also, please see Paul & Layne Cutright's biography at the back of the book.

SEXUALITY
Healing past issues, creating greater communication and intimacy

By Rebecca Marina

> *"The sacred meaning of sexuality is not located in sexuality itself, but rather in human mutuality. Sexuality is a mode in which mutuality is expressed."*
>
> *John Buehrens*

HOW DID YOU DECIDE TO FOCUS ON SEXUALITY AS ONE OF YOUR AREAS OF EXPERTISE?

I had been interested in helping people with sexual problems because of past experiences. Some of these areas included sexual and childhood abuse, battered women, hormonal problems and the emotional areas associated with sexuality. I was getting excellent results so I decided this was one area where I could make a real contribution in helping people, especially women and sexual issues.

WHY DO YOU THINK OUR CULTURE HAS DIFFICULTIES DISCUSSING SEX?

It's interesting because we're bombarded with fairly explicit sexual messages publicly in the media, yet many people are inhibited about talking about even basic sexual things with their partners. Being able to address sexuality in an honest and respectful way can positively transform many areas of relationships.

One of reasons I wanted to write this chapter was to encourage people to deal with any sexual issues they may have. Most sexual issues have strong underlying emotions at their core. EFT is a wonderful self-help tool for people to use to clear emotional blocks to enjoying a healthy sex life. I want to give a broad overview of the ways to use EFT for sexual issues because EFT is such a safe and gentle method.

Another reason for sexual "hang-ups" is that a lot of the commercials on television are made for men by men. They're putting sexuality out as a commodity. As far as women go, most women feel intimidated by the sexy women in the commercials. Women feel that they can never live up to that ideal. It's like men and women are on "different pages."

 ### How can EFT help with sexual issues?

We always say to try EFT on everything and this certainly applies to sexual issues. EFT can help with any emotional issue having to do with both sex and relationships. As examples, you can use EFT for sexual issues such as helping get in the mood for sex, increasing sexual drive, performance anxiety, invigorating the sexual organs, releasing pain or trauma, forgiving past events, and getting more comfortable with your body.

 ### How would you help somebody that's too busy or doesn't have time for sex?

Honey, I'll be candid. You've got to put it on your schedule. Sometimes that's the only way. You need to purposefully think about sexual intimacy and make time for it. Otherwise, you get so busy it becomes the last thing on your mind. For relationships, sex is very important and good sex is the greatest stress reliever in the world. Here are examples of EFT setup phrases:

 Even though it seems that I don't have time for sex, I deeply and completely accept myself.

Even though I may be avoiding making time for sexual intimacy, I choose to find a way for the right time somehow.

You get the idea. Use whatever EFT phrase is most authentic and feels comfortable for you.

WHAT ABOUT IMPROVING COMMUNICATIONS?

Along those same lines, one of the ways that I help women in their sexuality is to help them to understand that men cannot read their minds. As women find the courage to tell their partner what they like, what feels best and what doesn't, there is much less frustration on both sides. Ladies, men want to please us if they just know what we want.

Of course, it is important for both men and women to express their desires in a gentle, loving way. Specifically, EFT can help you alleviate any nervousness you have about bringing the subject up and speaking to your partner. Use EFT to give yourself the courage to say what's on your mind. Examples of EFT setup phrases that might fit include:

Even though I feel nervous about saying this, I deeply and completely accept myself.

Even though I feel nervous about talking to [person's name] about what I like and dislike, I deeply and completely accept myself.

Even though this is hard for me, I allow the perfect communication to flow.

CAN YOU USE EFT TO HELP GET INTO THE MOOD?

Sure, EFT is excellent for communicating with your body. I have found that if you use EFT to direct your body for desired results, your body is very happy to comply.

Even though I'm not in the mood for sex, I choose to allow myself to begin to get in the mood.

Even though I'm not interested in having sex, I choose to allow myself to do whatever feels right for me.

Even though I'm not in the mood for sex, I choose to allow my sexual hormones to flow in perfect balance.

When I hit upon the phrase of addressing the hormones and I actually did EFT to direct the hormones to be stimulated, it helped tremendously. I tried it with several clients. Everybody had really good results. You can even name the hormones because in EFT, the more specific you get, the better.

WHY DO YOU EMPHASIZE SAYING THE SETUP PHRASE WITH EMOTION?

I have found that emotion makes a big difference. Often, people say the EFT setup phrase with reticence. They're afraid to lose their dignity and hold back. I recommend putting the emotion of how you want to feel in your voice *even if you have to pretend or "fake it."* Your subconscious mind doesn't know the difference between real and fake so when you pretend, you get results. When you put emotion into your body and voice, you change your state.

With EFT setup phrases, I ask my clients to follow my lead, mimic me and use the voice inflections that I do. The results are much better because this helps clients let go of any feelings of embarrassment. When I do EFT with my clients, I put my whole heart into it, and I encourage them to put their whole self into it too. When we do that, the results are just spectacular!

HOW CAN SOMEONE USE EFT IF THEY HAVE HIGHER SEX DRIVE THAN THEIR PARTNER?

You honor or at least accept the other person as they are and you use EFT to change your energy if that is your desire. Pressuring another person just creates further discomfort for you both. You need to *own* your feelings about the situation. You might use setup phrases like the following:

Ann did not want sex or a relationship. What prompted her to see me was fear of being alone. She didn't want to die alone and have nobody remember her. Ann wanted some help in shifting her energy around sex and relationships. In fact, she had given up even trying to have a relationship.

I asked Ann for a SUDS level on her reluctance to become involved in a relationship again, and she said it was a 10 on two major issues. First, she believed that there was nobody out there for her and secondly, that even if there was, Ann would end up ruining the relationship. She also felt that she couldn't let her guard down and let a man near her heart.

After doing several rounds of tapping on different aspects, Ann felt really good. I could feel Ann's energy shifting to a more positive note. As we tapped on some positive choices, Ann became excited. She said that she even felt a little sexy. You could hear the difference in her tone. Her voice had a sparkle, and she sounded like a young girl who was eager to attract just the right lover and relationship.

Even though I'm frustrated, I choose to channel my sexual energy in other positive ways.

Even though I have a different sexual drive than [person's name], I deeply and completely love and accept myself as I am.

Even though I have a different sexual drive as [person's name], I choose to find the right balance for us both.

Even though I have a different sexual drive as [person's name], I choose to honor and respect us both.

Even though I only feel like having sex [time period such as daily, weekly, monthly], I choose to allow myself to begin to want it more.

I'M TOO OVERWEIGHT AND ASHAMED OF MY BODY TO FEEL SEXUAL. WHAT DO YOU SUGGEST?

One of the perfect ways to use EFT is to improve your body image or become more comfortable and less self conscious about your body. You might try an EFT setup phrase like:

> *Even though I have big fat thighs, I deeply love and accept myself.*
>
> *Even though I don't want [person's name] to see me, I deeply and completely accept myself.*
>
> *Even though I hate being [description], I deeply and completely love and accept myself.*
>
> *Even though I feel overweight, I choose to appreciate my body and be thankful for all that it does for me.*
>
> *Even though I feel ashamed of my body, I choose to feel love for my body in ways that I've never felt before.*
>
> *Even though I wish I had the perfect body, I choose to surprisingly discover what's beautiful about my body right now.*

I find that using EFT to send love, acceptance and appreciation to your body or the parts you *reject* makes you feel good about your body. Focus on the things about your body that you like. It's a great way to bring up some self love. Start by acknowledging the negative and then use EFT to create self love for your body.

Here are some more possibilities:

> *Even though I don't like my body, I choose to love myself anyhow, and I forgive myself for anything that I may have had to do with not liking my body.*
>
> *Even though I feel ashamed of my [body part], I deeply love and accept myself and I forgive myself for anything I had to do with it.*

Go through a round and then think of the positive choices. Look at a body part. Think of what you love and appreciate about that body part. There is a positive benefit although you may have to uncover what it is.

> *Even though I have a fat stomach, my stomach has protected me and kept me warm. I love and appreciate my stomach.*
>
> *Even though I have fat legs, I appreciate my legs for supporting me and carrying me around. I am grateful for everything that my legs do for me.*
>
> *Even though I'm bald, I appreciate my low maintenance hairdo and the savings on my shampoo.*

Let go of blaming your body or yourself for whatever you consciously or subconsciously had to do with creating your body's condition. When you send love and gratitude to your body while doing EFT, it's so wonderful. You'll start feeling much more appreciative of your body as it is.

It's like having a child. If you have a child and all you do is criticize and scold your child, how is that child going to feel? In particular, women too often look into the mirror and don't see anything to appreciate. They target in on the areas for criticism and that's very hurtful and self destructive.

In our culture there is so much of an emphasis on beautifying our physical exterior and very little on our interior selves, our inside beauty. When you change your inner feelings about yourself, it changes things around you. Use EFT to acknowledge how you feel and then shift that energy by tapping in some positives. Again, focus on things that you do like about your body. You'll feel a level of self love. When you feel more self love, you're certainly going to have better sex.

WHAT ABOUT USING **EFT** FOR PAIN DURING INTERCOURSE?

One of the main reasons that women often experience pain during intercourse is that when there are emotional issues bothering them,

Don contacted me about a male performance issue. He was 71 years old, had met a kind, beautiful lady on the Internet and had developed a relationship by telephone. Soon he was to meet his friend in person. Don's main concern centered on the pressure to perform and any sense of disappointment that might ensue. His intensity of feelings was an eight.

Once we got it down to a four we decided to tap in a positive choice, including taking small steps of change. Once Don's fear was down to a one, I decided to get to the root of the problem using different techniques. We discovered that the core issue dated back to when Don was 16 years old in high school. We tapped on that issue including some forgiveness and acceptance. At completion, Don reported having no anxiety at all. He just felt very loving and that everything would be okay.

Lastly, we used relaxed meditation to imagine and visualize future events. Although I never did see Don again, he did write me a letter and say that his rendezvous with his friend was fantastic and absolutely wonderful. He felt relaxed, completely comfortable and commented that in using EFT, even the most delicate and private things are easy to deal with.

they tense up and their muscles don't relax. You can use EFT to allow your muscles to relax. This in turn helps your body fluids to naturally flow.

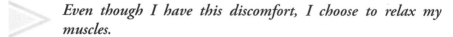

Even though I have this discomfort, I choose to relax my muscles.

Even though I have this pain, I send blood and oxygen to this area and ask it to relax.

WHAT ABOUT EFT FOR MENSTRUAL CRAMPS?

Yes, EFT is very good for menstrual cramps and regulation also. Here are some setup phrases:

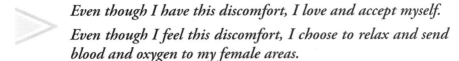

Even though I have this discomfort, I love and accept myself.

Even though I feel this discomfort, I choose to relax and send blood and oxygen to my female areas.

Even though I feel temporary mood swings, I love and accept myself and choose to enjoy the different moods.

WE'RE TRYING TO CONCEIVE A CHILD. HOW CAN I USE EFT FOR FERTILITY PROBLEMS? MORE SPECIFICALLY, HOW DOES STRESS AFFECT TRYING TO CONCEIVE?

Stress has a definite impact on trying to conceive a child. EFT is wonderful for tapping on stress and anxiety. Using EFT to relieve pent up emotions over having a child requires doing EFT regularly. You will want to tap on the different aspects such as feeling any anxiety and hopelessness. The key is to use EFT to release any fearful feelings.

To my way of thinking, anxiety and stress are the main reasons that block conceiving. Things are no longer spontaneous. The pressures to make it happen and watch the calendar, all create blocked energy. There needs to be room for allowing it to unfold.

With couples, there's so much pressure and blame — although not always consciously — on whose fault it is. The emphasis is on biological and physical issues. Emotions aren't taken into play. With younger couples, there's also a lot of social pressure.

I know of many instances where people have tried so hard, gave up and adopted a child instead. Soon after, many of them conceived children. It happens all the time. (EFT can also be used to transform the anxiety around adoption and the special circumstances that brings.)

Use an EFT setup phrase that fits best to your circumstances:

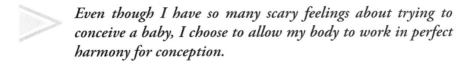

Even though I have so many scary feelings about trying to conceive a baby, I choose to allow my body to work in perfect harmony for conception.

> *Even though I am worried about conceiving a child, I choose to trust that it will happen somehow at the right time in the perfect way.*

Special setups can be used to encourage your body to cooperate.

> *Even though I feel anxiety about conception, I ask my body to come into perfect alignment, hormonally, emotionally, and be physically ready to conceive.*

When a couple desires to have a child and they've wanted a long time, sometimes *envy* comes into play. I've seen women who had such great difficulty going to a friend's baby shower because they feel envious. When they see someone else with a baby, it feels like twisting their heart into a knot. Envy eats away at you, creates a feeling of separation and lack. Whenever you tap on your feelings of envy, you transform it. Use EFT to release feelings of envy to open your energy and your heart.

> *Even though I feel envy because [person's name] is pregnant, I deeply and completely love and accept myself.*
>
> *Even though I feel I will never be a mother like [person's name], I deeply and completely accept myself.*
>
> *Even though I feel envy, I choose to feel thankful this person is showing me a picture of what motherhood looks like.*

WHAT ABOUT TEENAGERS DEALING WITH THE PEER PRESSURE OF HAVING SEX?

This is another area to use EFT. As I mentioned, television advertising as well as programs, movies and music have a focus on sexuality. Young people are under a lot of peer pressure, causing a conflict in personal values. Other people want them to have sex when they may feel they're not ready or they simply don't want to yet.

Dianna wanted to want to have sex with her husband but just did not have any sexual drive. According to Dianna, she had too many other things to think about. Often people are under such stress that they are mentally aware but not physically aware of things. They get wrapped up in their thoughts and aren't aware of what's going on in their body.

What worked successfully with Diana was that she used EFT to get out of her head, tune into her body and direct it using positive choices. Tapping on her non desire, in a short period of time, Dianna went from a SUDS level of nine down to a zero, and she felt her body tingling all over. She was amazed at the speed in which this happened. I finished the session with a meditation I created to awaken and tantalize all the senses. She was elated. What may surprise you is that Dianna is a lady in her fifties who has had a complete hysterectomy and subsequent hormonal imbalances.

EFT can make a big difference in your sex life. I encourage you to try experimenting with different setup phrases to find what works best for your situation. It is very helpful to find an experienced practitioner to assist you.

Teenagers and young adults benefit by realizing that they have control of the situation. Recognizing that they each have control over their bodies energy gives them the power of choice. Examples of setup phrases might include:

Even though I feel this peer pressure to have sex, I choose to stand up for myself and say no until I'm ready.

Even though my sexual hormones are affecting me, I choose to wait until I am mature enough to handle a sexual relationship.

Even though [person's name] wants me to have sex, I allow myself to do what is right for me, even if [person's name] doesn't like my decision.

CAN EFT BE OF USE IF I HAVE A DIFFERENT SEXUAL ORIENTATION?

EFT can be used by everyone for just about every issue, sexual and otherwise. In short, anything that bothers you or has a negative emotional charge. Use EFT to erase any hurt feelings or things that you want to *hide*. When you open yourself, you open your energy. Use EFT for fully expressing and accepting yourself. Here are just a few examples of setup phrases or create your own.

 Even though I'm afraid of what [person's name] might think, I deeply and completely accept myself.

Even though I feel uncomfortable about expressing myself, I deeply and completely love and accept myself anyway.

 I WAS SEXUALLY ABUSED. IS EFT EFFECTIVE FOR SEXUAL ABUSE ISSUES?

Based on past experience, it's important to focus on healing the feelings of anger, blame, and abuse, before even trying to inspire being sexual in the now. It has to be *safe* to feel sexual again. No one should attempt to force feeling sexual as long as feelings of *not being safe* abound.

One of the most effective treatments I use with people who have experienced abuse of any kind, is the "Volcano Technique." It's a way of healing the wounded inner child. I ask the client to get in touch with their *inner brat.* Many times sexual abuse started in childhood. The victim felt too frightened to allow their *inner brat* to stick up for them at the time. By getting in touch with that silenced *inner brat* and giving the client permission to "throw a tantrum" while tapping, the pain is alleviated and the person takes back the power that was stolen away.

For example, I might say "When you were six years old, what would you have liked to say to that person? Be as mean and ugly as you want." Once in touch with their *inner brat,* the client will have no problem telling me what they wished they could have said or done. I'll even ask them what physical thing they would have liked to do to the person. They might say that they would have liked to pull their hair and kick them in the shin.

When you give permission to get in touch with the childish brat, it's all in a childish context, yet it heals it at the level that it really happened. Then we use EFT and use the words they gave me. "Even though you hurt me so bad, I wish I could scream at you, you ugly, big horrible jerk." I even encourage them to cuss with anger issues. When you tap and say what you really wanted to say, what you were prevented from saying, you get in touch with the real, raw emotions. The release and healing is almost magical.

I had a client who was 55 years old. He was molested when he was five. When he got in touch with his inner brat, he had so much anger at that person. We tapped through it and included tapping on the anger at the people who should have been protecting him. At the end of the session, he was completely empty of the anger. There was no longer any emotional charge from that abuse, not a drop.

At the beginning of the session, he was in a lot of emotional torment. Afterwards, instead of having those intense emotions, he now was just a matter of fact about it. He felt so much better. You could see that his face was more alive. You could hear the change in his voice.

In this treatment, I encourage my client to get in touch with the personality that was wounded. The Volcano Technique and the inner brat give energy in expressing the hurt, anger and other feelings in a raw, honest and direct way that is very healing. By voicing the real emotions, the abused person takes their power back. People are healed on a deep level, feel empowered, and move from victim to victory over pain.

I also want to mention that you can't have someone tap in forgiveness when they're not ready. It's not right and the psyche will rebel. A person must release the negative feelings first. Take baby steps toward forgiveness. Most people are willing to move towards forgiveness or

190

be open to it somehow. Once you take off that anger, resentment and hurt, it's pretty much a *done deal*. Harboring hate and resentment is simply not as important anymore.

Another thing that I feel is important to address with abuse issues is what the *benefit* is that the person is still getting from hanging on to this pain. What's the *juice* someone could be squeezing out of hanging on to this issue? Sometimes clients have a really hard time with this. For example, perhaps they are getting sympathy or using the pain as an excuse to *not* move forward in their life.

It is important to tell clients that the *benefits* of keeping the pain are probably unconscious. If it was a conscious thing they would recognize it and release it. Sometimes, hanging on to the past is just a habit. Someone may have had the pain so long that they don't know any other way to be.

WHAT ABOUT SEX AND AGING?

Experience shows one benefit of sexuality is intimacy. Since sexuality increases intimacy, no matter what age you are, you can still be intimate and sexual. You can have a sexual life if that's what you desire. As we age, often the challenge is to get what's going on in our heads going on in our body too. EFT is a superb way to help align the desires of your mind and body.

> *Even though I'd like to feel sexual but I don't anymore, I deeply and completely accept myself. I forgive myself for anything I had to do with it.*
>
> *Even though my body has aged, I choose to feel as sexual as I did when I was [years] young, and I deeply and completely love and accept myself.*
>
> *Even though I may never feel as sexual as I did when I was younger, I choose to find pleasing ways to be intimate with my partner.*

As you'll note, I often use a "Choice" statement in the EFT setup phrases. After you learn the basics of EFT, you'll want to learn the *Choices* method. To find out more, go to www.emofree.com and search for "Dr. Carrington" or "choices." Also check Dr. Carrington's Website at www.eftupdate.com.

I recognize that I've been candid in discussing sexual issues in this chapter. My intention has been to give you practical ways that you can use EFT. I've given you a broad overview. If I can leave you with one key thing I'd like you to take away from this chapter, it's this.

Have the courage to try EFT on any aspect of your sexuality whether it's abuse, abstinence, peer pressure, body image, trying to conceive, physical symptoms, hormonal balances or whatever. Be kind and gentle to yourself. Go ahead and feel comfortable trying EFT. Relax, have a good time, be creative and use your intuition in using EFT to the fullest.

To contact Rebecca Marina, her e-mail address is
rebeccamarina@yahoo.com and her telephone number is 956-630-4930.
Visit Rebecca's Website at www.celebrationhealing.com. Also see Rebecca
Marina's biography at the back of the book.

SPEAKING & STAGE FRIGHT
Releasing the performance jitters and butterflies

By Angela Treat Lyon

> *"If you are distressed by anything external, the pain is not
> due to the thing itself, but to your estimate of it; and this
> you have the power to revoke at any moment."*
>
> *Marcus Aurelius*

WHAT IS THE CAUSE OF FEAR OF PUBLIC SPEAKING?

Any fear, anxiety or trepidation comes from a disruption in our energy system. From a purely energetic standpoint, it is postulated that when we have experienced a shock or trauma, it affects our brain and the cells in our body at a very deep level, resulting in the energy pathways becoming blocked, misaligned or even cut off. This results in the energy dynamic in the mind/body interaction changing out of its natural flow. The response to life itself thereby changes on all levels.

A shock or trauma may be entirely unnoticed consciously. The extent of an injury can also depend upon the emotional and energetic composition of the receiver, how he or she responds to the injury (both consciously and unconsciously), and upon how the people around us act towards us as, and after, we experience the trauma.

Causes of shock or trauma can be as gross as a car wreck, or as fine as a covert criticizing comment. One person may take a certain comment as nothing, whereby another might take it as a terrible insult. One person might sail through a horrendous injury; another might die of a small cut — according to his or her energetic/mental/emotional makeup, accumulated injury and past experience.

About two percent of our population is now being called the *Highly Sensitive Person*. These people have considerably less of the "tough skin" it takes to survive among the "normal" people around them. Fortunately, there is a trade-off: this HSP is also the one who is deeply creative — usually the artist, musician or genius who brings us cutting edge ideas, information and products. The HSP often sustains a higher intensity of *damage* than the ordinary person.

It's interesting to note that you can actually see energetic blockages in the brain and the cells themselves using CT (Computed Tomography) and MRI (Magnetic Resonance Imaging) scans.

Any shock, trauma or injury to the system will cause a distortion in the energy field. Imagine, if you will, a bent radio transmission wire. If the wire is bent slightly, the transmission will go through all right, although slightly distorted. Bent radically, or even disconnected, the wire can no longer function, and the result is static or no transmission at all. So it is with our energy systems.

The causes are as many as there are people who have it. I've seen people who were petrified of going onstage as a result of having been shamed or humiliated by teachers or parents, or even from a birth trauma resulting in the person feeling unwanted and not of value.

 WHAT IS IMPORTANT ABOUT THE SHOCKED OR DISTORTED ENERGY SYSTEM?

Until the distortion is corrected, our energy won't flow freely, and we will as a result feel restricted, limited, and not whole. Once the energy flows freely again, we will often forget what it was like to be ill or "off," and sometimes we can even forget that we had an issue at all. According to what experiences we have in our lives, and what stories we tell ourselves around the damage, we can go from feeling just slightly "off" to very, very ill — emotionally, physically, and mentally.

Whether caused by an emotional, mental or physical trauma, the energy system must be brought back to "blueprint" status for us to feel whole again.

WHAT KINDS OF STAGE FRIGHT ARE THERE?

I've seen fright of being on the stage, fright of people, fear of unsatisfactory performance, loss of approval, severe panic attacks, social phobias and agoraphobia. Manifestations of public performance fear are as varied as people. One person can have more than one different type of fear related to performing in public.

 ## HOW DO YOU KNOW YOU HAVE STAGE FRIGHT?

You might experience one or more of the following: wobbly knees, sweating, red or white face, heart racing and sweaty palms. Fear might be induced by the merest thought of going onstage to speak or perform — for any reason — to standing in the wings, waiting to go on and actually going onstage.

Some people, like singer Barbra Streisand, experience extreme nausea before going onstage. Others experience sweating, weeping and heart palpitations. They find it impossible to sleep the night before, finally falling into a deep sleep just before dawn and awaking an hour later, feeling absolutely fine.

Others experience a complete calm, almost numb, until they're on stage. But when they look out to the sea of faces, they become utterly paralyzed, go blank, and cannot speak even a whisper.

Then there are those who are fine until there is any disturbance in the audience — a heckler or an unexpected event. The speaker becomes so self-conscious that he cannot get back his previous state, and feels as if he will blow the whole thing. The resulting nervousness escalates.

Here is a list of the anxiety and performance issues my clients have defused using EFT:

My friend, Allen, is a doctor. He called me one day and asked me if EFT would work for his fear of consultations with his patients and would I please come right away? I had him start out in another room, and mentally walk through what would be the ordinary routine of going into his office with his patient. About ten feet from the door, his breath became ragged, his belly cramped, and his eyes bulged with panic.

I asked him what would be the worst thing that could happen to him if he messed up the consultation. He said, "I'd be laughed at. I'd lose respect — theirs and my own. I might even lose my ability to work."

Okay, and what will happen if you panic in the consultation room? He replied, "They won't believe me. They'll laugh at me, and I won't be good enough."

And right there he had a memory of his father laughing at him when he made a mistake as a nine year old. He started to choke up, and his face went sheet white. We tapped through all of the physical sensations, starting with his breathing.

Then we tapped on all of the above fears, and others that came up as a result of seeing through his nine year old eyes. At the end of our session, he suddenly realized that his dad hadn't been laughing at him. His dad had been laughing because he adored Allen and loved seeing him try so hard at something that was way out of his ability range. Allen had completely forgotten that his dad had hugged him and said, "It's OK, buddy, you'll be able to do it when you're a little older."

I asked him how he'd like to feel and be when he had to do consultations. He said, "I want to feel calm, confident, authoritative, believed, and happy to be serving my patients." We did more tapping to install his desired way of being, and his confidence and belief in himself.

When we re-walked through the routine of taking his patient to his office again, the panic wasn't there anymore, and he felt excited that this problem, which he had had for years, was gone. I checked back a week later. He'd had to tap a little once, but after that the panic never came back.

Physical sensations

- Sweating
- Belly ache/nausea
- Butterflies
- Knees shake
- Voice quivers
- Shortness of breath

Negative self talk

- I'm afraid to talk to people.
- I'm afraid I'll be too tired to remember my speech.
- No one will like me.
- No one will like what I have to say.
- I'm a failure before I begin.
- Onstage in front of everyone staring at me
- Onstage in front of everyone expecting more of me than I can give
- What if they don't clap?
- What if my introducer flubs it up?
- What if they laugh at me?
- What if I look stupid?
- What if they make so much noise during my talk that even I get distracted?
- What if I go blank and forget what I was saying?
- What if I can't get my audience involved?
- What if they ask questions I can't answer?
- What if I get heckled?
- What if I have onstage nerves?
- What if I get distracted or people get up and move around?
- What if people don't respond?
- What if people are whispering and chatting?
- What if I get emotional and want to cry during my talk?
- What if I get self-conscious?

What's a good example of a fear of public-speaking?

You've been asked to give a talk about your favorite subject at your local group meeting. Caught up in the moment of enthusiasm generated by the request, you agree, even though you have suffered from stage fright ever since Mr. Narrow put your oral book report down in third grade.

You drive to the meeting. You have dressed nicely. Your presentation is in order, and you're on time. But your hands feel like clammy, slippery eels. Your clothes are soaked from perspiration. Your heart is pounding so loud that you *know* it can be heard for blocks around. Your breath comes in rapid pants as if you were at the end of a marathon. Your stomach is full of not butterflies, but behemoths who threaten upheaval at any second, and you aren't even there yet.

This is exactly what happened to me 20 years ago when I was asked to make a presentation of my sculptures at a local artists' meeting. At first, I felt honored and excited. I put together my slides, organized my outline and made sure I had appropriate clothing, since many clients and gallery owners were to be there as well as other artists. If I was successful, it was possible to make enough sales and contacts at this one meeting to generate my entire year's income, as well as a lifetime of contacts and leads.

As I thought about this meeting, my initial excitement turned to outright panic. "What if" echoed inside my head until all I fantasized was disaster at every turn. My thoughts were, "Who am I to give a talk to this meeting? Who'd be interested in my work?" Every flaw in every piece of sculpture I had ever created came to mind. "Who would want to look at such imperfect stone, design and carving? What if so-and-so, an expert stone carver, was there? He'll laugh me out the door and out to sea. I'll be so embarrassed."

I was a wreck. I felt sick to my stomach and had a headache. Fully dressed, I fell onto my bed and cried myself to sleep.

I had just begun working with a public speaking trainer at the time — the incomparable Pam Chambers of Honolulu. I had just taken my first class. I called her in a panic after the first rush of excitement had ebbed away. She was out of town until after my meeting. I was on my own. If only I had known EFT then, it would have saved me days of anxiety and all of my fingernails.

I EXPERIENCE EXTREME NAUSEA. HOW DO I DEAL WITH THAT?

Nausea is an adrenalin reaction. It's possible to resolve it very simply. If you breathe in through your nose for one count, and out through your mouth for four counts repeatedly, you will easily gain your equilibrium back again. Make sure you don't breathe in through your mouth to avoid hyperventilation.

On the other hand, there may be other aspects to your situation. Once your nausea is cleared, you might feel other fearful feelings which can then be addressed with EFT.

HOW DO I GET RID OF MY STAGE FRIGHT?

Play "detective", or observer. Imagine you've been asked to give a talk, and notice the very little things that happen next. Are your hands suddenly sweaty? Did your heart start to pump rapidly? Did you break out in a cold or hot sweat? Did you suddenly remember how your teacher, Mrs. Pine, made fun of you the day you had to recite it in front of the whole school because you missed a line?

Were you like some women, who were happy, energized and talkative until their parents told then that little girls should be seen and not heard? Were you like many men, who were happy, energetic and talkative little guys until required to read aloud or recite something, didn't do well, and were told they were stupid or slow? Do you have thoughts of self-doubt, like "I'm stupid. I'm not good enough. Who will pay attention to or want to know about anything I have to say," and so on.

What do I do once I make note of my sensations, feelings, and thoughts and how they show up in my body? Here are two types of situations:

Surprise speech out of nowhere

In a situation where you have to go onstage and you can't prepare ahead of time, tap your Karate Chop points — one on each hand — together. You can also slap the insides of your wrists together. Use this for any anxiety.

This is a powerful way to calm yourself, and to simultaneously handle psychological reversals you might have towards wanting to be free of the fear sensations. I've seen too many cases where reversals weren't handled, and there was simply no progress even tapping ourselves silly.

Now you have gained a bit of composure. You can hear them calling your name, and you're not ready yet. What do you do? Stand still for a moment — as long as it takes for one to three deep breaths as you gently tap on your collarbone point six to ten times. Visualize your talk going smoothly. See yourself remembering all your lines or what you have to say, and being able to calmly receive any applause.

It doesn't take that long. If you go out there without doing it, the results may be far more painful than if you hadn't calmed yourself.

If collarbone tapping isn't appropriate for the situation, gently and slightly slap your hand against your thigh as if you were keeping time to some inner music. That's pretty unobtrusive, and can even be worked in while you speak. It will also act as a calming *anchor* or reminder to your body to be calm again.

Prepare for a talk in the future

As indicated, note what your sensations are. Especially notice your breathing. If you can only focus on any one thing, make it breathing.

Mary, a beautiful, healthy and vibrant 65-year old, was invited to sing with a group of women who circuit the world singing. Mary hadn't sung with them in 20 years, and she was terrified. She had gained a lot of weight and was embarrassed to think of herself as a fat old whale jiggling around on the stage. She had also smoked for years, and her voice was low, husky, and tended to break during inappropriate places as she tried to sing.

Since her invitation had come several months before the event, we had plenty of time for Mary to prepare. First, we used EFT to eliminate her smoking addiction. That was easy. We did it in two sessions. Actually, the second session segued into the being fat issue. We ended up tapping on that more than on the smoking.

In the end, Mary's fear originated with feelings about her mother who had passed away long ago and had never approved of Mary, hated her music, dancing and singing, and smoked like a chimney. Mary had become a good little girl for so long in order to please her mother that she didn't even know who she was.

We uncovered and tapped on several other issues. Mary's initial fear of being onstage disappeared in our first session. We worked another few months on her issues of becoming healthy and attractive, and refining her singing voice. Seven months after Mary was first invited to appear onstage with her friends, she weighed 30 pounds less and she had completely stopped smoking. Her voice was strong. She felt radiant, successful and happy.

Once your breathing improves and shifts, it signals your body to release the "Fight or Flight" syndrome. All of your systems can go back to normal again.

What you hear yourself saying

Listen. Your mind or self-talk will say something like: "Me? They want me to speak? I can't do that. I don't know how. I'll be a complete flop. I'll feel like a fool. I'll forget my lines. I'll blush. I feel so sick. Why did they pick me? I'm so scared. I'll lose my job if I fail this chance. I hate flying, and I have to fly there and back."

Each of these phrases is so normal, so everyday to us, they're easy to ignore or pass over. Be a good detective. Grab each one as it slides past your awareness. Each one is a perfect EFT setup phrase.

Do this:

As you strike your Karate Chop point, speak your setup phrases, like this:

Even though they asked me to speak, and I think they are nuts, I deeply and completely accept myself.

Even though I can't believe they want me to speak, I deeply and completely accept myself.

Even though I can't do that, I deeply and completely accept myself.

Even though I don't know how to give a speech, I deeply and completely accept myself.

Even though I'll be a complete flop, I deeply and completely accept myself.

Even though I'll feel like a fool, I deeply and completely accept myself.

Even though I'll forget my lines, I deeply and completely accept myself.

Even though I'll blush, I deeply and completely accept myself.

Even though I feel so sick, I deeply and completely accept myself.

Even though I can't figure out why they picked me, I deeply and completely accept myself.

Even though I'm so scared, I deeply and completely accept myself.

Even though I'll lose my job if I fail this opportunity, I deeply and completely accept myself.

Even though I hate flying and I have to fly to the event and back, I deeply and completely accept myself.

Alternate ways you can say the EFT acceptance phrase are:

Even though I [want to, would like to, learn how to, etc.], I deeply and completely love and accept myself

Even though [whatever the issue is], I'm a great kid. I'll be fine. I know it (or I'm okay).

Or you could use a "Choices" phrase instead of "I deeply and completely accept myself." What would you prefer? Make a list of what you'd prefer. And use a choice:

I choose to feel clear.

I choose to feel happy.

I choose to remember my talk (lines, routine, music, dance steps, etc.)

I choose to have a "cheat sheet" with me if I forget the order I wanted to follow.

I choose to feel excited.

I choose to feel calm.

I choose to feel inspired and ready to inspire.

I choose to feel in shape and ready to go.

I choose to feel receptive to the people around me.

I choose to handle questions and answers with complete ease and confidence.

I choose to easily pace myself to track time and end just a bit early.

I choose to remember to bring my business cards, brochures and other back-of-the-room material I need.

I choose to remain grounded after my talk.

I choose to easily interact with people before and after my talk.

Now that you have done the setups, and made a new choice, *speak your choices as you tap each of the EFT points.*

Although they're not "official" EFT points, you can also tap on the *Top of the Head* point (near the crown of your head) and the *Third Eye* point (between your eyebrows). Another recommendation is to slap or tap your inside wrists together as you speak your choices.

One hundred percent of the people I've worked with for stage fright — whether before or during performance — have easily used EFT for defusing their fear. They took the freed energy and made not just lemonade out of the lemon way they felt, but massive, awesome lemon meringue pie.

If you have a fear of public speaking, stage fright or performance anxiety, you're not alone. You're in good company. For example, one of the world's greatest swimmers, Australian Olympic gold medalist Susie O'Neill, has reported experiencing performance anxiety. So have actresses Kim Basinger and Courteney Cox, actors Sir Laurence Olivier and Peter O'Toole, plus singers Garry McDonald, Donny Osmond, Jonathan and Jordan Knight from the pop group *New Kids on the Block*, Kenny Rogers, Carly Simon and Barbra Streisand. If only they knew about EFT!

Now *you* have EFT — a simple, rapid, effective tool you can use daily. Make it a point to use EFT to feel comfortable and confident whenever and wherever you speak or perform in front of anyone — or anytime at all.

To contact Angela Treat Lyon, her e-mail address is lyon@pigees.com. Visit Angela's Websites at www.eftbooks.com or www.Rich-Radio.com.

SPIRITUAL GROWTH
The inner path to emotional freedom and a thriving life

By Rick Wilkes

> *"When a person takes one step toward God, God takes more steps toward that person than there are sands in the worlds of time."*
>
> *The Work of the Chariot*

HOW DO WE GROW SPIRITUALLY?

We begin to grow spiritually when we first become aware that there is *more to us than meets the eye.* As soon as we realize that there is a *non-physical* aspect to being alive, we are acknowledging a truth that is known by many names, including "God." All of us are always connected with this source of creativity, compassion, and well-being. Growing spiritually means we are making a *conscious* choice to deepen our awareness, experience, and trust of this innate part of *who we are.*

Our spiritual connection helps us to feel inspired, uplifted, joyful, guided, healed, forgiven, and loved beyond all description.

DO I HAVE TO USE THE NAME "GOD" TO DESCRIBE THIS SPIRITUAL CONNECTION?

I use the term God to describe what can and is called by many names, including "that which is nameless, faceless and beyond human comprehension." Alas, terms like God, trust, faith, and even love carry a lot of baggage sometimes — and limiting or painful beliefs. Here is the first place we'll use EFT to find some inner peace. Tap the following:

Even though I don't know what to call this spiritual connection I seek, and I'm not sure I like — and sometimes definitely do not like — what "God" has meant to me up to this point in my life, I ask to be guided through my spiritual connection to a name that feels right in my heart.

Even though others have defined what "God" means to me, I choose to be open to a broad range of new spiritual experiences. I want to grow. I choose to grow. I intend to grow. I love to grow.

As we go forward, feel free to use the name of your choice, one that resonates closest to your beliefs and your heart. God is known by literally hundreds of names including:

All That Is	I Am
Allah	Inner Being
Alpha & Omega	Jehovah
Beloved	Jesus
Christ	Lord
Creator	Messiah
Divine Intuition	Mother of All
Earth Mother	Savior
Goddess	Source
Godhead	Spirit
Heavenly Father	The Field of Infinite Intelligence
Higher Self	and Energy
Holy One	Universe
	Yahweh

It is my experience that God doesn't really care what name you use. We see evidence of this in all the names that have been used through the ages to connect with spiritual energy. Call Him Bob. Call Her Angel. Just call.

How can I start having spiritual experiences?

All roads lead to God, to Spirit, to Source energy. Some people will become aware of God as part of a peak experience; they feel so incredibly *Good* that they feel *God*. The experience leaves them feeling so alive that their hearts open in deep felt gratitude and appreciation. Indeed, if you have *ever* felt gratitude and appreciation, you have felt God.

Others will connect through misery and suffering — the "Dark Night of the Soul," when all is lost and we give up hope of personally resurrecting our lives. In surrender, we let go, expecting to fall, crash, and burn. We suddenly realize God is present and is uplifting and supporting us.

Some people are born with a clear awareness of God. Others will find it through simple, day-to-day events such as a friend's embrace, a lover's smile, or a flower growing where none could possibly survive.

Some will hear the voice of God within. Others will see a vision. Others will feel it in their body. Some simply know God's truth and have an abiding faith and love.

If you are feeling *left out* or are having a hard time believing such an experience is possible for *you*, try EFT with these statements — or make up your own.

> *Even though I don't feel God — and I am not even sure I want to — I choose to be open to a loving connection with all of who I am.*
>
> *Even though I feel left out because I don't know where God is in my life, I've decided to be open to spiritual growth anyway.*
>
> *Even though I feel hurt, and skeptical, and doubtful — and I have my reasons — I've decided to find out for myself, and I deeply and completely accept all of me.*

IS BLIND FAITH REQUIRED?

No. Indeed, I find spiritual growth the most *practical* of practices. It connects us with a greater wisdom. It lets us tap into a source of guidance that has a broader perspective and deeper knowing than our logical mind has on its own. It puts us into the flow of creativity with ample support to help us live our dreams. Spiritual experience manifests in wondrous ways across our entire life — physically, emotionally, mentally, and in our relationship to everyone and everything.

One measure of spiritual growth is how integrated it is into a person's day-to-day activities — work, play, family, and friends. God truly is in the *details*. Of course, early on in our spiritual practice, the growth is often occurring below the surface, just as some seeds germinate for a full season before sprouting visibly at the perfect time.

Spiritual growth is an emotional journey first. While faith helps, EFT can also assist us in releasing the fear, impatience, and doubt. Tap the following:

> *Even though I am afraid, and I fear what I'll find, or not find, I choose to be calm and confident as I embark on my spiritual journey.*
>
> *Even though I have little or no conscious experience of God, and I am not sure I'll know what to do and that makes me feel anxious, I choose to relax and allow spirit to guide me.*
>
> *Even though I have my doubts, and who wouldn't if they had my life experiences, I've decided to be open to the possibility.*
>
> *Even though I am impatient, because I need help now, I choose to allow my life and spirit to unfold at a pace that is perfect for me.*

DO I HAVE TO BECOME RELIGIOUS TO BE SPIRITUAL?

Religions are organizations with an *external* doctrine to guide and direct *internal* spiritual development. They provide community and context for spiritual growth. Spiritual development itself is, however, intensely private. Even poets are unable to express the beauty and intimacy we feel when loved unconditionally by All That Is.

If a religious organization or group meeting best serves you, wonderful. If silent meditation and prayer — alone in your personal, sacred space — serves you best, wonderful. Like any journey, some prefer to travel with a group — large or small. Some prefer the freedom to explore on their own.

Many people grow up or marry into a religious tradition and find later that God seems to be taking their heart in a different direction. That can create anxiety and fear. You may have dozens of different concerns if this is the case for you. I encourage you to write them down and use EFT on inner conflicts. Turn within to your own inner guidance on the best next step for *you*.

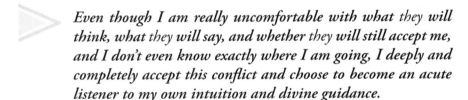

> *Even though I am really uncomfortable with what they will think, what they will say, and whether they will still accept me, and I don't even know exactly where I am going, I deeply and completely accept this conflict and choose to become an acute listener to my own intuition and divine guidance.*

For others, their experience of "God" has been hurtful, restricting, and even abusive. People have killed and worse "in the name of God." It is enough to make someone reject and turn away from their own inner source of well-being and guidance. If this is your situation, I'd like to offer you this thought and round of EFT.

What if "God" is not what *he* said, *she* proclaimed, or *they* insisted?

> *Even though I don't like his "God," and I can't stand her "God," and their "God" turns my stomach and leaves me cold, I am willing to open my heart to a true Source of well-being, a true friend, and a compassionate, forgiving, pervasive love.*
>
> *Even though I tried religion and it didn't work for me, I am open to a personal spiritual journey.*

Even though I am afraid I will become like them, *I've decided to discover the spiritual best of* who I really am.

Even though they hurt me, in the name of the "God" they said, I'd decided to introduce myself to the real God within me and trust my own heart connection.

So, how do I connect with God?

1. Ask and set a clear and strong intention.
2. Know that God always answers.
3. Allow yourself to experience God in your uniquely personal way.
4. Practice!

If you have doubts, which is completely normal, try EFT with this:

Even though I have many doubts, and I have my reasons, I deeply and completely accept myself, *and with all my being I choose to be open to the possibility that* God accepts me too, *and God will answer in a way that is perfect for me.*

How do I *ask* to grow spiritually?

Prayer is the most formal way to ask. Tapping while praying adds a physical component so that we align *body* with *mind* and *spirit*. Here is a simple prayer request. If your heart guides you to different words, by all means, use yours.

(Top of head point) Dear God,
(Eyebrow point) I want to grow.
(Side of eye point) I choose to hear you.
(Under eye point) I want to see signs of our connection.
(Under nose point) I am open to divine guidance to lead me on this path of spiritual growth.
(Chin point) I appreciate and am grateful for my life.

(Collarbone point) I relax and allow your love and comfort to flow into my heart.
(Under arm point) I accept your forgiveness.
(Top of head point) Guide me God to feel and to be closer to you, the Source of my well-being. Amen.

Let me add that by the very act of reading this, you have already asked to know your Spirit more closely. Nothing else is *required*. God knows that only sincere seekers read chapters on spiritual growth.

HOW CAN I KNOW THAT GOD ALWAYS ANSWERS?

That's easy. See, if you ever spent even a nanosecond *completely* disconnected from source energy — from God — you'd cease to exist. The intelligence that keeps your heart beating, your lungs breathing, and your tissues renewing is all God. It is our spiritual essence that animates us. It is what is present the moment before death that defines us as "alive" and that departs this bag of bones, organs, blood, and brains at the moment of death.

To develop spiritually is to grow and blossom in ways that may or may not be observable to the average person. Yet, we *feel* spiritual growth in our experience of life.

In other words, you are *already* spiritually connected whether you know it or not. The practice is to make it *conscious* and *intentional*.

But you may not feel God yet, so tap:

Even though I do not feel at all connected to God, I deeply and complete accept that there is more to me than meets the eye.

You may not believe God yet, so tap:

Even though I do not believe I am connected to God. I feel so alone. I feel so sick. I feel so poor. I feel so fearful. I deeply and completely accept all my feelings.

You may not trust God yet, so tap:

> *Even though I do not* trust *God, and I have my reasons, I choose to be open to trusting all of me, including any or all of me that might be connected to God consciousness.*

You may think God isn't *in you* yet, so tap:

> *Even though God must be "out there" (point up or away from you) and not "in here" (tap over your heart), I've decided to find God* wherever *I look, touch, hear, and smell, and I look forward to feeling Spirit flow within me and through me to bless my life and the world.*

How do I *allow* myself to experience God and grow spiritually?

Notice that the key word is to *allow*. Most people forget that we are human *beings* not human *doings*. To grow we must allow our spiritual connection to rise to our conscious awareness from deep within us.

To *allow* means relaxing, opening, expecting, and patiently receiving. I remember meditating for several months before I started receiving clear communication from my inner guide. The more I tried to force it, the more I tried to *do something* instead of allowing myself to *be who I am already*, the more distant God felt. During the natural unfolding process — which never ends by the way — EFT can help considerably to address feelings of doubt, fear, impatience and "not doing it right." Here are tapping phrases.

> *Even though I have all these doubts, I choose to relax and allow spiritual growth to unfold for me.*
>
> *Even though I have these fears because I don't know what to expect or even what it is going to be like, I choose to be calm and confident and allow myself to relax and be open.*

Even though this isn't happening fast enough for me, I have decided to relax and enjoy the process without rushing because I am an eternal being after all.

Even though this isn't working for me, as usual, I'm open to allowing myself to feel the way God does — accepting, patient, forgiving, and unconditionally loving of who I am becoming.

Even though I have to do it now, I have to do it right, and I definitely have to be the perfect spiritual student, I've decided to "let go and let God."

Another technique is to simply tap through the points alternating expressions of spiritual energy. For example, start at the top of the head, say one of these choices, and then move to the next EFT point and the next choice. Or, tap a full round on whatever word or phrase allows you to feel spiritually connected:

Relaxing
Allowing
Connecting
I choose peace
Let go and let God
Listening
Trusting
I am forgiven
Be still and know
I am
Grace
Kindness
Love
Appreciation
Gratitude

WHAT SHOULD I EXPECT TO FEEL AS I *ALLOW?*

Well, have you ever used EFT to go from a 10 to a zero? At the end of those rounds, what did you feel? What words do you use to describe the feeling? For me, there is *relief.* There is *peace.* There is a calm, patient *stillness.* There is the sensation of being a part of the *flow of well-being.* Those are just some of the qualities of God that we tap into with EFT.

DOES SPIRITUAL GROWTH REQUIRE MUCH PRACTICE?

That depends. Do you want more peace, joy, and well-being in your life? Do you want to *thrive* rather than just *survive?* If so, intending spiritual growth and being in a state of spiritual awareness will bring those, and more, *much more.*

WHAT ARE SOME OF THE PRACTICES I CAN USE FOR SPIRITUAL GROWTH?

The truth is, almost any human experience can be used for spiritual growth. There are, however, some that have been shown through time to be fruitful across many traditions. Two of these are meditation and mindfulness.

HOW DOES MEDITATION HELP?

Meditation is the cornerstone of my practice because it helps quiet my mind so I can hear my spirit. Even 10 minutes of sitting and *being* in meditation can be of great help. (Note: I did not say *doing* meditation.)

I typically meditate any chance I get. When I was starting out, I sat comfortably in a straight-backed chair for 20 minutes, twice a day, focusing on the breath. Within just 30 days the level of inner chaos had already started to shift.

Can you allow yourself to sit still and simply listen to your breathing for 20 minutes? If you are feeling resistance to the idea, you might try tapping:

> *Even though there is no way I can sit still and do nothing because it's a waste of time, I have too many responsibilities, there are things to do and places to be, and there's that show I want to watch on TV, I deeply and completely accept my busy mind and give it permission to take a short meditative rest and renewal break.*

In my experience, 20 minutes of meditation yields the equivalent benefits of rest and renewal as two full hours of sleep. You *have* the time to meditate. Just get up 20 minutes earlier.

WHAT ROLE DOES MINDFULNESS PLAY IN SPIRITUAL GROWTH?

You may find that *mindfulness* practices, bringing focused awareness into the *now* and becoming fully present with whatever you are doing, takes you deeper into your spiritual connection. Conveniently, daily meditation practice leads naturally to greater mindfulness in our everyday lives.

So imagine for a moment that you have a dirty dish to wash. You are going to be completely present and mindful as you *just wash that dish* with all your attention. You feel the warm water, you smell the slippery soap, and feel your hands grip the hardness of the dish. You feel appreciation and gratitude for being alive to feel these simple sensations.

If you are like most people, when doing "autopilot" tasks like dishwashing, your mind is consumed with other thoughts and worries. If so, you can use EFT to help your energy system focus on the present:

> *Even though there are so many worries demanding my attention, I choose to simply be in the present moment and allow myself the pleasure of God's company.*

Remember: God's present to you is the present moment.

What is the role of prayer?

If meditation is listening to God, our prayer time is an opportunity to express our feelings to God. Sure, most people pray when they are suffering and want divine intervention and relief. Do that and tap along with the prayer if you want to add a body component.

In addition to prayers that make a request, I also want to encourage you to prayerfully offer appreciation and gratitude. Appreciation and gratitude are such *healthy vibrations*. Practice them every day. I often take a short "gratitude walk" where I notice and give honest thanks for what is in my life that feels good to me.

It may be nearly impossible to reach all the way to gratitude on some days. *And that's okay.* On the really tough days, the gratitude might be as minimal as, "Well, at least tomorrow is another day." You will find that offering even a modest acknowledgement of gratitude brings relief. I assure you, as you grow in your communion with God, you will find that Spirit helps you notice all around you the many blessings that are in your life. And by the Law of Attraction, the more you consciously appreciate, the more you will have in your life *to* appreciate. Tap:

> *Even though things don't seem to be going perfectly well for me now, and I feel more wrung out and beaten than grateful, I choose to beat the drum of appreciation for my life and for the loving support God offers to my heart.*

Where do I go from here?

Your spiritual path will be unique to you. The good news is that the perfect teacher is *always* with you, right there in your heart. Know that God speaks to all of us through our emotions. The thoughts that feel good and peaceful are the thoughts closest to where God's emotional guidance system is directing us. With practice you will learn to discern the difference between your inner critic and your divine inner guide. Once you do, your life will be transformed.

You will notice that books, coaches, friends, and opportunities "show up" at the perfect time. Rather than exhausting yourself in struggle, you will *allow* God to take care of so many of the hard details, so you can relax and play in the river of abundance and well-being. You will find it easy to appreciate both what you love in your life and the opportunity that challenges bring to grow and dream.

It has been my honor to share with you these thoughts and the energy that EFT can bring to our spiritual growth. My prayer for you is a thriving life filled with joy and co-creation in partnership with God. I welcome your stories and look forward to hearing from you.

I close with these simple instructions my teacher shared with me:

Go within. Listen. And follow your heart.

To contact Rick Wilkes, his e-mail address is Rick@Thrivingnow.com. Visit Rick's Website at www.Thrivingnow.com. Also, please see Rick Wilkes' biography at the back of the book.

SPORTS PERFORMANCE
From healing injuries to improving your game

By Stacey Vornbrock

> *"If you think you can, you can. And if you think you can't, you're right."*
>
> *Henry Ford*

ARE PROFESSIONAL ATHLETES WILLING TO USE **EFT**?

Absolutely! I explain the use of EFT to professional athletes from a biochemical standpoint. Every cell in our body has up to one million cell receptor sites. It is the job of these cell receptors to take in nutrients, proteins, vitamins and minerals to nourish each cell and keep it in balance.

When an event happens — that event can be a thought we have, something that happens to us, something we witness happening to someone else, an injury, etc. — the hypothalamus in the brain releases a cascade of chemicals that are called peptides. These peptides are short chain amino acids that we experience as an emotion. Every chemical/emotion has a specific cell receptor that it fits into. For example, there are cell receptors that will only allow the chemical of fear to dock onto that receptor. No other chemical/emotion peptide would fit into it.

Once that chemical/emotion has docked onto its specific cell receptor site, nutrients, proteins, vitamins and minerals can't enter that receptor to nourish the cell and keep it in balance. If the chemical/emotion isn't processed out of the receptor site, over time the receptors will shrink up and die.

When the cell divides there are more receptor sites for that same chemical and fewer receptor sites for nutrients, proteins, vitamins and minerals. That's also why over time it can feel like a problem is getting worse. That's not your imagination. That is truly a biochemical response your body is having.

Through this series of taps on end acupressure points, these chemicals are released from those cell receptor sites and the cells return to a state of balance. This balance allows your body and mind to do what it knows how to do and allows you to perform at your optimal levels.

Professional athletes, doctors, athletic trainers, physical therapists, coaches and sports massage therapists easily understand and relate to this biochemical explanation of EFT.

Is EFT BENEFICIAL IN HEALING INJURIES QUICKLY?

EFT will speed up the healing time of injuries significantly. Whenever you are injured there are three areas that need to be addressed. The first area is the trauma to the body itself. Let's say you sprain your right ankle. That trauma immediately settles into the cell receptors and will just stay there unless you signal the receptors to release that trauma. This can be done with the setup phrase:

> *Even though I'm holding this trauma in every cell of my right ankle, I deeply and completely love and accept myself.*

Repeat this three times. Then as you tap one point say:

> *(First point) I'm holding this trauma in all the muscles of my right ankle.*
>
> *(Next point) I'm holding this trauma in all the ligaments of my right ankle.*
>
> *(Next point) I'm holding this trauma in all the tendons of my right ankle.*

Use this same wording and go through joints, bones, cartilage, tissues, nerves, fascia, membranes, skin, fibers and fluids while moving to a new EFT tapping point every time. Then end this sequence by saying on a tapping point:

> *(Tapping point) I give my right ankle permission to release this trauma from every cell.*
>
> *(Next point) I give my right ankle permission to relax and let go of this trauma.*
>
> *(Final point) I give my right ankle permission to release this trauma from every cell receptor site.*

The second area is all the emotions that you experience as a result of the injury. I call it the "oh damn" moment where you realize what you've done and there is a cascade of thoughts and feelings about what this means to you. For example: pain, fear, anger, frustration, fear of death, fear of re-injury and sadness are common emotions that get stuck in the cell receptors. It's critical to tap on each of these chemicals/emotions using the above format to release them from the cell receptor sites.

Finally, whenever you are injured, the body immediately forms a memory of protection to keep that part of the body safe. You begin to hold yourself in a certain way and the body begins to adapt around the injury. Once that injury heals, nothing signals the body to release the memory of protection. Your body then never returns to a state of balance but remains in that adaptive state.

Through the use of EFT, it's easy to signal the cell receptors to release this memory of protection. You would start with the setup phrase:

> *Even though I'm holding this memory of protection in every cell of my right ankle, I deeply and completely love and accept myself.*

Tom is a major league baseball pitcher who has been out on the disabled list for months. He had a torn ligament in his left shoulder from throwing. He came to see me to work on confidence issues related to pitching. In the course of our work together, Tom decided to have surgery on his shoulder after an alternative treatment failed to produce the results he was looking for. Before the surgery we tapped on issues about the surgery: worry, doubt, and fear around rehabilitating his shoulder. I wanted to make sure that he went into surgery without any chemicals or emotions sitting in those cell receptor sites.

Tom's surgery went very well. His surgeons discovered two tears in his ligament. We had an EFT session after his surgery. We tapped for: the trauma, pain, fear, his body not being in harmony with the screws they inserted into his ligament, the anesthesia, doubt he would recover his range of motion, scar tissue, and memory of protection. At his first rehab session Tom could reach his left arm completely across his chest. His physical therapist said, "I don't understand this. I've never seen anything like this."

The therapist explained that it would normally take four weeks for someone to achieve what Tom was doing on his first day of rehab. It normally takes 16 weeks to rehabilitate from this surgery, and we had already cut that time by 25 percent. Approximately one month later, the physical therapist took range of motion measurements and told Tom that some of his measurements were better than normal. Once again, the therapist couldn't understand how. Later, Tom saw the doctor who performed the surgery. The doctor told Tom that his range of motion was excellent and Tom's recovery from this surgery was ahead of schedule.

Repeat this three times.

(First point) I'm holding this memory of protection in all the muscles of my right ankle.

(Next point) I'm holding this memory of protection in all the ligaments of my right ankle.

Use this same wording and go through tendons, joints, bones, cartilage, tissues, nerves, fascia, membranes, skin, fibers and fluids while moving to a new EFT tapping point every time.

Then end this sequence by saying on a tapping point:

> *(First point) I give my right ankle permission to release this memory of protection from every cell.*
>
> *(Next point) My right ankle no longer needs to hold onto this memory of protection and can choose to relax and let it go.*
>
> *(Final point) I give my right ankle permission to release this memory of protection from every cell receptor site.*

Substitute *right ankle* for the part of your body where you have the injury. It is important to be as specific as you can for the best results. You will be amazed at how using this process of EFT will speed up the healing time of injuries and insure a complete recovery.

What about old injuries?

I have discovered that old injuries never fully heal because the trauma, emotions and memory of protection have never been released from the cell receptor sites. Most athletes who have been injured have a deep fear of re-injury and this significantly affects their performance. They end up holding back to protect their body either unconsciously or consciously. Once the old trauma, emotions and memory of protection are removed, they report an ability to give 100 percent to their performance. Many have reported that aches and pains they've had for years are completely gone once we go through the above process.

How can I use EFT to increase my range of motion?

It seems that whenever we're injured it reduces our range of motion (ROM). Whenever I tap with an athlete addressing trauma, emotions and memory of protection (as described above), their ROM dramatically and quickly increases.

If you haven't experienced an injury of any kind but are just tight or lack flexibility you can still use EFT to increase your ROM. The first approach to take is to tap directly on the tightness itself. For example, let's say you have a tight hamstring on your left side. You would use the setup phrase:

> *Even though I'm holding this tightness in every cell of my left hamstring, I deeply and completely love and accept myself.*

Repeat this three times.

Then as you tap one point say:

> *(First point) I'm holding this tightness in all the muscles of my left hamstring.*
> *(Next point) I'm holding this tightness in all the ligaments of my left hamstring.*
> *(Next point) I'm holding this tightness in all the tendons of my left hamstring.*

Use this same wording and go through joints, bones, cartilage, tissues, nerves, fascia, membranes, skin, fibers and fluids while moving to a new tapping point every time.

Then end this sequence by saying on an EFT tapping point:

> *(First point) I give my left hamstring permission to release this tightness from every cell.*
> *(Next point) I give my left hamstring permission to relax and let go of this tightness.*
> *(Final point) I give my left hamstring permission to release this tightness from every cell receptor site.*

If you have little or no result after tapping directly on tightness, or whatever word you would choose to describe how it feels, that tells me that there is something else you are holding in that hamstring. The most common

John is a discus thrower who competed in the 2004 Olympics and placed within the top nine in his event. He felt drained after the Olympics and took some time off. Once he resumed training he felt mentally flat. The men's track and field program at his college had been cut. John was feeling alone because all his friends left when the program was cut. In addition, he lost his coach. John was feeling shocked and fearful. Needless to say his performance was suffering considerably.

We used EFT and tapped on: abandonment, anger, feeling betrayed, feeling alone, shock, confusion, fear he couldn't train on his own, and doubt in himself and his ability. Within a couple of sessions, John started training and throwing again. He reported feeling really free, very confident and feeling like this was the most motivated he's ever been.

things are stress, anxiety, anger, fear, guilt and frustration. Ask yourself what was going on in your life when that tightness in the left hamstring started and guess at the feeling that may be locked in there. Then use the above tapping protocol to address each emotion stored in that hamstring.

I have found that a lack of range of motion is often a barometer for one's emotional state. I know that if I'm not processing my emotions out of my cell receptors, my sciatica joint will act up and let me know. The low back seems to be a common area for many people. They hold stress and tension there on a regular basis. It's a great feedback system — your body will always let you know when there are unprocessed chemicals sitting in those cell receptor sites.

How can I use EFT to improve my golf game?

You can tap for everything related to your golf game — mechanics, weather conditions, course conditions and any emotional states. This includes anxiety or lack of confidence, any mental state such as not being able to commit to a club or not being able to focus over the ball, and past performance traumas. Also, use EFT for limiting beliefs such as "I've never been good getting out the sand" or "I'll never play as good as my best friend," specific holes you've had trouble with and putting your body in harmony with your golf clubs.

For example, let's say you're having trouble with your short game, chipping shots to be specific. The two most common errors are the fat chip (chunker) that goes nowhere and the thin chip (skull) that shoots across the green.

To address the problem of the fat chip you could use the setup phrase:

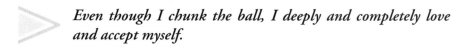

> *Even though I chunk the ball, I deeply and completely love and accept myself.*

Repeat this three times. Then at each point use some of these phrases:

> *(First point) I hit the ground and the ball goes nowhere.*
>
> *(Next point) I'm afraid of hitting the ground.*
>
> *(Next point) I'm trying too hard to get the club under the ball.*
>
> *(Next point) I try to scoop the ball.*
>
> *(Next point) I can't relax and let the club lift the ball.*
>
> *(Next point) I feel like I have to help the ball.*
>
> *(Next point) My arms and hands are tense as I try to help the ball.*
>
> *(Last point) I try to hit up at the ball to lift it.*

To address the problem of the thin chip you could use the setup phrase:

> *Even though I skull the ball, I deeply and completely love and accept myself.*

Repeat this three times. Then at each point use some of these phrases:

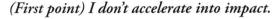

(First point) I don't accelerate into impact.

(Next point) I'm afraid of hitting the ball too far.

(Next point) I'll hit the shot past the hole.

(Next point) I'll hit the shot over the green.

(Next point) I try to slow the club head down prior to impact.

(Next point) I'm afraid I'll hit into the trap.

(Next point) This is too delicate of a shot for me.

(Next point) I'm afraid I won't hit accurately.

(Last point) I strike the top of the ball with a rising leading edge.

How can I put my body in harmony with my clubs?

Every golfer has problems with one or more clubs at some point in time. There are certain clubs you don't like using, other clubs that just don't feel right, and even some clubs that are your favorites, but then one day you wake up and even one of those favorite clubs doesn't feel right. With EFT there is a quick and easy remedy for all these circumstances.

Every living and inanimate thing has a certain frequency it resonates at. For example, all the molecules of a table are moving. They just move so slowly that they appear solid to our eyes. The same would apply to golf clubs.

Imagine you and your clubs are like two radio stations and your clubs are broadcasting at a frequency of 99.9 and your body is broadcasting at 98.7. They are not in harmony or resonance with one another. This would cause a lot of confusion and static for your body if you tried to tune in or listen to both stations at one time. But if you can align these two frequencies with one another, you will experience clear reception and your body will be much calmer while "listening to the radio."

The same is true for your clubs and your body. When your body is not in harmony or resonating with your clubs, it causes a lot of static and confusion in your body. You end up feeling anxious and not confident when using certain clubs, or the club just doesn't feel right and sometimes you can identify why and sometimes you can't put your finger on the problem.

Here is the protocol for putting your body in harmony with your clubs. Take one club at a time and first take a couple of swings with it to get a "before" feel, and then lay it across your lap while you tap. Fill in each blank below with the club you are tapping on. For example:

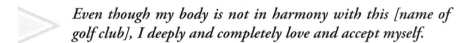

> *Even though my body is not in harmony with this [name of golf club], I deeply and completely love and accept myself.*

After you have gone through the entire sequence with your driver, take an "after" swing to feel the difference. People report a variety of things, such as "the club feels lighter" or "the club feels more solid" or "I feel more comfortable with this club now."

Move on to the next club and do the same thing, substituting that club to fill in the blank. Do this with every club in your bag, even the ones you don't use that often.

Don't worry if these statements aren't true for you or they feel exaggerated. We are speaking to your body and intentionally exaggerating the words to clear the blocks on the cellular level.

Tap on your Karate Chop point and repeat three times:

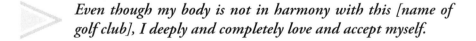

> *Even though my body is not in harmony with this [name of golf club], I deeply and completely love and accept myself.*

Now say one phrase per tapping point as you run through the sequence:

My body is not in harmony with the grip on this [name of golf club].

My body is not in harmony with the length of this [name of golf club].

My body is not in harmony with the angle of this [name of golf club].

My body is not in harmony with the degree of this [name of golf club].

My body is not in harmony with the weight of this [name of golf club].

This [name of golf club] doesn't look right to my eyes.

This [name of golf club] doesn't feel comfortable to my body.

This [name of golf club] doesn't feel good in my hands.

My hands tense and tighten when I hold this [name of golf club].

My arms feel tense and tight when I swing with this [name of golf club].

As soon as I take this [name of golf club] out of the bag, I start to feel anxious.

My body is not in harmony with this [name of golf club].

I sometimes dread using this [name of golf club].

I'm holding this anxiety about using this [name of golf club] in all the cells of my body.

My mind is not in harmony with this [name of golf club].

The cells of my body are not in harmony with this [name of golf club].

I have discovered that it was possible to tap for:

- Any kind of equipment: training devices, balls, etc.
- Clothing: shoes, gloves, shirt, etc.
- Course conditions: fast or slow greens, bunkers, water hazards, trees on the left or right, etc.
- Weather conditions: wind, rain, cold, heat, etc.
- Golf partners you're playing with: slow play, giving you advice, too competitive, annoying behavior, etc.

230

Joe is a tennis player with a ranking of 4.5. He came to see me because he was double-faulting his serves. Angry and frustrated, the harder he tried to correct his serve the worse things got. I discovered he had a past performance trauma from a doubles game where he double-faulted every single point. Joe felt like he'd let his tennis partner down. He was embarrassed and angry about it.

We tapped on his past performance trauma. At the next session, he reported a 60 percent increase in getting in his first serves. He said, "I feel more relaxed and I'm not over analyzing things. If I double-fault, it's not a big deal now. I'm not worried about what others may say." His first serves continued to improve, and we moved on to other issues.

Tapping for any of these has produced great results for all my golfers. This works for every sport and all the equipment connected with that sport. There is nothing you can't tap on to put your body in harmony with it. Try it and see what happens.

Can I use EFT to make mechanical changes?

This is an area I have been working on extensively with my athletes with great success. I've discovered that you can make mechanical changes very quickly with the use of EFT. The standard belief in golf is that it can take up to a year to change a golf swing and in baseball the belief is that it can take up to 5000 swings to change a batting swing. Well, not anymore!

When you are attempting to make a mechanical change, you're fighting against a habit that is literally held in every cell membrane of your body. Every time your body makes the new movement your cells fight to re-establish the old pattern. It feels hard and uncomfortable because you're not only fighting the habit that is trying to re-establish, but also you're directing your body to make a new movement it isn't used to or comfortable with. With EFT it's easy to give your body the instruction to release the old habit and easily adapt to the new movement.

Here's an example of what I did with one of my major league baseball players. His batting coach was asking him to lower his hands to waist level at bat and his normal stance was to have them at shoulder level. This was a significant change and would normally take quite a bit of time to get used to. This is what we tapped on:

- It feels awkward with my hands lowered.
- My arms feel uncomfortable lower.
- I can't keep my arms parallel to the ground.
- I'm holding this habit in every cell of my arms to move them up.
- I can't trust myself to keep my arms down there.
- I don't like my hands there.
- I can't step into my swing with my arms lowered.
- My arms and hands feel tense and tight when I hold the bat lower.
- My arms and hands fight against holding the bat lower.
- It feels natural and comfortable to hold the bat at shoulder level.

The next session he reported the following, "My new batting position feels really natural. I have more squat in my stance and I'm able to explode with my legs with no fear. I'm swinging good and my grip is looser and feels very comfortable." We never had to tap on that mechanical change again.

With one of my Senior PGA Tour Players we worked on the mechanical issues of not getting the club across the line and not taking the club inside. Here's what we tapped on:

- I'm not getting the club across the line.
- I'm not getting my hands inside.
- It doesn't feel comfortable to take my hands inside.
- I do it perfectly and then I revert back to the old way.
- Every cell membrane is holding the habit of not taking the club across the line.
- I take the club outside to avoid hooking the ball.

- Taking the club inside feels unusual and uncomfortable to my body.
- I'm holding this habit of taking the club outside in every cell of my body.
- My body is more comfortable taking the club outside.
- It feels so new and different to take the club inside.
- It feels awkward to my body to take the club inside.

By the next session he reported a considerable difference in his ability to take the club inside and across the line. He was pleased with his rapid results.

IS IT BAD TO FEEL ANXIOUS IN COMPETITION?

I think it's very important to distinguish between anxiety and what I would call a state of "heightened awareness." Every good athlete needs a certain amount of adrenaline and energy to perform well, which creates a heightened awareness. When it becomes excessive, then it turns into anxiety.

The good news is that with EFT you can tap to eliminate the anxiety or you can tap if you feel "flat" and need to increase your intensity. Sometimes athletes have a passive attitude or give in when they play poorly. Tapping can help to clear that passivity or flat feeling and create a "fight back" feeling and attitude, thereby creating the heightened awareness necessary to compete.

Too much anxiety on the other hand will interfere with performance. Adrenal stress hormones constrict the blood vessels in the forebrain, reducing its ability to function. Stress signals will diminish conscious awareness and reduce intelligence. Physical sensations can include a pounding chest, sweating, dry mouth, reduced vision, shortness of breath, tightness in arms and legs, butterflies in your stomach, irritability, the jitters, confusion and loss of concentration.

All of this leads to an inability for the body to do what it knows how to do and perform at peak levels. EFT can easily eliminate anxiety but you must be persistent and consistent with your tapping. You'll have a superb tool for increasing your sports performance.

To contact Stacey Vornbrock, her e-mail address is stacey@breakthroughperformance.net and her telephone number is 480-945-9750. Visit Stacey's Website at www.breakthroughperformance.net. Also, please see Stacey Vornbrock's biography at the back of the book.

STRESS
Preventing damage from overload and burnout

By Ron Ball

> *"The greatest weapon against stress is our ability to choose one thought over another."*
>
> *William James*

WHAT IS STRESS?

Although it may seem otherwise, stress is always an inside job. Stress is our internal response, psychologically and physically, to something real or imagined in our environment. Our perception triggers our internal thinking and feeling, setting off a cascade of chemical processes in our bodies. Stress is subjective. What causes stress for one person may not create stress in another. Stress is a state of being polarized because of internal conflicts or resistances.

In a different way, we might describe stress as retaining negative energy in our bodies or creating a disruption in our energy system. Instead of being in a state of energy flow, stress causes physical tension and compression. It's like having our foot on the gas peddle and brake simultaneously. There's energy trying to move us forward and also energy holding and stopping us in our tracks.

The demands, expectations and pace of modern life have increased our levels of stress. People are being bombarded with constant demands for attention. Stress manifests as anger, irritability, worry, addictive behaviors, nervousness, fatigue, memory loss, pains and illnesses.

236

 WHAT IS "EMERGENCY MODE" OR THE "FIGHT OR FLIGHT" RESPONSE?

Genetically, we're wired to have a way to escape from physical harm. The fight or flight response is based on prehistoric times when there was a threat or danger. It was necessary for survival. In a stressful situation, the cerebral cortex sets off an alarm to the hypothalamus, located in the midbrain, starting a series of about 1500 chemicals cascading in our body, activating neurotransmitters, releasing hormones and metabolizing nutrients.

Our body both expends and conserves physical energy to escape the stressful situation. Some body systems accelerate to generate more energy, while others slow or shut down to conserve energy. For example, our heart beats faster to pump more blood so we can escape the situation, while our gastrointestinal system slows down operations until after the emergency is over and we can safely digest things.

Most stress today is psychological or social so we really don't need the fight or flight response. Unfortunately, we're wired for it. The byproducts of the stress response continue to circulate in our body and have the potential to create physical illnesses. We do have another option. We can learn ways to better interpret and flow with the situation. Using EFT and tapping when stressed can help release negative energy and emotions to help get into a neutral or flow state.

 ISN'T STRESS JUST A NORMAL AND NATURAL WAY OF LIFE?

Observe any infant or child and you'll see your answer. Babies are completely open to their environments. Kids play and experiment with situations. They naturally find fun and joy in the things around them. Also, they observe, learn and mimic how adults respond. If you respond in stressful ways, most likely your child will too.

If you're out and about in the world, it's unlikely that you won't have any stress in your life. In fact, a certain amount of stress is positive. What's

Steve is a successful businessman, entrepreneur and millionaire. He has built and sold several businesses. He came to me because he was worried about a new commercial property he had purchased and was developing with two other business partners. Steve was feeling stressed because of a negative cash flow regarding the property. He didn't have enough tenants yet, and he said that he couldn't get the problem "off his chest." That's just where the physical sensation of his stress was — right in his chest area.

We did several rounds of EFT, incrementally releasing the blocked emotions and energy. In less than five minutes, the stress Steve felt in his chest area was completely gone. He was truly amazed at the results. He didn't understand how something so simple could be so powerful and effective. As we often say, "To some people, EFT is a seemingly ridiculous method that surprises people with its undeniably wondrous results."

important is learning how to use tools such as EFT to change your emotional reactions to situations that you might perceive as stressful. You can change and control how you choose to respond to stress.

The real problem is chronic stress or stress overload. It's where people's minds race along almost robotically, not being aware of the continual negative self-talk and not tuned in to paying attention to the feelings in our bodies. We don't rest and relax enough so our bodies don't have time to rejuvenate. Imagine driving your car during peak traffic hours days on end without stopping. Eventually your car will break down.

The other thing to remember about stress is it's often focused on the past or the future. We need to retrain our minds to tune more into the *now*.

WHAT IS CHRONIC STRESS?

Our bodies are well equipped to handle stress for short periods of time. The real danger to our health and well being is prolonged stress that just grates on us. Chronic stress is having multiple stress responses that don't let up. What's worse is that the stress continues to mount up.

With chronic stress, excessive amounts of stress hormones like cortisol have adverse effects, damaging cells, tissues and organs. With chronic stress, the fuse is burning and the clock is ticking. If people don't do something to relieve chronic stress, there is plenty of medical evidence proving that it's just a matter of time before stress negatively affects their health and well being.

 ## Is all stress bad? Is there good stress?

Actually, we need some stress to keep us energized. Moderate amounts of stress stimulate and motivate us to do things. Stress really becomes a problem when stress overload and burnout occur. Stress overload makes a person feel out of touch and out of control.

The word eustress means *good stress*. It comes from the Greek *eu* which means well or good. Eustress is a healthy level of stress, giving a feeling of fulfillment. Eustress is the amount of positive energy that motivates, excites and moves a person to achieve something. Moderate levels of stress help you produce your best performance. Most positive events in life, such as getting married, doing well on a test or finishing a marathon, although stressful, also create states of eustress.

Eustress is the opposite of distress — the feeling of being overloaded. As mentioned, too much stress, which is far too common today, can create stress overload, leading to fear, frustration and a wide range of other negative emotions and physical issues. On the other hand, eustress is positive, stimulating experiences or events.

What effect does stress have on my mind and body?

Stress is a state of dis-ease. There is mounting evidence on how stress causes or contributes to numerous diseases. Stress can affect and damage almost every system in your body, including the circulatory, digestive, endocrine, immune, lymphatic, musculoskeletal, nervous, respiratory and reproductive systems. Chronic stress is linked to cardiovascular problems, depression, diabetes, memory issues, overeating, reproductive problems, sleep disorders and even accelerated aging.

What many people simply don't understand is the tremendous damage stress can cause. It is far reaching because the damage incrementally builds up over time. With chronic stress, your adrenal glands secrete corticoids which inhibit your bodily systems and keep them from functioning at optimal and healthy levels. Our bodies don't have enough time to recuperate and return to a normal state.

WHAT EFFECT DO OUR BELIEFS HAVE ON CAUSING STRESS?

Our beliefs have everything to do with stress because our beliefs are the underlying foundation behind stress. Our beliefs have a major impact because stress is our perception, our internal response or reaction to outside events. Whether we feel stress or not depends on our beliefs about how things *should* or *should not* be:

- Beliefs about work
- Beliefs about family
- Beliefs about money
- Beliefs about how people should be
- Beliefs of the way things should or shouldn't be

The important question to ask yourself is what underlying beliefs do you have that might contribute to stress in your life?

HOW DOES STRESS AFFECT CHILDREN AND TEENAGERS?

This is perhaps the most disturbing aspect about stress in our culture today. We're passing on the habitual stress lifestyle to our kids at an early age. Younger people are under increasing levels of stress at school

> Imagine being a superintendent of schools, handling budget problems, plus dealing with issues with teachers, students and parents. It nets out to long hours and resolving a lot of conflicting issues. When Don came to see me to learn EFT, he was worn out. He had been unsuccessfully battling stress for over seven years. Although he had tried other techniques, he wasn't getting much stress relief.
>
> In learning to do EFT when he felt stressed, Don found EFT to be incredibly effective. The first time he did EFT for stress, he said that he felt a calmness that he hadn't experienced in years. People with chronic stress are often unaware what it feels like to be without stress. Don knows that if the evidence of stress returns, he now has a real, practical and effective approach to handle it.

and at home. One of the harmful things about teenagers and young children experiencing more stress is that it can have an adverse impact on a child's development.

Childhood stress can affect skeletal growth and may even be the foundation of future adult diseases. Chronic stress can also affect a child's self-esteem and lead to a wide range of health and social problems.

 WHY AREN'T MORE PEOPLE DOING SOMETHING ABOUT STRESS IN THEIR LIVES?

In fast changing, competitive cultures, a lot of people, consciously or unconsciously, don't want to get rid of their stress. In EFT, we say they are getting a *secondary gain*. Stress is politically correct in our society. In a strange way, stress is almost revered. It defines us. For many, stress equals success. There's a pervasive belief that the more busy and stressed out a person is, the more successful they must be. People are on a stress treadmill until stress takes its toll and manifests in health problems, work issues and family or relationship conflicts.

There are people who are afraid of giving up their stress because they believe they'll lose their drive to get things done. Actually, that's not the case. Initially, stress does arouse the sympathetic nervous system, pumping up performance. However, if stress levels aren't reduced, mental, emotional and physical exhaustion set in. Have you ever worked on a project so long that you felt exhausted and started making mistakes? Usually you didn't discover the mistakes until the next day when you felt rested and refreshed.

Some people have become resigned to having stress in their lives even though they know intuitively that stress can negatively influence their jobs, relationships, finances and health. They're coping with it because they feel stuck. It's like they're caught in a web or maze and don't know how to get out.

For other people, they are stressed because they're unhappy in their work. They're not in jobs they like or love. They may be making a lot of money, but they're not happy. They're loaded down with things they *should* do instead of what they *want* to do. They're following other people's definitions of success instead of defining success for themselves.

Perhaps the biggest reason people are so caught up in stress is that they haven't learned any methods for managing stress. Or they don't think they have time to learn how to manage it. It follows that old saying, "Pay me now or pay me later." Learn how to handle the stress in your life or you'll suffer the consequences later.

CAN I REALLY CONTROL MY STRESS?

It's not about controlling your stress. It's about releasing or relieving stress. EFT is an effective tool for erasing and letting the negative feelings of stress go. The first step is to believe you have the power or ability to do something about chronic stress or stress overload.

Linda couldn't stand working with one of her co-workers. The mere thought of the other person made her feel stressed. Just by doing three minutes of tapping, she was able to reduce her stress level from an eight to a zero (SUDs). In fact, afterwards she felt downright giddy. The thoughts and feelings about the person causing her internal stress were no longer intense. She felt calm about it. Linda said that even though she was familiar with various complementary healing modalities, she'd never been able to diffuse stress quite so fast and effectively until she experienced EFT.

Stress is an indicator that you are resisting something. What are you resisting? Could you make the decision to just let go of it? When you let go of resisting it, what happens and how differently do you feel?

WHY IS EFT SO GOOD FOR STRESS?

EFT helps interrupt and release negative feelings and energy. EFT changes emotions and attitudes. When you do tapping with EFT, you positively change your body's electromagnetic fields. With EFT, the method is quick and simple, and the relief is usually immediate. Once you clear the negative feelings that are causing stress, you can then instill positive feelings to energize and recharge your batteries.

HOW CAN I USE EFT FOR STRESS RELIEF?

There are several ways you can use EFT for stress relief. The first and best way is preventative. Get into the positive habit of doing EFT for tapping to release stress in the morning and particularly in the evening before going to bed. In the morning, tap on anything that you imagine might be stressful for you coming up during the day.

Try the funnel approach. Start with general, global setup phrases. If you get good results, that's great. If not, funnel down to something narrower and more specific.

Morning

What thoughts or feelings do you have in the morning? Here are some examples:

Even though I'm stressed about all that I have to do today, I deeply and completely accept myself.

Even though I have to do everything myself, I deeply and completely accept myself.

Even though other people don't work as hard as I do, I deeply and completely accept myself.

Evening

In the evening before you go to bed, do EFT and tap on the stressful things that happened during your day. This will help you let go and release any negative or frustrating feelings and can often help you sleep easier. Here some examples. Be as specific as you can:

Even though I was angry at Ted for the way he erupted and got upset at the meeting, I deeply and completely accept myself and I choose to forgive Ted.

Even though I worry about having enough money to pay the bills, I deeply and completely accept myself.

When you're in a stressful situation:

What do you do if you're stressed about something right now? You can change how you feel quickly. The key is to recognize what is foremost in your consciousness right now:

- Is your mind racing with thoughts?
- Are you experiencing strong emotions?
- Is there a physical sensation or tension?

Go with whatever is dominant. Don't think or analyze. Trust your intuition.

If your mind is zooming thoughts, use an EFT setup phrase like this:

> *Even though my thoughts are out of control, I deeply and completely accept myself.*
>
> *Even though my head is in the clouds, I deeply and completely accept myself.*
>
> *Even though I have all of these thoughts racing in my mind, I deeply and completely accept myself.*
>
> *Even though I don't know how to turn off my thoughts, I deeply and completely accept myself.*
>
> *Even though I feel overwhelmed by my thoughts, I deeply and completely accept myself.*
>
> *Even though I want to quiet my thoughts, I deeply and completely accept myself.*

If feelings are strong:

You can release a lot of stress by going right to the feelings that are the roots of your stress. As you tap, take deep breaths at each point. Really feel your stress.

> *Even though I feel so much [whatever the feeling or issue is], I deeply and completely accept myself.*
>
> *Even though I'm frustrated that I'm not getting enough done, I deeply and completely accept myself.*
>
> *Even though I'm pushing myself too hard, I deeply and completely accept myself.*
>
> *Even though I feel [whatever the feeling or issue is], I choose to release these feelings and free my energy.*

If you're feeling stress or tension in your body, where is it? One of the following setup phrases might be appropriate:

> *Even though I have a headache at the back of my head, I deeply and completely accept myself.*

Even though I have tension in my back, I deeply and completely accept myself.

Even though I feel like I'm carrying the weight of this job on my back, I deeply and completely accept myself.

Even though I want to get my boss off my back, I deeply and completely accept myself.

Even though my back is to the wall, I deeply and completely accept myself.

Even though I don't want to shoulder this responsibility, I deeply and completely accept myself.

Even though there's tension in my neck, I deeply and completely accept myself.

Even though I don't want to stick my neck out, I deeply and completely accept myself.

Even though I'm up to my neck in projects, I deeply and completely accept myself.

Even though I'm having trouble keeping my head above water, I deeply and completely accept myself.

Even though I'm tired of lending a helping hand, I deeply and completely accept myself.

Even though one hand doesn't know what the other is doing around here, I deeply and completely accept myself.

Even though I'm tired of putting my best foot forward, I deeply and completely accept myself.

Even though I want to put my foot down, I deeply and completely accept myself.

Even though I wouldn't touch this job with a 10-foot pole, I deeply and completely accept myself.

Even though I want to keep this person at arm's length, I deeply and completely accept myself.

Even though I'd like to give him a piece of my mind, I deeply and completely accept myself.

Even though I'd like to have peace of mind, I deeply and completely accept myself.

Try this for general stress issues:

Of course most people would consciously dispute that there is part of them that *wants* to be stressed. Subconsciously, however, we may want to feel stressed. We get some kind of subconscious "positive" benefit from it — a benefit we are most likely not even aware of. Again, this is called *secondary gain.*

> *Even though I feel stressed out about [whatever the feeling or issue is], I let go of wanting to be stressed and I deeply and completely accept myself.*

Is relaxing the issue? People talk about making themselves relax. That's an oxymoron. You know how to relax. What prevents you from feeling relaxed? Relaxation is a state of *being*, not *doing*. Allow it to be. Try one of these setup phrases or whatever is appropriate for you:

> *Even though I'm afraid to let go of my stress, I deeply and completely accept myself.*
>
> *Even though I've forgotten how to relax, I deeply and completely accept myself.*
>
> *Even though I don't know how to relax, I deeply and completely accept myself.*
>
> *Even though I won't relax, I deeply and completely accept myself.*
>
> *Even though I shouldn't relax, I deeply and completely accept myself.*
>
> *Even though I shouldn't let up, I deeply and completely accept myself.*

When you're stressing, your body is setting off tension or pain alarm bells to tell you what's wrong and where it is. Your body is communicating. Stop, feel and listen. If you imagine that the stress in your body could talk to you, what would it be saying? Pay attention to sensations in your body. Tune in to feelings or tensions. Where specifically do you feel the stress? What conflicting beliefs might be causing your stress?

Empowering questions

Another important thing to do with stress is to ask yourself empowering questions:

- How might I approach this stressful situation in a playful way?
- Where is the stress in my body and how am I *creating* it?
- How might I find humor in this dilemma?

Shift to positive feelings

A powerful technique is to make a shift and boost your energy by consciously tapping on feelings of gratitude, appreciation, thankfulness and other positive emotions. These feelings will generate positive chemicals and endorphins in your body.

> *Even though I feel [whatever the feeling is], I choose to feel [the feeling you'd like to have].*

EFT and music

Tune into feeling good using music. Put on your favorite piece of music and use EFT as you tap along to balance your energy. Sit in a chair or lie down. As you listen to the music, start tapping and doing rounds on the EFT points. Tap on each point as long as you want, and then move to the next point. If a particular point feels good, stay on that point until you're ready to move on. Do this until you feel the right time to stop. Pay close attention to your breathing while doing the tapping. Relax. Everything's all right.

Do the Nine Gamut Procedure

The Nine Gamut Procedure looks a little unusual and is excellent for reducing stress. First, you need to locate the Gamut point on the back of either hand. It's right at the crease in the tendons where the little finger meets the ring finger and about a half inch back.

1. Tap on the Karate Chop point on the bottom of either hand for 10-15 seconds to correct for any psychological reversals.

2. *Continuously* tap on the Gamut point in a steady rhythm while doing the following in sequence.

3. Close your eyes.

4. Open your eyes.

5. Quickly look down to the right toward the floor *while holding your head steady.*

6. Do the opposite and quickly look down to the left toward the floor.

7. Roll your eyes clockwise in a circle like your nose was in the center of a clock and you were trying to see all the numbers in order.

8. Now roll your eyes counterclockwise in the same manner.

9. Hum a few seconds of your favorite song.

10. Count rapidly from one to five.

11. Hum a few seconds of your favorite song again.

12. Take a deep breath and notice how you feel.

13. Repeat if necessary.

Here are a couple of other related techniques for relieving stress:

Forehead Release

Lightly place your fingertips and palm of your hand on your forehead. Focus on whatever's stressing you. Keep your hand on your forehead from 3-5 minutes.

Third Eye Point

Close your eyes and place whatever fingertips feel right for you on the point between the middle of your eyebrows. Breathe slowly and deeply for 3-5 minutes.

These are some of the ways that you can you EFT to release and manage stress. The wonderful thing about EFT is that once you learn it, you have a tool at your disposal to relieve not only stress but anything that drains your energy or causes negative emotions. You owe it to yourself to discover the myriad of benefits that EFT offers.

To contact Ron Ball, his e-mail address is reb@eftblog.com. Visit Ron's Websites at www.eftzone.com, www.eustress.net, and www.stress-sucks.com. Also, please see Ron Ball's biography at the back of the book.

TRAVEL

What to do when... leavin' on a jet plane

By Betty Moore-Hafter

"We must travel in the direction of our fear."

John Berryman

WHAT ARE SOME TRAVEL-RELATED ISSUES THAT CAN BE TREATED WITH EFT?

The most common travel issue that we treat is a fear of flying. EFT has often produced remarkable results with this problem. There are many stories of EFTers who, during a plane trip, have noticed the tension and anxiety of a stranger sitting beside them and have offered to show the person a "simple stress-relief technique."

Not only does EFT help on the spot, but often an e-mail arrives later to the effect, "I don't know what you did but the rest of my flights were easy for me too. Wow!" Better still is thorough work with EFT before actually taking a flight. Often the fear is so completely released that tapping while on the plane is unnecessary.

Other travel-related issues include jet lag, motion sickness or seasickness, adjusting to food and climate (if these are significantly different), sleeping in hotels, and simply the general anxiety we may feel about disrupting our routines and getting ready to travel. EFT works well with all of these. As a matter of fact, an excellent way to approach a trip would be to write down all your worries, everything about the trip that makes you anxious, and then tap for each thing on the list.

As layers of anxiety slide off, you would probably feel clear and focused and able to get ready to go with ease. Remember, EFT balances and aligns our energy system. It's as if you would be aligning your energy with the trip, getting in the flow, so to speak. And chances are that the whole trip would go better with that simple preparation.

 ### How would you get started in treating a fear of flying with EFT?

Fear of flying is actually different for each individual. For some people, it's about fear of heights and the terror that the plane will fall out of the sky. For others, it's more of claustrophobia, fear of being in that enclosed space and not being able to get out. A common theme is "I'm not in control." For most people who fear flying, a sense of dread and a feeling of anxiety occur when they simply think about getting on a plane.

I like to begin by having people notice how they are experiencing this general fear in their body. When you think about flying, what happens? Does your stomach tense up? Do you find it hard to breathe? Does the fear surge through your whole body? One way to begin is to rate the intensity of what you feel on a scale of 1-10 (SUDS) and tap as follows:

> *Even though I have this fear of flying and I feel it in my stomach, I deeply and completely accept myself.*
>
> *Even though I have this fear of flying and I can hardly breathe, I deeply and completely accept myself.*
>
> *Even though I have this fear of flying and I feel it all over, my whole body tense, I deeply and completely accept myself.*

Three or four rounds of tapping will generally release much of this pent-up fear in the body. So it's good to begin with the global issue of "fear of flying" and tap for how your body is holding that fear. Usually, there is a huge sense of relief and then it is easier to talk about the issue in more detail and zero in on the specific aspects to tap for.

Grace had been a flight attendant but had quit her job eight years previously after having a panic attack on a plane. Since then, she had only flown once, and she had to be heavily drugged to get through the flight. Now she wanted to be able to fly so they could take a family trip. In one session of EFT, we collapsed her fears by using the EFT "movie technique" which is making a short, specific mental movie. Grace mentally went through the scenario of taking a flight imagining the "feelings of dread" she would experience just thinking about the trip, to the "sense of impending doom" when she saw the plane, to the actual experience of being on the flight.

We tapped for the trauma of the panic attack she had once experienced while in the air. Finally, she felt calm about it all and no longer feared a panic attack while traveling. She felt secure that if she should have any anxiety, she could tap to relieve it. She felt in control and empowered for the first time in eight years.

The test, of course, was the real thing. I called Grace several months later. She reported that the trip had gone beautifully. She had been completely relaxed and enjoyed the flights. She commented that, as a former flight attendant, she knew that roughly a third of the people on any plane are probably uncomfortable with flying and, in her words, "I wish they all knew that they can get this freedom so easily with EFT."

WHAT SPECIFIC THINGS COULD I TAP FOR? WHAT SETUP PHRASES MIGHT I USE?

Get in touch with what bothers you the most about flying. As I mentioned, fear of flying is very individual. What is so scary about it for you? Is it being up so high? Fear that the plane will fall from that height? Or is it that you couldn't get out if you wanted to? Do you hate being in that small space with all those people, breathing the same air?

Do you dread the bumpiness of the turbulence and the way your stomach turns over when that happens? What scary thoughts or images come into your mind when you're on a plane? Think about what you see, hear, think and feel. What bothers you most about flying?

All of the details you may come up with are aspects to be tapped on. Here are some examples:

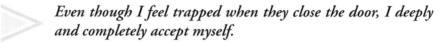

Even though I feel trapped when they close the door, I deeply and completely accept myself.

Even though I hate the way the plane shakes when it's taking off, I deeply and completely accept myself.

Even though all the noise makes me nervous, I deeply and completely accept myself.

Even though I can't stand the feeling of being confined, I deeply and completely accept myself.

Even though it feels like I have no control, I deeply and completely accept myself.

Even though turbulence really scares me and I'm afraid we're going to crash, I deeply and completely accept myself.

Even though I can't look out the window, I deeply and completely accept myself.

Even though I saw a terrible plane crash in a movie, I deeply and completely accept myself.

Let's say that what bothers you the most is being 20,000 feet up in the air. You could begin by tapping as follows:

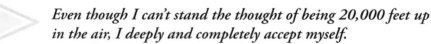

Even though I can't stand the thought of being 20,000 feet up in the air, I deeply and completely accept myself.
Reminder: Fear of 20,000 feet

Tap all the EFT points for either:

20,000 feet up in the air
Fear of being at 20,000 feet
Reminder: Fear of 20,000 feet

Take a deep breath and see if anything has changed. The very thought of "20,000 feet" may seem more neutral to you. You can continue tapping for "*remaining* fear of 20,000 feet," or you can take things further by adding reframing and creative language.

WHAT IS REFRAMING AND HOW WOULD YOU USE IT WITH EFT FOR FEAR OF FLYING?

Reframing has to do with seeing things differently and looking at the problem from different angles. It is often a reality check. When you tap while reframing, this seems to loosen the old inner programming within us where limiting beliefs and fear-based emotions are all intertwined.

As Gary Craig says, reframes "land better" when we do them while tapping and we accomplish a much deeper shift in perspective. Abundant examples of creative language and reframing while tapping are to be found on Gary Craig's "Specialty Series" and "Borrowing Benefits" DVD sets available from www.emofree.com.

Here's an example of a reframe:

> *Even though I can't stand the thought of being 20,000 feet up in the air, the truth is, thousands of people go up there on planes every day and come down safely. It's safer than driving a car. There's more room up there than on the streets.*

The above is the setup phrase. Then while tapping through the EFT points, you can be creative. For example:

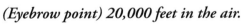

> *(Eyebrow point) 20,000 feet in the air.*
> *(Side of eye point) but people go there on planes every day.*
> *(Under eye point) and come back safely.*
> *(Under nose point) 20,000 feet in the air and all my feelings about it.*
> *(Chin point) but planes go there every day.*
> *(Collarbone point) and come back safely, etc.*

Kevin had been limited all of his adult life by an irrational fear of being away from home. Every time he traveled, he felt that he was forcing himself against his will. He was filled with anxiety until he got home again. Kevin came to me because his extended family was planning a trip to Ireland. He really wanted to join them but only if he could enjoy the trip.

When I asked how long he had felt the dread of being away from home, he remembered that as a boy, he had hated having to go to summer camp. Although nothing traumatic had ever happened there, he felt lonely and uncomfortable and never seemed to fit in. He was always greatly relieved to get home again.

I asked him to imagine being "12 years old" again and to get in touch with his feelings about summer camp. We tapped on all his general feelings and also on several specific incidents until it all seemed neutralized. We then did EFT with some choice statements such as, "Even though in the past, I was anxious about being away from home, that was then and this is now. Now I choose to feel excited and enjoy myself. We're going to have such a good time in Ireland."

Kevin did indeed go on the family trip and was thrilled to be free of the old anxiety. He let me know that he was ecstatic to be able to travel at last and had already begun to plan another trip.

One of my clients said that what bothered her most was the thought of "nothing but thin air under that plane." I did a reframing as follows:

"Even though it seems to me that there is nothing but thin air under that plane, the truth is the plane is moving so fast that the air is like solid bricks under it. The plane has an aerodynamic shape, and, when it's moving, this creates solid bricks of air underneath. Even a paper airplane can't fall through thin air. There is no thin air under a moving plane."

We tapped the points alternating "afraid it was thin air" with "now I know it's solid bricks of air." This seemed to "scramble the brain" enough that she no longer saw "thin air" under the plane at all and the next time she flew, she felt quite secure traveling on those solid bricks of air. Her fear of "dropping out of the sky through thin air" was gone.

Perhaps my favorite opening phrase for reframing is, "the truth is...." With any irrational fear, there is a reality check that we need to integrate. We've all been told that, statistically, flying is safer than driving. This fact may make little difference unless you tap it in.

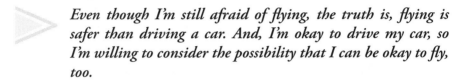

> *Even though I'm still afraid of flying, the truth is, flying is safer than driving a car. And, I'm okay to drive my car, so I'm willing to consider the possibility that I can be okay to fly, too.*

How would you tap for the claustrophobia issue in the fear of flying? Being enclosed on the plane is a big part of the problem.

One client told me he hated being stuck in the "tube" of the airplane with all the other people "trapped" in there, "like in a coffin." Obviously, the very language being used here is anxiety provoking. And that's the way our minds work. So much of the phobia is literally "in the mind," in the way we are perceiving the situation. And where the mind goes, the body and emotions will follow. This way of seeing it immediately causes physical tension and anxiety as the body reacts to the perceived danger.

In the case of claustrophobia, it would help to become aware of how you're perceiving the experience of being on a plane and do some reframing as well as tapping for the fears. For example, you could start by tapping for the fears alone:

> *Even though I feel stuck, I deeply and completely accept myself.*
>
> *Even though there are too many people in this small space and I feel uncomfortable, I deeply and completely accept myself.*

Even though we're all breathing the same air and that bothers me, I deeply and completely accept myself.

Then you might do some reframing, perhaps including a "Choices" statement. (For more information on this technique, visit www.emofree. com and do a search on "choices" or "Dr. Patricia Carrington.")

Even though I've thought of the airplane as a coffin, I choose to see it differently. The truth is, I don't think of my car as a coffin. It's just a vehicle, and the airplane is just a vehicle. And, I'm going to have such a good time when I reach my destination. I choose to feel safe and comfortable during the short time I'm in this vehicle. We'll arrive so soon.

Even though it seems we're cooped up, breathing the same air, I choose to see it differently. The truth is the airplane has an excellent ventilation system. It is a perfect small environment. I choose to relax and enjoy the trip.

DO YOU NEED TO KNOW THE CAUSE OF YOUR FEAR OF FLYING? AND IF YOU DO KNOW WHEN IT STARTED, DOES THAT HELP TO MAKE THE EFT MORE EFFECTIVE?

We don't have to know the cause to treat an issue effectively with EFT. Sometimes the cause is never revealed and yet the block in the energy system can still be released with tapping. Other times, a surprising root cause may come to our consciousness as we tap. Once I worked on fear of flying with a client who got images of Will Rogers in his mind as we tapped.

At first, neither of us knew what that was about. Then he realized that Will Rogers had died in a plane crash, which brought him to the memory of a film he had seen as a boy about Will Rogers' life. The plane crash at the end of the film had upset him greatly.

As he got in touch with this, it occurred to him that he must have identified with Will Rogers — "because I liked to make people laugh. I wanted to be like Will Rogers when I grew up." This brought tears. He began to understand that somehow plane crashes had come to symbolize the death of things he held dear, "the destruction of love and laughter in the world."

We tapped creatively, "Even though I had all this associated with planes and plane crashes, the truth is, love and laughter live on." This man had not flown in 10 years but the results of our session were such that he took a flight within six weeks and called to say he had done fine. "I even enjoyed it," he marveled. "Is that normal?"

It is always important to ask the question, when did this start? When did you first become afraid of flying? Sometimes there is a clear cause. If a person has had a traumatic flight experience or has known someone who died or almost died in an airplane accident, then of course it would be essential to treat those experiences with EFT. The best method would be to tell the story and tap for all the feelings and fearful thoughts. I once worked with a client whose issue was not fear of flying but fear of heights.

As I asked him when it started, he said that it began in the service when he had to jump out of airplanes with a parachute! That could certainly contribute to a fear of heights. But as we went deeper into the story, he realized that the parachuting had not bothered him until a day when they'd had a close call and it appeared momentarily that the plane was going to crash. "I thought I was going to die," he said.

We tapped many times for the extreme terror and fear of that moment. His fear of heights was released. Interestingly, he had not developed a fear of flying. The subconscious is not rational and we may not know how the subconscious has processed an experience until we tap for it and notice what arises.

I have often found that EFT "stirs things up" and information we didn't consciously know can come to awareness through tapping. It is good to sit for a moment with your eyes closed after a round of tapping and just see what comes to mind. What thoughts or images pop into your mind? What feelings do you notice? Does this remind you of anything? How far back do you remember feeling this way? What associations come to mind? You may find a "cause" that you had never thought of before.

 ONCE YOU'VE TAPPED ON ALL THE ASPECTS AND ALL THE CAUSES YOU CAN FIND, WHAT ELSE CAN YOU DO TO MAKE SURE YOU'RE READY TO FLY BEFORE YOU BOOK A TICKET?

I recommend a mental rehearsal. Vividly imagine calling or going on-line to book your plane ticket. Is this anxiety provoking? If so, tap for it. When it feels comfortable, take your scenario or mental movie further. Imagine packing for the plane trip. Does that bother you? If so, do a round of tapping on:

 Even though I still feel nervous about packing to take a plane trip.

When packing seems peaceful, imagine arriving at the airport, checking in, waiting to board, and so forth. Can you see or imagine yourself in the waiting area calmly reading a magazine? Or do you see yourself tense and dreading getting on the plane?

Tap for each stage of the scenario until it seems more peaceful and neutral. Finally you imagine getting on board and fastening the seat belt. Does it bother you to see them close the door so that you can't get off the plane until you land? You can imagine everything, the take-off, the noise, the turbulence, the view from the window, etc.

If you've already done a thorough job with EFT, you may be amazed at how easy it is to imagine all of these things and see yourself remaining calm. It may be hard to get the fear back even if you vividly play the scenes in your mind.

Another excellent test is to visit an airport. Watch the planes taking off and landing. Watch the passengers checking in and going through security. Does anything you see make you think, "It's okay for them but not for me!" If so, tap for your thoughts and feelings right there, on the spot, until you feel that you could "join the crowd" and comfortably board a plane.

HOW DO YOU TAP IN PUBLIC WITHOUT DRAWING ATTENTION TO YOURSELF?

This is a personal matter. People do so many things in public now, talking loudly on cell phones about private issues, taking their office into public areas as they work on a computer, bopping with their music on headphones. So many people are in their own worlds that tapping may not draw the attention that it would have a few years ago. I find it possible to tap very discreetly. You can rest one hand on your belly or knees and drum the fingers of the other hand on the Karate Chop point so that it looks like a simple nervous habit.

You can rub or press the points on the face rather than tapping and it just looks like you're trying to relieve a slight headache. And then one can always go to the restroom for a few moments. However I've often tapped lightly in public and never found that it attracted stares. It is also true that simply imagining the tapping may help. Go through the verbal process in your mind as you breathe deeply and imagine a gentle hand tapping all the points. Sometimes this alone can bring surprising relief.

Of course, one of the great things about EFT is that you can tap during the flight if you need to. This "insurance policy" means that you no longer have to feel powerless or out of control. With EFT, you are in control and can feel better fast no matter what feelings may arise during your flight. If you feel self-conscious, just tell your neighbor you're doing a simple form of acupressure to relieve stress. If you're feeling friendly, you can add, "Want to learn it?" You may find yourself teaching EFT to a stranger.

HOW WOULD YOU TAP FOR JET LAG?

There are many ways to approach it. The simplest way is to use EFT for the obvious issues:

 Even though I'm not sleepy yet, I accept myself, and I choose to adjust to the time change.

Even though I'm not hungry yet, I accept myself, and I choose to eat and adjust.

Even though I'm waking up too early, I accept myself and I choose to adjust to the time change.

Even though I'm still tired, I accept myself.

I like to "inform the body" and make gentle, incremental adjustments by tapping during the flight. Let's say you are taking a flight from the East Coast to the West Coast, which will involve a 3-hour time change — your body needs to adjust to "three hours earlier." A third of the way through the trip, you could change your watch from 11 am to 10 am and tap:

 Even though my body still thinks it's 11 am, I accept myself, and I want my body to know that it's 10 am now.

Tap all the EFT points, saying:

 Adjusting to the time change, it is now 10 am.

Go through the same process two-thirds through the trip, and again near the arrival. The same wording is very effective anytime:

 Even though my body still thinks it's [the old time], I want my body to know it is now [the new time].

Tap through all the points saying the words:

Any problems adjusting to the time change.

Then go through the points again stating the new time:

I want my body to know it's now [the new time].

I sometimes think of EFT as "rebooting our system" much as we have to reboot our computers when they get stuck. Tapping for jet lag will help your body rebalance itself more quickly when you have to adjust and function in a different time zone.

WHAT SETUP PHRASES COULD YOU USE FOR OTHER TRAVEL ISSUES?

Very briefly, here are some possibilities that come to mind:

Even though my body's not used to this food (or this weather), I deeply accept myself.

Even though my stomach is a little upset, I deeply accept myself. I appreciate my body. It can make this adjustment.

Even though it's hard to sleep in this hotel, I deeply accept myself, and I choose to relax and get a good night's rest. It's okay to be here.

Even though there are unfamiliar noises and they bother me, I choose to ignore them and drift off to sleep.

To contact Betty Moore-Hafter, her e-mail address is betty@risingsunhealing.com and her telephone number is 802-860-7286. Visit her Website at www.risingsunhealing.com. Also, please see Betty Moore-Hafter's biography at the back of the book.

264

WEIGHT LOSS
Removing self-sabotage from the weight loss equation

By Carol Solomon

> *"You must begin to think of yourself as becoming the person you want to be."*
>
> *David Viscott*

WHY EFT FOR WEIGHT LOSS?

You can lose weight simply by eating when you are hungry and stopping when you are satisfied. For most people, however, it is not that simple. Stress, emotions and limiting beliefs get in the way. People turn to diets, drugs and even surgery to help. However, these strategies do not teach you how to control your emotionally driven appetite.

EFT is a perfect tool to use to fill the gap. You can use it to reduce immediate cravings, neutralize the emotions that drive overeating, eliminate self-sabotage, manage difficult situations, increase motivation for exercise and improve body image.

EFT is safe, simple and easy to use. There are no known side effects. The only thing that can happen is that as you tap for one problem, other issues, memories or feelings can come up. You may start feeling a different emotion, or the feeling you have may shift or change in some way. Experiencing these feelings may or may not be painful. There is an upside to this process. As you become more aware of events, you can use EFT to manage them.

So just notice if other issues come up or if you are feeling any differently when you use EFT. You may want to keep track of your experiences in a journal. It is important to become an observer of your own thinking, feelings and behavior. Many people make the mistake of focusing too much on external events (what other people do and say) as opposed to their own internal reactions to the events.

 ## WHAT IS INVOLVED IN USING EFT FOR WEIGHT LOSS?

"I want to lose weight, but I can't stop eating." It's the same story with the same frustrating and circular theme. If you feel like you are running in circles, you are not alone.

Controlling your weight is so much more than counting calories. If we only ate when we were hungry, few of us would have any weight concerns. To be truly successful with weight management, you must understand that the problem has little to do with the foods we eat. It is absolutely not about the food — rather it is about what we use food for.

Overeating is a coping behavior. If you struggle with weight issues, chances are you are using food to satisfy needs other than hunger. Many people use food to regulate their mood and energy levels. Think about it. Either you are trying to calm down, as in self-soothing, or you are trying to raise your mood and energy levels using food.

Here's what I mean. Let's say you've had a long day at work and you are feeling very fatigued. As soon as you walk in the door, the kids hit you with all of their demands and needs. You look for something to eat, even though you are more tired than hungry. In this instance, food is more about soothing stress than relieving hunger.

Here is another example. It's 3 pm. You have a long afternoon ahead of you and your energy level is low. Even though you don't feel physiologically hungry, you find yourself at the vending machine, wanting something that will lift your energy to make it through the rest of the afternoon. You have a true need for more energy. It just isn't a food need.

The problem with overeating is that we typically invest too much time and energy in the external process of what we should or shouldn't eat or

In my office I taught my client, Connie, how to use EFT for food cravings. The next week, she came in and reported that she had had two extreme moments where she felt like she just had to eat and it had nothing to do with hunger. Connie simply had a strong urge to eat even though she knew she was not physiologically hungry. She had been having a stressful week and knew that she was probably just feeling overwhelmed and exhausted when the urge to eat hit her. After performing the EFT procedures, Connie said that for some reason, she just didn't get up off the couch to go to the kitchen. EFT had worked perfectly.

how many calories or carbohydrates foods contain, etc. We don't spend enough time or energy on the internal process of discovering what feelings are driving our eating behavior. We give very little focus to *how* different foods make our bodies feel. We settle for the temporary comfort that can be achieved.

Deprivation diets fail because they do not address the emotions and stress that are driving our eating. Diets do not teach us how to eat less and exercise more. They do not address the emotional issues. It is clear that the diet mindset hasn't worked for most people. Otherwise, we would not continue to struggle with weight problems. Ninety-five percent of people who lose weight by dieting regain the weight within two years.

A successful long-term weight strategy requires a shift in focus, dropping the diet mindset, and breaking out of the vicious cycle of diet/deprivation/binge/guilt, etc. You can then focus on learning new techniques to guide you through challenging situations that arise each day.

HOW CAN EFT BE USED MOST EFFECTIVELY FOR WEIGHT LOSS?

For EFT to be most effective, you need to differentiate between and address the different aspects of the problem. Aspects represent different layers of the same problem. Most problems have a number of different aspects. For example, aspects for fear of flying can be fear of turbulence, claustrophobia, fear of taking off, fear of landing, fear of not being able to breathe, fear of having a panic attack, fear of dying, etc.

There can be a lot of different pieces to the puzzle. Gary Craig uses the metaphor that a problem is like a table top. It is held up by all the feelings, beliefs and experiences that are the "legs" of the table. By reducing the emotional intensity of these past experiences, it is like knocking out some of the legs of the table. When you knock out enough of the legs, the table (problem) eventually collapses.

Some tables may have literally hundreds of legs. It is not usually necessary to find and neutralize every single one in order to get significant relief. But it may take using the techniques persistently and diligently in order to get results with complicated problems.

At a bowling alley, you don't have to directly hit every pin to get a strike. Just like hitting a few pins will knock down other pins, some aspects will collapse other aspects as well.

If it seems that you will be tapping day and night because you have so many issues, don't worry. It is most important to use the technique regularly. If you do that, you will make consistent progress.

On the other hand, some seemingly very difficult problems are sometimes cleared away very quickly and easily. There is *not* a direct correlation to the difficulty of the problem and how long it takes to resolve it.

For weight loss, aspects can be food cravings or just the urge to eat when you aren't hungry. They can include feelings of deprivation or boredom, the fear of success, the fear of failure, or the fear of being back in the same cycle again. Sometimes it is just feeling tired and wanting to eat, or feeling anxious, stressed or overwhelmed. You can also use EFT with specific events, if you think they have contributed to your problem.

Janet felt overwhelmed at work. She often was faced with more work than she could do, and no energy to do it. She tried to psyche herself into it using food. Janet reached for food to cope in the late afternoons. Once she started using EFT, she found that her energy was steadier throughout the day, and she was better able to pace herself. Janet also became more reasonable in her expectations. When she cleared away some of the pressure caused by her overwhelmed and burdened feelings, she got more done. She began to lose weight slowly and steadily.

How can I use EFT for specific events?

For instance, you may have been forced to eat, told you were fat, ridiculed by kids at school or worse by family members. These experiences may have contributed to the overall attitudes you hold about yourself in regard to food and weight issues. Most likely, they are still affecting you now.

Think about the experiences you have had in your past that contribute to how you feel about yourself now. Did others tell you that you needed to lose weight? Did your parents put you on a diet at a young age or take you to a doctor to lose weight?

Take each one of these specific events and tap for that experience.

Even though [name of person] told me I was fat, I deeply and completely accept myself.

Even though I had to sneak chocolate as a child, I choose to be open to forgiveness.

Often, in the case of someone making a negative remark to you, it is not what the other person said to you, but what you said to yourself. It becomes your negative belief about yourself. If you tap on what they said to you, you will feel calmer about that experience.

How can I use EFT for food cravings?

Imagine yourself in a situation where you might have a craving or just the urge to eat when you aren't hungry. You might think about a food that tempts you or even have that food right in front of you. Rate how strong your craving is on the SUDs scale (0-10).

You might use statements like:

> *Even though I have the urge to eat, I deeply and completely accept myself.*
>
> *Even though I really want [whatever the food or craving is] right now, I choose to feel indifferent toward it.*

To be most effective, don't wait until the last minute to work on some issue that you know is a problem for you. In other words, don't wait until you are on your way to Ben and Jerry's® for an ice cream to start tapping.

What can I expect when I tap for food cravings?

If you have ever had an acupuncture treatment, you know that there is a deep relaxation effect. The same is true for EFT. That sense of relaxation alone may help you to move away from the kitchen.

When you tap for food cravings, sometimes they suddenly disappear as if by magic. Sometimes the shift is more gradual, the desire to eat becomes less or you just view it in a different way, feeling more in control.

Sometimes, you still eat the food, but you eat less of it or it just doesn't taste the same. What you thought were your favorite foods can actually taste differently (usually less desirable) to you. Gary Craig explains this by the fact that your body knows what is good for you and after you balance your energy system with EFT, foods that are not good for you may not taste the same.

When teaching EFT in a teleclass, I asked the participants what foods they brought to the call. One woman replied, "Chocolate covered peanuts are my favorite, and I knew you were going to make me dislike them, so I brought Oreo® cookies instead."

Often you are just able to distract yourself more easily. You find yourself not getting up to go to the kitchen during TV commercials, when you might have automatically done that before. You may not really understand why, but you are just able to make a different choice.

EFT restores *choice* to the process. You may do something else besides eat or leave the room and forget about it entirely. Don't discount these *subtle* shifts. They may seem minor, so that you don't even attribute the change to the tapping, but it is working.

Sometimes you may feel so overwhelmed with a high degree of emotional intensity or many aspects (layers) that you need to sit down and work through some of the emotional aspects first. It is well worth working on these issues whenever you notice them.

How can I identify the emotional issues?

With emotional issues, it pays to sit down and do some homework first. Find a quiet place and ask yourself these questions. Really think through it — writing and journaling about the process will help sort it all out.

Think about what emotions you are trying to tranquilize or avoid with food. Try to learn about the emotional roots of your overeating behavior.

Talking things over with a trusted friend, relative, therapist or coach can be extremely helpful as well. Don't be afraid to ask for the support you deserve. What emotions are driving your behavior? What is the downside of losing weight? (And don't say there isn't a downside.) There is always something positive, a benefit about keeping things the same. Some people feel they need the extra weight to feel protection from life or from feelings.

Terri's difficult time of the day was just as she arrived home from work. She had an intense, demanding corporate job and it required working a lot of hours. Terri often arrived home mentally fatigued, yet she still needed to prepare dinner for her family and respond to the needs of her children. She used food to manage her exhaustion.

Terri learned to use EFT prior to leaving her office. After doing EFT, she would arrive home feeling fresh, calm and ready for the evening. Her own temptation to overeat at that hour disappeared, and her weight started moving in the right direction.

You simply don't keep doing the same thing over and over again unless there is a benefit. For many people, the desire to keep things the same (comfort) rather than risk making a change (discomfort) is the greatest motivator of all.

What is the upside of keeping things the same? How would you feel without your favorite comfort foods? What emotions are you trying to tranquilize or avoid with food?

 WHAT ARE SOME COMMON EMOTIONAL STATES THAT LEAD TO OVEREATING, AND HOW CAN I ADDRESS THEM WITH EFT?

Fatigue. It can be as simple as feeling fatigued or mentally exhausted. It is often difficult to distinguish hunger from fatigue. You may have such an automatic response of reaching for food when you are tired that you don't even realize you are doing it. It can feel almost like you are hard-wired to eat when you are tired. Remember, you have a true need, but it is a *nonfood* need. Try this setup statement:

 Even though I am exhausted and I just want to eat, I deeply and completely accept myself.

Anxiety. EFT is particularly helpful for anxiety. Fear often shows up as anxiety and/or tension in the body. You may go through the day with physical symptoms, *e.g.* a nervous stomach, a backache, a tension headache or difficulty focusing. Anxiety is typically a fear of something bad happening in the future. It is often associated with a specific event, like a test you have to take, a public presentation or a particular challenge at work.

Anxiety can also be experienced as worry or apprehension. Worry is like a porch swing. It gives you something to do, but it doesn't get you very far. It is wasted energy. When addressing anxiety with EFT, try to be as specific as possible.

> *Even though I feel anxious, I deeply and completely accept myself.*
>
> *Even though I feel worried about my test, I deeply love and accept myself.*

Deprivation. From years of dieting, many people live with an inner sense of poverty and deprivation. You may simply feel that there is not *enough*. Try these EFT setup statements for feelings of deprivation:

> *Even though I feel deeply deprived, I profoundly and completely accept myself.*
>
> *Even though I feel like there will never be enough and I will never be enough, I deeply and completely accept myself.*

Anger and resentment. Everyone gets angry, but people who hold onto anger and resentment suffer most. The actress Carrie Fisher once said "Resentment is like drinking poison and waiting for the other person to die." There are many ways to resolve anger and let go of resentment. It is important to find one (or more) that work for you and use it regularly. EFT can help.

> *Even though I can't stop feeling angry, I deeply and completely accept myself.*
>
> *Even though I feel like I can never forgive, I am open to the possibility of forgiving myself and anyone else who may have contributed.*

Hopelessness/defeat. These feelings and attitudes often accompany attempts to lose weight and can be difficult to modify. For example, you can be doing everything right and not see the difference on the scale. Or you can eat just enough to sabotage your weight loss efforts. These patterns easily lend themselves to feeling hopeless and getting right back into the vicious cycle. Experiment with these setup statements:

> *Even though I feel that it is hopeless to try, I deeply and completely accept myself.*
>
> *Even though I feel defeated, I deeply love and forgive myself.*

How can I use EFT to stop sabotaging myself?

The roots of self-sabotage are ambivalence (mixed feelings) and conflicting intentions. Part of you wants to change and part of you doesn't. I once heard someone standing at the side of a pool say "the problem is I want to join the others in the pool *and* I want to stay dry." Sometimes we want what we want and we want what we have. Therein lies the dilemma.

Part of you wants to lose weight and part of you wants to keep things the way they are. You may want to lose weight, but you're afraid of what you would have to give up. While you may not fully understand why you do this, it may help to tap on this issue directly. Then try to break it down and identify the reasons for your mixed feelings.

> *Even though I sabotage myself, I deeply and completely accept myself.*
>
> *Even though part of me doesn't want to change, I deeply love and forgive myself.*

How can I use EFT when I am feeling stuck?

At times, we all meet our own resistance to change. If you are feeling stuck, chances are you are feeling resistance to doing what you know it takes to get what you want. This is part of a normal change process.

> Cheryl was a teacher who had difficulty getting past all the goodies in the teacher's lounge without overindulging. When she learned to use EFT, Cheryl found that she was able to go into the lounge to socialize and do her work while passing up on all of the temptations. Cheryl was surprised how quickly and easily this pattern shifted for her. She felt much more in control of her eating.

You may feel trapped in an emotional loop, unable to move out of the vicious cycle. It is a matter of *acknowledging your resistance*, accepting where you are in the process and figuring out a way to work through it, rather than giving up.

In my teleclasses, when people are not doing the homework assignments or are too busy to follow through on what they said they wanted to accomplish, I talk about resistance. It often helps just to speak it out loud, acknowledging it to yourself and/or others.

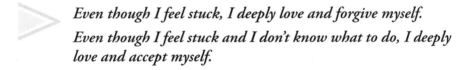

> *Even though I feel stuck, I deeply love and forgive myself.*
> *Even though I feel stuck and I don't know what to do, I deeply love and accept myself.*

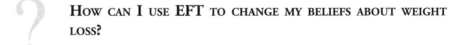

How can I use EFT to change my beliefs about weight loss?

Limiting beliefs can interfere with weight loss. Your beliefs can be subtle or not-so-subtle in exerting influence over your actions. The extent to which your beliefs guide your life is the extent to which they can interfere and lead to self-sabotage.

There are limits, of course to what one can achieve. But these limits are usually far fewer than most people think. Limiting beliefs counteract or mitigate the effectiveness of EFT or any technique you may apply to help yourself.

For example, if you believe that you are insatiable, why would you undertake a process to change? Why would you even bother to make the effort? If you believe that you will never be able to lose the weight you want, or that you won't be able to keep it off, why bother?

These beliefs are counterproductive to a weight loss plan. Some people try to protect themselves from disappointment by holding onto such pessimistic beliefs. A certain amount of skepticism is understandable since you may have tried many times and don't want to fail again.

But when you hold negative beliefs, you are actually working against yourself. You are not allowing yourself to be in the best frame of mind to succeed.

Limiting beliefs can be difficult to uncover because, for the most part, they are invisible. For instance, try this exercise. Get quiet and go inside. Ask yourself how much you really believe that you can lose weight and keep it off permanently. Notice the thoughts that arise and use EFT to address them.

Even though everyone in my family gains weight as they get older, I deeply and completely accept myself.

Even though I don't believe I can lose weight after age 40, I choose to love and accept myself.

Even though I don't believe that I can keep the weight off, I deeply love and forgive myself.

These are expensive beliefs, and they are costing you!

HOW CAN I USE EFT TO STAY MOTIVATED IN MY WEIGHT LOSS PLAN?

Everyone wants to wake up two sizes smaller *yesterday*. EFT can be used to manage the impatience and frustration that accompany your efforts to lose weight. Sometimes you can be doing everything right and still not see the results on the scale right away.

Healthy change often follows an established physical or developmental plan, just like when a baby has to crawl before walking. Experiencing frustrating plateaus and having to wait for the scale to change is enough to sabotage your efforts.

 Even though I feel frustrated and impatient, I choose to find a creative way to wait for my results.

Let's face it — losing weight can be discouraging, even demoralizing at times. You can go through a lot of ups and downs and a lot of trial and error before figuring out what is going to work for you. Stubborn plateaus can last for weeks or months at a time while your metabolism resets. Or you can sabotage yourself by eating just enough to keep your weight the same instead of decreasing.

EFT can help you get through these discouraging times and help you stay motivated to hang in there and stick with your program.

 Even though I feel discouraged, I deeply and completely accept myself.

Just *knowing* that you are now able to calm yourself in *any* situation can be incredibly comforting. You now have a tool that you can use to calm and soothe yourself whenever you have the urge to eat. You will be able to relax easily within minutes and stop self-sabotage. Now that is emotional freedom.

To contact Carol Solomon, her e-mail address is Carol@LoseWeightWithEFT.com and her telephone number is 847-680-0272. Visit Carol's Websites at www.LoseWeightWithEFT.com, www.MoreMoneyWithEFT.com, and www.EFTtips.com. Also, please see Carol Solomon's biography at the back of the book.

BIOGRAPHIES

Gloria Arenson

Gloria Arenson, MS, MFT, is a Marriage Family Therapist in practice for over twenty-five years. She specializes in using EFT to treat eating disorders, stress, anxiety, panic, trauma, phobias and compulsive behaviors. Gloria is an internationally known charismatic teacher and speaker. Her innovative classes and workshops have helped thousands of people overcome self-defeating behaviors, raise self-esteem, and improve relationships. She provides professional training for psychotherapists, teachers, and health professionals.

Ms. Arenson has appeared on major radio and TV shows including *The Home Show with Gary Collins*, *Montel Williams Show*, *Leeza Gibbons*, *AM Los Angeles*, *CNN News*, and more than fifty radio call-in shows throughout the United States and Canada.

Her extensive knowledge of eating disorders and compulsive behaviors led her to write four books: *How To Stop Playing The Weighting Game*, *A Substance Called Food*, *Born To Spend* and the award winning book about meridian therapy, *Five Simple Steps to Emotional Healing*. She is Past President of the Association for Comprehensive Energy Psychology, an international organization promoting the uses of Energy Psychology. She lives in Southern California and is available for phone counseling.

Contact Information

Gloria Arenson
805-563-1140
glotao@cox.net

www.GloriaArenson.com
www.meridiantherapy.net

Ron Ball

Ron Ball, EFT-CC, EFT-ADV, has had an eclectic career, proving you can do whatever you set your mind to. An entrepreneur, Ron is a professional speaker, author, trainer and stress expert. In his work life, he's also been a professional photographer, syndicated broadcast interviewer, radio producer, copywriter, and business executive. He is a contributor for stress tips to *Business Week Online* and other publications.

As a vice president of marketing in several high technology companies, Ron sought out a breakthrough method to help employees handle the fast-paced schedules, demands and stress of the world of hi-tech. In his quest, he discovered EFT (Emotional Freedom Techniques), an amazingly simple and powerful method.

He immediately understood its value and potential in the business world. People can tap into EFT at work, in play and everyday life. Ron's company, Inroads LLC, specializes in teaching business executives, employees and other people how to learn EFT to relieve and manage stress. EFT is a tool anyone can use in a myriad of ways to enhance their lives.

In addition to EFT, he's made a lifelong study of self-help and peak performance tools including NLP, the Sedona Method and HeartMath. He publishes a popular blog on EFT called the EFTzone. He's a member of the Association for Comprehensive Energy Psychology. Part of Ron's mission is to help bring the simple, elegant and powerful method of EFT to the general public. Ron Ball resides in the Washington, DC area.

Contact Information

Ron Ball
reb@eftblog.com

Inroads, LLC
P.O. Box 357
Fredericksburg, VA 22404-0357

www.eftzone.com
www.eustress.net
www.stress-sucks.com

Gwenn Bonnell

Gwenn Bonnell is South Florida's foremost trainer in EFT, offering private and group training in advanced uses of EFT and Energy Medicine since 1999. She shares simple, powerful, and transformational personal energy methods with people locally and globally through her private consultations, workshops, web sites, eBooks and digital programs. Her works have been translated into six languages and are available worldwide.

A member of the Association for Comprehensive Energy Psychology, Gwenn has trained in EFT, BSFF (Be Set Free Fast), TAT (Tapas Acupressure Techniques), Touch for Health, Energy Medicine, Reiki and Huna. The author of *The Foundational Energy Psychology Training Manual* and *Tap Away Those Extra Pounds: Lose Weight Forever with EFT & Energy Medicine*, and her articles have been published in *Natural Awakenings, Miracle Journeys*, and *Quality Life* magazines.

Some of Gwenn's case histories can be found on Gary Craig's EFT website support list. Visit Gwenn's website, for valuable and insightful information about EFT and Energy Medicine, and sign up for her free newsletter.

Contact Information

Gwenn Bonnell
954-370-1552
gwenn@tapintoheaven.com

www.tapintoheaven.com
www.tapawaypain.com
www.tapawaystress.com
www.EFTslim.com
www.Chakrativity.com

Paul & Layne Cutright
EFT Master Practitioners

Paul and Layne Cutright are authors, speakers, trainers, and coaches. They've been professionals in the human potential field since 1976 and have been in a successful romantic and professional partnership for close to 30 years.

As a team, they're a force of creative energy, authoring books, courses, and a variety of other educational products, including the Amazon bestseller, *You're Never Upset for the Reason You Think: Secrets and Strategies to Resolve Any Upset Quickly and Easily*. They're innovators in their field, always keeping their eyes on the horizon for new ways to help transform the way people relate.

Both serve on the faculty of Barbara Marx Hubbard's Foundation for Conscious Evolution in Santa Barbara, California. Paul and Layne are also recognized as pioneers in the emerging field of energy psychology, in which they've developed relationship energy repatterning.

They are also creators of the Integral Relationships Coach Training and online EFT training. For more information on their educational and training resources, visit their Websites.

Contact Information

Paul & Layne Cutright
505-474-6018
partners@paulandlayne.com

P.O. Box 32268
Santa Fe, NM 87594

www.IntegralRelationships.com
www.EFTTrainingOnline.com
www.PaulandLayne.com
www.enlightenedpartners.com

Lindsay Kenny
EFT Master Practitioner

Lindsay is a Life Coach and an EFT Master Practitioner in the San Francisco Bay Area. She is also the Founder and Director of the National Alliance for Emotional Health: www.NAFEH.org. NAFEH is a free resource for those seeking emotional support or searching for a competent EFT or Energy practitioner.

"My mission in life has always been to help other people. I knew when I was 12 years old that that's what I wanted to do in life. Life Coaching gives me a great opportunity to achieve that goal and EFT has given me a powerful tool to accomplish it. For me, nothing is more rewarding than to know that someone is a little better off as a result of my teaching them how to use EFT."

Lindsay also conducts EFT workshops and regular EFT teleclasses. She attributes her success to the fact that she genuinely cares about her clients and is willing to do just about anything to help them experience relief. Lindsay brings over 30 years of counseling experience to her work. Lindsay strives to provide great client support, follow-up, and guaranteed satisfaction. Through her commitment, and caring, Lindsay establishes relationships with her clients that she hopes will last a lifetime.

Contact Information

Lindsay Kenny
888-449-3030
LKcoaching-Linz@yahoo.com

www.LKCoaching.com
www.EFTworkshops.org
www.EFTtele-classes.com

Dr. Alexander R. Lees

EFT Master Practitioner

Dr. Alexander R. Lees goes by the credo that… "People are not broken and in need of fixing. Most people are just fine. They simply need a tune-up." Dr. Lees has been in private practise for 20 years, as a counsellor, therapist and personal coach. He is a Registered Clinical Counsellor with a Doctorate in Clinical Hypnotherapy. Dr. Lees also presents seminars internationally on a wide variety of topics, including EFT, NLP, and the Mind/Body Connection.

Dr. Lees' goal is to assist people to achieve a higher level of emotional well-being, so they can live their lives with a feeling of joy and contentment. He became a psychotherapist so that he could help people to realize that they have the power within themselves to overcome adversity, and Dr. Lees' is no stranger to adversity. When a devastating accident left him bound to a wheelchair with a poor prognosis for recovery, he harnessed the energy of his mind and used its power to achieve his goal -- to walk again.

Whether presenting a seminar or in private practice this energy is apparent. With passion and humour Dr. Lees strives to provide an atmosphere where individuals can fully realize the power they have within themselves. He wants to introduce you to the real healing guru - Yourself!

Dr. Lees is the author of *EFT — Emotional Freedom Techniques — What is it and how does it work*? He is also a member of the EFT Advisory Board and a Contributing Editor to Gary Craig's newsletter *EFT Insights*.

Contract Information

Dr. Alexander Lees
604-542-6277
lees@dralexlees.com

Dr. Alexander R. Lees & Associates Inc.
17265 – 2nd Avenue
Surrey, BC V3S 9P9
Canada

www.DrAlexLees.com

Carol Look
EFT Master Practitioner

Carol Look's specialty is inspiring clients to attract abundance into their lives by using EFT to clear limiting beliefs, release resistance and build their "prosperity consciousness." Before becoming trained in numerous *Energy Psychology* methods, Carol was trained as a Clinical Social Worker and earned her Doctoral Degree in Clinical Hypnotherapy. She was among the first group of practitioners in the world to be certified by EFT founder Gary Craig as an EFT Master.

Dr. Look worked as an addictions specialist for eight years at Freedom Institute, an out-patient substance abuse facility, and currently maintains a private practice in New York City. As a leading contributing editor to EFT founder Gary Craig's newsletter, *EFT Insights*, Carol has written dozens of articles to support fellow EFT practitioners in their work.

Carol teaches EFT workshops around the country on the topics of attracting abundance, anxiety relief, and weight loss. She has been invited to teach EFT classes for organizations such as the National Guild of Hypnotists (NGH), the Association of Comprehensive Energy Psychology (ACEP), the National Institute for the Clinical Application of Behavioral Medicine (NICABM), the Toronto Energy Psychology Conference (Toronto-EPC) and the Center for Spirituality and Psychotherapy (CSP).

While Carol is no longer accepting new clients due to her extensive waiting list, she offers a wide variety of *Attracting Abundance with EFT* teleclasses, "live" seminars, and a new *Abundance Package* for clients who are ready to break through any barriers to prosperity and expand their comfort zones.

Carol's new book, *Attracting Abundance with EFT*, is also available as an e-book with companion audio recordings. Carol is the author of two of the field's classic EFT training manuals, *How to Lose Weight with Energy Therapy* and *Quit Smoking Now with Energy Therapy*. She is the senior author of the new computerized EFT program, *The Key to Successful Weight Loss* with co-authors Dr. Patricia Carrington and Sandi Radomski. Carol is the host of the popular internet radio show *Attracting Abundance: The Energy of Success*. Archives of her interview shows with leading EFT experts may be heard by visiting her web site.

Contact Information

Carol Look
212-477-8645
Carol@CarolLook.com

5 East 22nd Street, Suite 23-B
New York, NY 10010

www.CarolLook.com

Angela Treat Lyon

Angela Treat Lyon is an International EFT practitioner/trainer and Accelerated Freedom Tools trainer, Wealth and Success Trainer, author, professional graphic and fine artist (see www.Lyon-Art.com and www.TheLandofAmmaze.com), and sought-after public speaker on personal wealth and energy management. She also edits, constructs and publishes eBooks and print books.

Angela is the author of *Change Your Mind! with EFT* (the very popular comprehensive EFT manual), and the shorty, *Illustrated EFT Guide* (which is also available in Spanish), *The REAL Money Secrets, The Six Little P.I.G.E.E.S. Learn the Amazing Money Multiplying Methodde*, and *The Six Little P.I.G.E.E.S. 90-Day Daily Millionaire MindSet Guide*.

Angela conducts individual and group trainings, and twice-weekly P.I.G.E.E.S. Treasure Tele-Classes about creating and maintaining a high level of personal health and wealth.

Angela interviews and records wealth, health and energy experts to bring the best of the best people, instruction and products to help people find and live their most outrageous dream. Find it all — 24/7 listening at www.Rich-Radio.com.

Angela spent 40 years as a professional fine artist in porcelain, stone, bronze and oil painting. She has extensive experience in advertising, graphic design and marketing. In her free time, you'll find her at the beach.

Contact Information

Angela Treat Lyon
Lyon@PIGEES.com

www.EFTbooks.com
www.PIGEES.com
www.Rich-Radio.com

Rebecca Marina

Rebecca has an intense desire to share EFT because she has used these techniques to heal so many areas in her own life. Raised as one of eight children in the back roads of Alabama, Rebecca experienced childhood poverty and the feelings of inferiority that often come with it. Because, she learned how to use energy therapy to transform these energy patterns in her own life, she delights in helping others do the same. There is no greater way to become an expert than to learn to apply a healing technique because of personal need.

Rebecca feels especially blessed to pioneer the use of EFT in intimacy and relationship issues. There is such satisfaction in helping others have happy, healthy, loving, intimate, relationships. Rebecca enjoys an international private practice and teaches others how to use the unique EFT techniques she has pioneered. She lives with her husband, children and five canine friends in deep South Texas.

Rebecca is the author of *30 Angel Steps to Prosperity* which combines powerful spiritual principles with energy therapy for simply divine results. Also, the DVD, *The Power of Emotions in Our Blood*, was created by Rebecca and provides visual evidence that our emotional states affect our blood and how EFT can assist in creating rapid, positive changes. The video actually shows live blood cells under a dark field microscope responding to Rebecca doing EFT.

Contact Information

Rebecca Marina
956-457-5568
rebeccamarina@yahoo.com

www.celebrationhealing.com

Betty Moore-Hafter

Betty is a certified hypnotherapist and EFT practitioner in Burlington, Vermont. Her work helps people reach the subconscious levels of the mind where emotional patterns are rooted and core beliefs held. She works with a wide range of issues including inner child healing, regression therapy, relief from phobias, weight and eating issues, removing blocks to success, and more. She believes that with the right tools and support, everyone can create and realize his or her own vision of wholeness and well-being.

A former teacher, Betty values the opportunity to teach others how to use EFT effectively for their issues. As people learn to trust their own healing process, they are empowered to continue this work on their own. She specializes in EFT phone sessions and, upon request, offers the additional support of a personalized hypnotherapy or "guided tapping" CD.

Betty is the author of *Tapping Your Amazing Potential*, a sourcebook for using EFT creatively, and also offers a unique series of EFT/hypnosis CDs. She maintains an international e-mail forum for sharing EFT ideas and stories, the Rising Sun EFT Group. All of these EFT resources are available through her website.

Contact Information

Betty Moore-Hafter
802-860-7286
betty@risingsunhealing.com

Rising Sun Healing Center
35 King Street, Suite 7
Burlington, VT 05401

www.risingsunhealing.com

Carol Solomon

Carol Solomon, Ph.D. PCC is a psychologist, author and personal coach. With 25 years experience in helping people find solutions and make positive life changes, Carol is a natural teacher and coach. She enjoys a thriving coaching practice and is passionate about helping others succeed. Carol has a warm and genuine personal style and an enthusiastic love of learning.

Carol was selected as a trainer in the Authentic Happiness Coaching program led by Dr. Martin Seligman and Dr. Ben Dean, and is on the faculty of Mentorcoach™. She is the author of *Lose Weight Now… Stay Slim Forever*, a practical how-to manual for learning to lose weight without dieting. Register for her free email newsletter at www.StressEating.com

Carol is highly proficient with EFT which can stop immediate food cravings, reduce binge eating, and decrease the intensity of emotions that lead to the urge eat. She is the author of *How To Stop Food Cravings and Lose Weight With EFT* and *More Money With EFT* available on her websites.

Contact Information

Carol Solomon
847-680-0272
Carol@LoseWeightWithEFT.com

128 Newberry Avenue
Libertyville, IL 60048

www.LoseWeightWithEFT.com
www.MoreMoneyWithEFT.com
www.EFTtips.com
www.StressEating.com

Loretta Sparks

Loretta Sparks, MA, MFT, is the Founder and Director of the Center for Energy Psychotherapy and TAAP Training Institute. She is a licensed psychotherapist and practitioner of Emotional Freedom Techniques. As an author, educator and trainer, she has trained mental health professionals and as well as the public, nationally and internationally, in EFT for more than a decade.

Even though, Ms. Sparks has trained extensively with the developers of a number of energy psychotherapies, she has chosen to focus her work on EFT not only because of its effectiveness, but also because of the ease with which it can be accessed and be learned.

In addition to her private practice, Ms. Sparks has worked for a number of years in the Addiction Medicine Department of a large HMO. Where she developed her interest in the application of EFT to addiction and its root causes. She is a Certified Addiction Specialist (CAS), an Advanced Certified Relapse Prevention Specialist (Cenaps), a member of the American Academy of Psychotherapists and a charter member of the Association for Comprehensive Energy Psychology.

Ms. Sparks maintains a private practice and is available for consultation and training workshops. California CEs are available for MFTs and LCSWs (BBSE #467), RN and LVNs (BRN CEP #12768).

Contact Information

LsparksMA@aol.com

www.energypsychotherapy.com.

Mary Stafford

Mary E. Stafford, M.Ed., EFT-ADV, is a Licensed Professional Counselor, in the state of Arizona, with 24 years experience. She is a member of the American Counselors Association and the Association for Comprehensive Energy Psychology. Counseling is a second career, for Mary. In her first career she attained a Ph.D. in biochemistry from the University of California at Irvine. She did bio-medical research for ten years before making a career change to counseling, a field she felt would be more fulfilling. At that time she went back to school and earned a M.Ed. in counseling and guidance from the University of Arizona.

Since 1981, she has worked as a counselor in various settings including as a crisis counselor for a state agency. She routinely had clients in extreme states of distress. In 1996, she was looking for a counseling approach that would be more effective and efficient. She became trained in Thought Field Therapy, (TFT), the approach which first used energy meridians. She experienced amazing results, using TFT, and trained with its originator, Dr. Roger Callahan, so she could also train professionals. Six months later, Mary learned of Gary Craig's development called Emotional Freedom Techniques (EFT), and began training professionals in EFT, as well.

In recent years, Mrs. Stafford has focused on EFT, using it for clients and training others in its use. She is pleased with how empowering EFT is for clients, since the same tapping procedure is used for a multitude of issues. She was privileged to present EFT to the Arizona School Counselors' Conference in Mesa, Arizona in March, 2005. Her dream is that someday all school children will learn to use EFT to let go of anger, hurtfulness, sadness, fear, and guilt and then go home and teach their parents. Young people today would not have problems with drugs and violence, if they were taught how to manage their emotions.

Contact Information

Mary E. Stafford
520-575-1497
mstafford@mindbodytherapy.com

MindBody Therapies
9941 North Placita Papalote
Oro Valley, AZ 85737

www.mindbodytherapy.com

Carol Tuttle

Carol Tuttle is an energy psychologist, best-selling author, and an incredibly successful speaker. She has appeared on hundreds of radio shows and made numerous local and national television appearances. She and her husband, Jon, reside in Salt Lake City, UT and utilize these energy clearing techniques in their everyday lives with their five children.

Carol's best-selling book, *Remembering Wholeness* and her other products have helped transformed the lives of hundreds of thousand of people. They are available on her website. In addition she has launched *The Carol Tuttle Healing Center*, an interactive website utilizing these techniques for clearing literally hundreds of issues. You can learn more about this website and EFT at www.YourEmotionalHealing.com

Contact Information

carol@CarolTuttle.com

www.CarolTuttle.com
www.YourEmotionalHealing.com

Stacey Vornbrock

Stacey Vornbrock, M.S., Sports Performance Pioneer, helps elite and amateur athletes turn blocks into breakthroughs. She has worked with athletes in golf, baseball, football, discus, shot put, tennis, Aussie football, and a variety of other sports.

Stacey has her Masters in Counseling from the University of Nebraska and worked as a psychotherapist from 1977 until 2003 when she began working with athletes. She has been using EFT since 1999 and believes it is the most powerful tool she has found in her entire career.

Stacey helps elite and amateur athletes achieve breakthrough performance by increasing range of motion by at least 20 percent completing the healing of old injuries, speeding up the healing of recent injuries, clearing past performance trauma, eliminating sports related anxiety and accomplishing mechanical changes in weeks instead of months.

Stacey's number one commitment is getting results for her clients. She guides elite and amateur athletes to release the cultural constraints inherent in their sport and rapidly breakthrough blocks, opening up her clients to their full performance potential. Stacey is an innovator in the sports performance field. Most notably, she has pioneered the application of EFT with range of motion and sports-related mechanical issues.

Contact Information

Stacey Vornbrock
480-945-9750
stacey@breakthroughperformance.net

www.breakthroughperformance.net

Maryam Webster

Maryam Webster holds both Bachelor and Masters degrees in Counseling Psychology and has been in private practice for over 20 years. A graduate of Coach University, Maryam has been an Adjunct Faculty member of The Graduate School of Coaching, and is current Communications Director of the Association of Comprehensive Energy Psychology (ACEP). A certified Master of Neuro-Linguistic Programming (M.NLP), through NLP California, Maryam holds Dr. Pat Carrington's EFT-CC certification and has been trained in Provocative Energy Techniques by Steve Wells and Dr. David Lake.

After incorporating Coaching and Energy Psychology with her clients, Maryam developed and currently serves as Director of The Certified Energy Coach Program, which teaches energy coaching to helping professionals. Visit the CEC website and download the first week of training free: certifiedenergycoach.org. For public training in how to use these techniques, visit Maryam at: quantumflow.com and download the free Quantum Flow Bioenergetics Energy Therapy CD: snipurl.com/FreeEnergyCD.

Maryam's popular book and 2-CD set, *Quantum Flow Bioenergetics: Be Your Own Healer*, features EFT as a primary energy therapy and teaches you through videos, audios and 100 pages of interactive tutorial, over twenty different energy therapy interventions to use in your own life. This and more are available at the Quantum Bazaar: quantumflow/shop.html.

Contact Information

Maryam Webster

quantumflow.com/contact.html

Rick Wilkes

Rick Wilkes is an Emotional Freedom Coach, Certified Massage Therapist, and Ordained Interfaith Minister.

For the past fifteen years, Rick has been exploring energy therapy combined with spiritual inner guidance to promote healing from chronic stresses and pains. This exploration lead him to become nationally certified in therapeutic massage and bodywork. During his hands-on work with clients, he became intrigued with the ways the body stores emotional pain in physical tissues. For Rick and most other energy touch therapists, emotions are palpable just as a muscular knot or spasm is. Intuitive guidance often lead him to rub, tap, and flow energy intentionally between specific points on the body to bring physioemotional relief and allow the body to heal itself.

Rick discovered EFT several years ago, and it immediately felt like an "old friend." The energetic relief clients felt on the table can now be experienced over the phone and the internet using systematic tapping -- even for painful core issues, traumatic memories, and limiting beliefs. Rick loves the fact that EFT can be used for ongoing emotional *self-care*, and he has devoted himself to spreading the word about EFT and teaching people around the world how to transform their pain into optimal health so they can truly feel *good* in the present moment.

That is the essence of *Thriving Now*. To feel good in the present moment is to literally feel the spiritual presence of God. Body, mind, *and* spirit are integrated with EFT in Rick's holistic approach to emotional freedom coaching. As an ordained interfaith minister, Rick naturally respects and honors the individuality of each person's spiritual path and religious traditions.

Rick also leverages his 27 years of technology experience on his website. Visitors will find many hours of freely available audio coaching sessions to tap along with, hundreds of articles, an EFT quick start guide, and a free email newsletter. Also available is the Thriving Now Team Membership which includes group coaching and other services for a very affordable monthly fee.

Contact Information

Rick Wilkes
Thriving Now LLC
Rick@Thrivingnow.com

www.thrivingnow.com

Brad Yates

Brad Yates, C.Ht. is a member of the Association for Comprehensive Energy Psychology, the National Guild of Hypnotists and the American Counseling Association. He was trained and certified at the respected Hypnosis Motivation Institute in Tarzana, California where he served on staff. Combining this background with training in energy psychology and various schools of thought in the area of personal growth and achievement, he coaches groups and individuals in achieving greater success, health and happiness in their lives.

Brad has worked with a diverse group of clients, ranging from CEOs to professional and NCAA athletes, award-winning actors and clients in homeless and rehabilitation programs. He conducts ongoing teleclasses that are attended by participants from around the world. He has also been a presenter at the past three International Energy Psychology Conferences.

Brad is recognized around the world as a leading practitioner of EFT, known for the effectiveness of his work as well as the sense of humor he brings to it. His eclectic background includes touring internationally as an actor and being a graduate of Ringling Bros. & Barnum & Bailey Clown College. He lives near Sacramento, California with his wonderful wife and their two magnificent children.

Contact Information

Brad Yates
916-729-0347
brad@bradyates.net

www.bradyates.net
www.golfbeyondbelief.com

Jan Yordy

Jan Yordy is an educator and a child therapist who has been working with children and families for over twenty-five years. Working first as an elementary teacher and later as a child counselor and play therapist she holds a Master of Education, a Master of Social Work and certification in Play Therapy with the Canadian Association of Child and Play Therapist. More recently she has become a certified Brain Gym instructor, EMDR and Energy Psychology clinician.

In the last several years Jan Yordy has developed a therapeutic game called *Energy Connection* and produced a video/DVD on Indigo Children called *Indigo Child, the Next Step in Evolution*. Writing a children's book called *Becoming the Boss of Your Feelings, EFT for Children* is her most recent project. Jan Yordy is a popular workshop presenter and conducts workshops locally as well as internationally sharing her innovative tools and insights about working with children.

In the last year Jan, along with two partners, has opened the Integrated Centre for Optimal Learning where they are helping children who learn differently to optimize their learning potential. To find out more about Jan Yordy, her workshops and her innovative resources you can visit www.energyconnectiontherapies.com

Contact Information

Jan Yordy
519-664-3568

P.O. Box 35
St. Jacobs, Ontario
Canada N0B 2N0

www.energyconnectiontherapies.com

GLOSSARY

Apex Problem: Explaining, giving credit, attributing the changes produced by EFT to something else within the person's belief system.

Aspects: Another part of an issue or different issue that comes up when tapping.

Basic Recipe: Classic, long version of EFT doing rounds of tapping. Consists of the setup, the sequence, the Nine Gamut Procedure and the sequence again.

Collarbone Breathing: A corrective technique used when the body's energy system is so disorganized that it doesn't respond to treatment.

Discovery Statement: The cause of all negative emotions is a disruption in the body's energy system.

EFT-ADV: Administered by Pace Educational Systems, Inc., the Advanced EFT Certificate of Completion is available to those who, after passing the exam for the Basic Certificate (EFT-CC), have in addition passed the EFT-ADV examination that is based on Gary Craig's advanced videos, *Steps Toward Becoming The Ultimate Therapist.*

EFT-CC: Administered by Pace Educational Systems, Inc. the Basic EFT Certificate of Completion is available to those who have passed the EFT-CC examination based on Gary Craig's foundational series of videos, *The EFT Course.*

EFT Master: Program authorized by Gary Craig and administered by Ann Adams. The premier level attainable for an EFT practitioner, EFT Masters have achieved the highest standards of excellence and passed a rigorous qualification program. EFT Masters specialize in EFT on a full time basis and have demonstrated their ability to deliver EFT at the highest creative levels.

Energy Medicine: Based upon the belief that changes in the "life force" of the body, including the electric, magnetic, and electromagnetic fields, affect human health and can promote healing.

Energy Psychology: Applies principles and techniques for working with the body's physical energies to facilitate desired changes in emotions, thoughts, and behaviors.

Energy System: The total system of energy pathway meridians that course throughout the body.

Energy Toxins: Electromagnetic, chemical, food or other toxins that disrupt the body's energy system.

Gamut Point: The point on either hand located a half inch behind the midpoint between the knuckles at the base of the ring finger and little finger.

Karate Chop Point: Point located at the center of the fleshy part of the outside of either hand between the top of the wrist and the base of the baby finger.

Movie Technique: Getting specific about an event by making a short mental movie with a beginning, a crescendo and an end. If a person can't make a specific movie of their problem then the problem is too globally stated.

Muscle Testing: A way of checking with the subconscious mind by applying a consistent force to a muscle in the body, in the presence of a defined stimulus, and observing the response of the muscle to the stimulus. Applied kinesiology is a way of discovering if there are blockages or reversals by testing whether the response is strong or weak.

Nine Gamut Procedure: Simultaneously thinking of the bothersome issue, tapping on the Gamut point on the back of the hand and going through the nine different actions.

Palace of Possibilities: Each of us has our own limiting beliefs and emotions. We also live within a Palace of Possibilities. EFT can help erase limiting factors and install empowering beliefs. For more information on this, check out the set of videos with this title at www.emofree.com

Personal Peace Procedure: The Personal Peace Procedure involves making a list of every bothersome *specific event* in one's life and systematically doing EFT to take the *sting* out or eliminate any negative emotional impact. By diligently and systematically doing this, we can help eliminate major causes of our emotional and physical ailments.

Polarity Reversal: Means that the energy in the body is reversed or going in the wrong direction. The polarity is reversed.

Psychological Reversal: An unconscious block that occurs when the body energy system changes polarity. Self-sabotaging thoughts and beliefs.

Reminder Phrase: Short phrase used when tapping to describe the issue.

Round: Doing a complete sequence with each of the EFT points.

Secondary Benefit Syndrome Reversal: Reversal that occurs because the subconscious mind perceives it is better or safer to keep an issue than to eliminate it.

Sequence: Tapping on the EFT end points of the major energy meridians on the face, torso and fingers.

Setup: Part of EFT where person rubs the Sore Spot or taps the Karate Chop point while simultaneously repeating the setup or affirmation phrase.

Setup Phrase or Affirmation: Phrase used in the setup that describes the problem and is a neutralizing affirmation.

Shortcut Technique: Most often used, short version of EFT that skips the finger points and the Nine Gamut procedure.

Sore Spot: Spot located on upper left and right portions of chest. Used in the setup. The Karate Chop point performs the same function and is used more often.

Subconscious: The part of the mind below the level of conscious perception.

SUDS: Subjective Units of Distress Scale. Used in EFT to gauge the intensity of an emotion and measure changes typically using a scale of 0-10. Zero means no intensity. Ten is very intense.

Surrogate Tapping: One person acts as a surrogate by tapping on themselves with the intention of doing it on behalf of another person. (Also done with pets or animals.)

Testing: Checking to see if the result holds or lasts.

Tail Ender: The often unrecognized inner reservation or resistance that comes up when making a positive affirmation. It's the mental "yes, but" that can block the effectiveness of the affirmation.

Visit the Freedom at Your Fingertips website:
www.fayf.com

Quick Order Form

3 Ways to Order Additional Copies of This Book

1. You can usually order additional copies of this book from one of the co-authors. Check the biography section for information on their Websites.
2. Order from your favorite bookseller or online from Amazon.com.
3. Order directly from the publisher.

Fax Orders: (540) 972-1071. Please copy and send this form.
Postal Orders: Inroads Publishing
                 P.O. Box 357
                 Fredericksburg, VA 22404-0357

Title	Quantity	Price (USA)	Extension
Freedom At Your Fingertips		19.95	
Subtotal			
Sales Tax: Add 5% for books shipped to Virginia addresses			
USA Shipping: First book $4.50; $2.00 for each additional book			
TOTAL			

For International orders or volume discounts to professionals and organizations, contact the publisher at info@fayf.com or call (800) 930-7434 Ext. 702

Name: _____

Address: _____

City: _____ State: _____ Zip: _____

Telephone: _____

E-mail: _____

Payment:
☐ Check
Credit card: ☐ Visa ☐ MasterCard ☐ Amex ☐ Discover

Name on Card: _____

Card Number: _____

Expiration Date: _____/ _____/ _____

Card Verification No. _____ (On back of Visa, MC, Discover. Front of Amex.)

Signature: _____

Quick Order Form

3 Ways to Order Additional Copies of This Book

1. You can usually order additional copies of this book from one of the co-authors. Check the biography section for information on their Websites.
2. Order from your favorite bookseller or online from Amazon.com.
3. Order directly from the publisher.

Fax Orders: (540) 972-1071. Please copy and send this form.

Postal Orders: Inroads Publishing
P.O. Box 357
Fredericksburg, VA 22404-0357

Title	Quantity	Price (USA)	Extension
Freedom At Your Fingertips		19.95	
Subtotal			
Sales Tax: Add 5% for books shipped to Virginia addresses			
USA Shipping: First book $4.50; $2.00 for each additional book			
TOTAL			

For International orders or volume discounts to professionals and organizations, contact the publisher at info@fayf.com or call (800) 930-7434 Ext. 702

Name: _____

Address: _____

City: _____ State: _____ Zip: _____

Telephone: _____

E-mail: _____

Payment:

❑ Check

Credit card: ❑ Visa ❑ MasterCard ❑ Amex ❑ Discover

Name on Card: _____

Card Number: _____

Expiration Date: _____/ _____/ _____

Card Verification No. _____ (On back of Visa, MC, Discover. Front of Amex.)

Signature: _____